MESA

PAM CAMERON

LUMINARIA PRESS

Published by Luminaria Press
First Printing May 1998

For information contact:

LUMINARIA PRESS

Luminaria Press
P. O. Box 4249
Pagosa Springs, Colorado
U.S.A. 81147

ISBN 0-9657104-0-8

Cover Art by Andrew Normington
Cover Design by Raven Graphics
Chapter Graphics by Paul Bond, Art & Soul Design

Published in the United States of America

ACKNOWLEDGMENTS

This is a true story which explains some of the changes occurring in our world as we are being presented with the opportunity to understand reality in new ways. This is my story; but there are many other people involved, each with a story of their own. Names have been changed to protect the anonymity of my friends. I wish to extend my love and a special acknowledgment to Jeanne, Cathie, Robyn, Kathy, Lisa, Beth, Andrew, Ian, Kari, Gene, Deborah, Cheryl C., Michael Ann, Jo, Eunice, Crea, Eric, Christine, Karen, Joyce, Bev, Ann, Cheryl W., Nancy, Gail and Brooks.

Special thanks and love also to Jayn Stewart, Morgan Caldwell and Susan Tinkle for their assistance.

To Fred

The possibility exists for each of us to manifest Heaven into our lives now! The restrictions have been lifted and the potential of a new reality is present. We may bring it here now with courage and with joy. Everyone who is present on the planet at this time has agreed to be a part of this process. We may choose our role. And we may choose our experience and our expression.

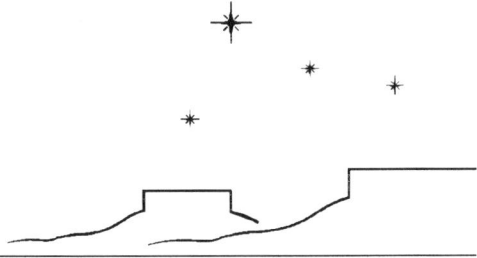

PROLOGUE

Into ordinary lives can come very extra-ordinary events – events which propel us forward into new discoveries about who we are and how we perceive the world. Just such an event happened to me in September of 1990, when a vision penetrated my consciousness and altered the course of my life. This book is the telling of that story.

It is the story of a sequence of events which occurred over one year's time. As the story began to unfold, I was asked to keep a record of everything that transpired. It is only by virtue of having followed this advice from Spirit that I have been able to relay such a detailed account. It is now the end of 1996, and I still continue to more fully comprehend the importance of what occurred on Earth six years ago. There was a global quickening in consciousness as many souls began to *remember* a sense of union – and our view of reality began to shift.

My life was pretty "normal." I had two teen-aged children, two step-children, and all the usual concerns of parenting. My husband and I had our own computer software development company where I was Vice President of Sales and Marketing. We lived in a suburb of Silicon Valley in California with our children, 3 dogs, a cat, a rabbit, 18 chickens and a horse. My greatest joy was working in my garden, where I spent every free moment.

While taking some college courses in the early '70s, I was awakened to the probability that we create a viewpoint of reality which we construct around us like a box. And it was only after having the sides blown out of my box that I realized the shell surrounding my own cocoon of awareness had expanded. I wanted to understand more, so I began studying and exploring. I learned about meditation at the Presbyterian Church. I changed my college major from English to Psychology. And life went on as usual.

But events in the world were changing things around all of us, asking us to wake up. There were dramatic events occurring on the planet which affected everyone, whether or not they had an awareness of metaphysical thought. These events came in the form of hurricanes, fires, earthquakes, and floods. None of us touched by these things could any longer take the certainty of life for granted. For me and my family it was the 1989 Loma Prieta earthquake which shook our foundations to the core. It dismantled our complacency and made us reevaluate our priorities.

After that, thoughts began to come into my head, unbidden. Thoughts which were seeds planted so that I would begin to listen. I became aware of the concept of Ascension, and was introduced to the process of channeling. I had made a conscious decision to expand my understanding about Spirit, so my intention created the opening which allowed me to begin to hear.

I am still trying to understand more, as my world continues to expand. I know that our greatest source of strength must come from within us as we each reconnect with Source. It is with this divine connection that we can each access a greater understanding. And it is only by listening to this inner guidance and by following Spirit unhesitatingly that we can even approach an understanding of the truth of our existence.

I do not profess any particular religious philosophy. What I do profess is the imperative that we each establish a direct connection to Spirit. Right now there are changes occurring on the planet, and in our galaxy, that we are all participating in – whether we are aware of it or not – just because we're here. For many years, I have been hearing all sorts of predictions about this coming time: the new age, the end of the millennium. The predictions have become current events as history unfolds all around us. Many people are in confusion; many are afraid of the changes which they can no longer deny.

I have gained an awareness about a shift presently underway which is going to alter everyone on the planet emotionally, physically, and spiritually, and I share this story in the hope that it will somehow help others understand things which are occurring in their own lives. If I can give one person the courage to listen to their spiritual guidance, if I can help one person understand their confusion, then releasing this story will have been worthwhile. For the time has come when each of us is going to be asked to stand in our own truth.

This story is much greater than I and the others in it. It is about the fulfillment of ancient prophecies. It is about the Light Activation of planet Earth. It is about a shift which is occurring in our solar system and in our universe, for all things are connected and all things are changing, as they must.

Even you.

Pam Cameron
January, 1998

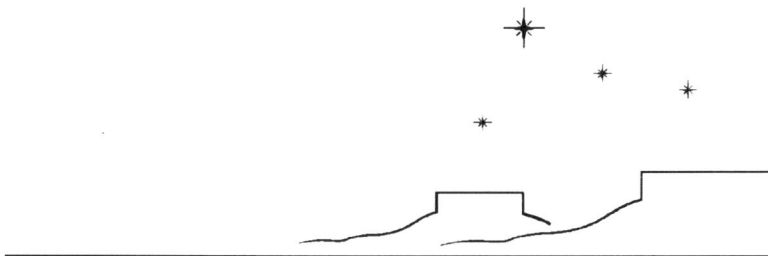

VOICES

"Go you to the desert of the great Southwest!"

My slumber was broken by the commanding words which jerked me back to consciousness. They came with the forcefulness of a ship's captain commanding his crew. My eyes, wide open from the startle of being awakened by the power of this voice, looked at the clock – 3:00 a.m.

Just a dream. I shrugged it off and rolled over to go back to sleep.

"Go where the sky is pink!"

There was that voice again, looming over me and disrupting my sleep. I remained calm as I watched a surrealistic sunset paint vibrant pink hues across the screen of my half-conscious mind. And then, I was awake.

I didn't know what it meant, but I knew this wasn't a usual dream – the unraveling of subconscious thoughts or fears. This was different. In fact, it didn't really seem like a dream at all. It was more a vision than an ordinary dream. In the darkness, I reached over and picked up my journal to record what had happened. I scrawled the mysterious words I had heard across the page. Now burned into my memory, these words would come to haunt me – to change my life, as well as the lives of many others with whom I would share them.

Once again, I closed my eyes in an attempt to return to sleep. This time a number wrote itself across my viewing screen:

"65,000 people there."

I was not awake, yet not asleep, but somewhere in between as I asked for a sign to know where this information was coming from or what it was about. Part of me wanted to dismiss it, but a stirring curiosity made another part begin to question: Who was this speaking? What was this about? Why should I go to the desert? Why should I care?

Then, as I began drifting off again, another number wafted into view and quickly faded. It was very faint. Only the numbers 9 8 4 were certain; the rest was veiled from my consciousness. The harder I tried to grasp what I was seeing, the more elusive it became. Was it 2 4 1 1? Was it a telephone number? Was it some sort of a key intended to help me understand the instructions I had just received?

What was all this about?

Perhaps it was nothing – nothing at all. I tried to reassure myself as I felt conflict between curiosity and disbelief. I decided to put these thoughts away, but, deep within, I knew that something significant had just happened.

When I awoke that morning, it seemed like any other day. The sun was shining across a California sky, the woodpeckers were tapping on the roof above my head, the kids were already up and getting ready for school, the dogs were barking at the neighbors on their early morning walks. It was the same as every other morning. Nothing was different.

I picked up my journal from the floor where it had fallen the night before and opened it, my heart pounding faster as I read the awkward scrawling:

Go you to the desert of the great Southwest.
Go where the sky is pink.
65,000 people there.
984-????

My eyes remained fixed on the page as I wondered why I was having an emotional reaction to the words. Then, my eyes rested upon the last line:

Sign = Sananda

"What is this?" I spoke the words aloud.

I didn't remember writing it.

I thought back.

Yes, I had asked for a sign so that I could understand where the message was coming from. Seeing these words jogged my memory. I recalled seeing the vague image of a man in my mind. He had a gentle smile, shoulder-length brown hair, and was dressed in a long white robe. I knew without question that this was Sananda, an Ascended Being of Light known as Jesus on Earth. Could it be that the one I knew as Christ was behind these messages? The implications of this sign had been too great to accept, and I had closed my memory to the words.

A voice in the night had interrupted the silence of my slumber and given me a message. I didn't know what it was about: pieces of a puzzle delivered by a phantom – just pieces. I filed them away in a corner of my mind and went out to the kitchen.

"Good morning," I greeted my son, Drew, who was already at the kitchen counter eating a bowl of cereal. I wanted to share my experience from the night before with someone and told him, "I sure had some strange dreams last night."

He walked over to the sink to wash his bowl. "Yeah?" and then he turned, "I gotta go now. I'm late for class." He brushed his blond hair out of his eyes as he grabbed his books and headed for the door. "I'm going surfing after school."

And he was gone.

It didn't matter that my 18-year-old son wasn't interested, for my mind was full of my own questions. What was I supposed to do? It was unsettling.

As I dressed for work, the vision continued to haunt me. When I arrived at the office in town where my husband, Fred, and I had our software business, I found him already working. I gave him a kiss on the cheek and sat down in the leather chair beside his desk. "You left early this morning. Do you have a big deadline you're working on?"

"No," Fred turned away from his computer and looked at me. "I'm trying to work on the logic for a new program and I had an idea. I just wanted to get started."

"I had some incredible dreams last night. There was something unusual about them. I actually heard a voice speaking to me."

We were interrupted by our secretary's voice over the intercom as Fred's telephone buzzed, "There's a customer on line ONE whose computer just crashed. Sounds like they're in a real panic!"

Fred said, "I'll have to take this."

"Okay. I need to get started with my day anyway."

I was disappointed. But how could anyone else understand the compelling sense of urgency I was feeling from hearing that voice in the night? How could anyone else feel driven by the message? I felt as though I had a secret. This was for me alone to figure out.

I walked down the stairs to my own office and looked at the pile of papers on my desk. Owning this business was like having another child which we were caring for and nurturing, for our dedication to it was great. Throughout the day I attempted to put the mid-night message out of my mind, but the voice lingered and the vivid sunset remained. I was preoccupied with the meaning of the vision as I looked at the pile of paperwork surrounding me. Finally, I surrendered to the persistent call from within and excused myself from work.

Once back at home, I was overcome by a blanket of sleepiness and, in response, lay down on the living room sofa. As I closed my eyes, I felt myself begin to drift away. I was awake, yet my consciousness seemed to be in some far away place. I wanted to know if there was more information for me, and I struggled to stay alert as I drifted in and out of consciousness. Slowly, words began forming in my mind, _"The Indians. Proud. Strong. The spirits of the Sun, Moon and Earth – all focused."_

I saw a Native American standing on a mesa as the words continued to form, _"The Indians upheld their truth. The Indian Chief protected this spot because he knew it was sacred. This land was saved for a special purpose. It will be used. The time is now."_

As I watched the Indian looking out from where he stood on the mesa, I kept hearing the word _"Apache"_ over and over again: _"Apache. Apache. Apache."_ And, then, I saw an eagle launch itself from the mesa, soaring smoothly overhead.

Although it seems brief as I record it here, receiving these messages took nearly an hour of focused attention on the images appearing in the silence of my mind. I felt as though they were another piece to the puzzle, and I tucked them away with the messages from the voice in the night.

Days passed. From time to time a message would leak through – dreams and messages I couldn't understand. One evening I told Fred, "You know, there is something unusual going on here. Do you remember me telling you about the voice which came in the night and woke me up?"

He nodded and I continued, "Well, there's more. I've been keeping a record of the messages I've been receiving. Can I share them with you?"

"Of course." Fred was intrigued and waited as I went to retrieve my journal. He listened in silence as I read. Then, after a few minutes of quiet thoughtfulness, he said, "Why don't we take a trip?"

I was surprised by his reaction, "Do you mean it?"

"Sure. There's a convention coming up in Arizona next month. We've both been wanting to go to the Southwest. Let's go. There are some business contacts we need to make and some relatives we could visit. We'll make a vacation out of it."

"And look for a sunset?" I urged him on.

"Who knows what we might find. It'll be fun!"

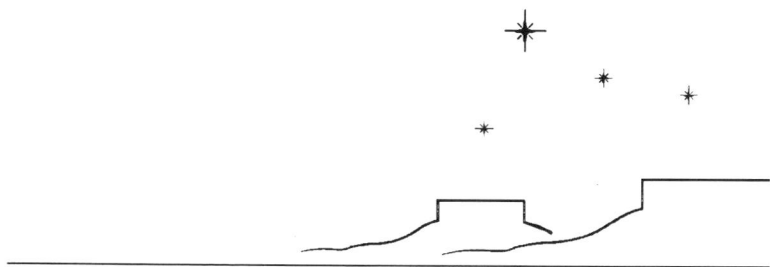

ASHTAR

So, we began making plans. We had more than an idle curiosity. There was a stirring, a force which drew us forward. On the surface we were making an ordinary trip, but intrigue was whispering in our ears with the compelling message that there was some thing, some place, some reason to be found. We would go. We would do it. A vision quest to find one spectacular southwest sunset and its meaning had begun.

One night shortly after receiving this vision, words again came into my head, unbidden, as I was drifting off to sleep. I picked up my pen and began to write, "*This is Ashtar.*" I could see him in my mind's eye. He was a handsome being, seven feet tall with light brown slicked back hair. His lean body had a peaceful strength, and his piercing blue eyes were full of kindness and wisdom.

Ashtar continued, "*I assist and direct many spiritual beings from many places in the universe which are currently on and about planet*

Earth. We are working in brotherhood to assist the people of your planet under the guidance of the one you know as the Lord Jesus-Sananda. He is our inspiration." My thoughts returned to the night this all started. I had wanted to know where the voice was coming from, and to understand the nature of the vision. When the image of the one known as both Jesus and Sananda appeared, my mind had been put at ease. The message continued and there was no time now for my own thoughts, "*Although we are beaming down information, there are few who are ready to accept it. You must fight away your limited perceptions, for we would like to call upon your assistance, as you have an important role to play if you choose. You are an instrument and we need you in the Plan.*

"*You must not delay because time is of the essence now. The stars will soon be in the proper alignment for the fourth dimension to pass on fully into the fifth. Your beautiful planet is anxious, and the process cannot be stopped. It is bigger than you and bigger than Earth. It is the Divine Plan for the galaxy unfolding.*

"*Get ready for a wondrous dream, for we shall lift the veil. You and Fred are a part of it now.*

"*The bell is ringing, and many are being awakened.*

"*It is the death knell for those who do not listen.*

"*I, Ashtar, am here to help you!*"

Now, I would ask that you bear with me here. I know that this may sound strange. It certainly seemed strange to me at first. This is the story of how I came to know beyond any doubt that these things are true. The information I was receiving was direct communication from beings in another dimension! Although it began in dreams, the link expanded and soon began coming in the form of channeled messages. This guidance has always proved to be "right on" and full of love and caring for humankind.

In the beginning, my attempts at receiving these communications felt awkward, as though I was receiving the messages through an electrical circuit with too many resistors. But the messages were too compelling to ignore. So, together, Fred and I persevered and learned to listen.

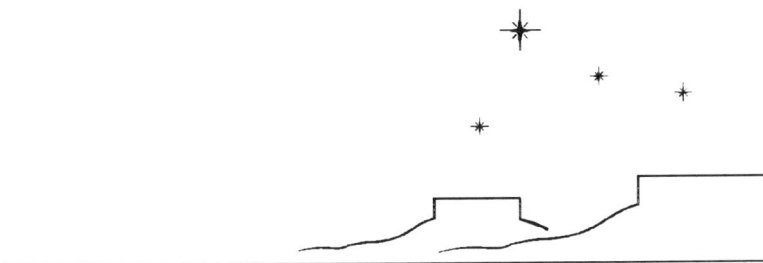

CRYSTAL

I sat holding the crystal which my dear friend Kate had given to me. It was a six-inch, double-terminated crystal of rare purity and beauty. This crystal had been her constant companion for several years, giving her comfort and support. Its importance to her was so great that it seemed to have taken on its own identity. She had even named it "Crystal" referring to it as a *her*.

I thought back to the day Kate had given the crystal to us. I saw how difficult it had been for her as she handed it to me saying, "I was meditating last week and a thought came into my head that I could give 'Crystal' to Pam and Fred. I said, 'No, I don't think so.' But each day since, the same thought was always there. So, I finally understood that it would be a good thing to do." Kate was tearful as she passed her treasure to us and I sensed deeply the importance of the gift.

The crystal in my hand glistened in the sunlight, reflecting a spectrum of rainbow colors. I pondered my confusion as the departure date of our quest drew near. It was difficult to comprehend that a message from a "space commander" or a spiritual being from another dimension had been validated by a sign from Sananda, that they were in alliance, and that it might have something to do with me. I viewed having received this treasured crystal as a sign of the significance of our quest; I felt both honored and humbled by this trust. Like Alice in Wonderland, everything had suddenly taken on an unexpected meaning. My senses were keen as we approached this great adventure. Everywhere I turned there was another mystery revealed.

My attention returned from my daydream and I rose, telling myself, "Now, you really must end all of this idleness and get back to the office." I placed the crystal on the window sill where it could catch the rays of the afternoon sun and went to get the mail.

We lived in the coastal mountains of California near Santa Cruz, and I was always filled with a sense of peace as I walked down the long driveway to the mailbox by the road. I was aware of the subtle forces of nature surrounding me as I listened to the wind gently blowing through the pine needles as it danced across the treetops. The joyful songs of birds filled my heart, and the moist coastal air caressed my cheeks. Two cottontail rabbits who lived in the woods nearby came out to greet me at the end of the driveway and then scampered away into the brush.

A large envelope was waiting in the mailbox, containing tourist information from the Chamber of Commerce gathered by a friend who had recently visited Santa Fe, along with a note: "Thought you might want to have this." The package included maps and brochures on things to do and see. One booklet particularly attracted my attention and I opened it immediately. As I looked intently through the pages, I remembered the phone number shown to me on the night I received the vision. There had been no area code. Could it have been a Santa Fe exchange?

I read every phone number in the brochure ... some of them began, "9 8 4 - ." My hands began to perspire as I looked at the numbers, and a feeling of recognition began to surface. I thought, "It could be Santa Fe. There could be something we're supposed to find there." I wondered how many other cities also used a 984 prefix and quickly pulled out our own telephone book to check the numbers. I scanned the listings. No "984" numbers here.

That evening, as Fred and I sat together looking through the travel literature, I told him casually, "984 is a Santa Fe exchange." I wanted to share with him the mystery which was beginning to unravel in my mind, even though I still wondered how much of it was only my imagination.

There was something else in the travel guide which attracted my attention. It drew my eye each time I flipped through the pages. Some land was for sale – a huge ranch. The description sounded magnificent! And I couldn't ignore the name of the place.

It was called Apache Mesa Ranch.

There was that name again: "Apache." Could this land be connected to me? Or, was I connected to it? My powers of reason were being challenged. Some general directions were given in the advertisement but not a specific location, so we pulled out the atlas to see what we could figure out. As we looked at the map, my attention was drawn to a small town outside of Santa Fe but, since I couldn't understand the attraction, I attempted to dismiss it. I was finding it difficult to acknowledge that these subtle feelings were my own intuition trying to be heard. The small voice of inner knowing I had artfully denied for so many years was struggling to come to life.

Fred and I both knew that we were embarking upon an adventure and prepared for our trip with great anticipation. We had carefully planned our agenda. The arrival and departure times at each city were fixed by an airline schedule, but the spaces in between were open blocks of time left free for discovery. We packed an eclectic assortment of things for the trip. We would be leap-frogging across the Southwest, making stops in the desert and in the Rockies, taking six flights before our return. It was the time of changing seasons, so we needed to anticipate almost any kind of weather. It would still be warm in Arizona, but Colorado could surprise us with an early October snow. We packed business attire and blue jeans, hiking boots and shorts, swimming suits, ski sweaters, and tour books.

I stopped packing and turned my attention to the crystal, picking it up as I sat down. What was it about this crystal which made it so special to our friend? I didn't understand. I heard Ashtar's voice again, now responding to my questions, "*Yes, dear one, the crystal is important. You will use it on your trip. You will know when and why. Do not question it. Keep it with you at all times from this day on, for it will bring you protection. It is a symbol to you of your connection, and you will know that we are with you.*"

It didn't matter where the thoughts came from, for I was aware that there was much I didn't understand. It had been just a month since I was given that first message about taking a trip somewhere. I turned my attention back to my task of packing and tucked the crystal away in my handbag. Fred and I felt ready for anything, two explorers with a treasure map in our minds, setting out in search of mysterious treasure. Who could know what we might find?

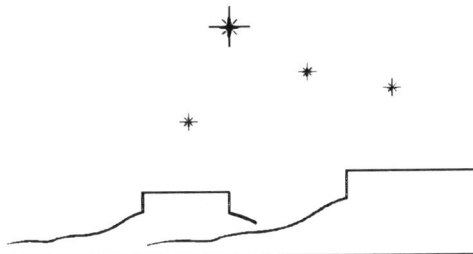

RUNNING DEER

I sat down on the edge of the bed in our hotel room in Mesa, Arizona. As I took the crystal from its green velvet pouch and placed it on the headboard, I remembered being here just a year ago at a convention for health-related products, a little side-business of mine. Something quite unusual happened to me on that trip which I had completely forgotten, and the memory of it now flooded back.

Fred and I had broken away from the business meetings and gone to spend the night with an aunt and uncle who lived in the town of Payson, about an hour's drive away. I was wakened that night feeling that a bolt of lightning had just shot through my body. The voltage ran through me in surges as I tried to steady my breathing. Was I having convulsions? Was this a heart attack? I gasped for breath as I wondered what was happening. Fred slept peacefully by my side, unaware of my struggles.

I had experienced something like this about ten years earlier when I was attending a communications workshop sponsored by the electronics firm where I was working at the time. We had been given an assignment to attempt to contact someone in the class telepathically when we went home and report on the results at the next session. I had experienced an electric sensation which seemed to have been the result of merging energies – but nothing like that was going on this weekend. I told myself that I was safe and that the feelings would soon pass.

The next morning, I told Fred about the energies I had experienced.

He leaned over and said, "You know, we are in Comanche territory. There are Indian reservations all around here. Maybe it was an Indian spirit trying to make contact with you." I realized that he was serious and, although I didn't really believe him, his explanation seemed as plausible as any. We didn't yet understand much about the spirit world. Could this be?

For the next three days, we participated in a whirl of convention activities. We dutifully attended product meetings, reunited with old friends, and made business acquaintances. We went shopping and out to dinner. All the while we were waiting for the scheduled hour when we could slip away and begin exploring.

Saturday afternoon finally arrived and Fred asked me, "Do you want to stay for the closing activities?"

I looked up at him, sensing his impatience with the meetings, knowing it was a mirror of my own eagerness to begin our adventure. "Uh uh," I shook my head, "Let's go."

Fred smiled in return. And we both spun around, mid-step, changing direction to go to our room where we quickly packed for our departure.

Soon we were driving north across the desert. Giant saguaro cacti dotted the landscape along the highway, and I felt a keen sense of anticipation. As soon as we turned off of the main highway onto the road to Sedona, the scenery abruptly changed. Instead of dry desert and barren land, green trees appeared and the pale shades of the desert turned to a deep red palette. The scenery was spectacular!

I started looking in the changing landscape for a mesa like the one shown in the vision as I nervously watched the first major rock formation come into view. There was a vibration here, an energy which quickened my internal flow and I could sense it with my entire being. This area was well known for its energy centers, known as vortexes. Many tourists came to marvel at the land. Others came to seek out the phenomena of unique energies from the earth reported in the area.

We both wanted to experience these energy centers to see what mysteries may be revealed. We bought a vortex map to help us explore the area and spent the next several days hiking around the rocks, sitting in meditation, and taking in the beauty of this unique area. Everywhere we went, I carried the crystal with me in its special pouch without understanding why.

We spent our days outside in walking communion with the earth and with each other, waiting for a sign that we were on course. Every evening we went to the edge of the mesa where we were staying to look out over the valley below, to watch the sun set, and each time wondering if this would be the sunset of my dreams.

On the last morning that we were in Sedona, we decided to hike to the top of one of the energy vortexes, Airport Rock, to watch the sun rise. It looked like a simple climb over one large rock by the side of the road.

We were bundled in our warmest sweaters as we began our trek in the chill of the pre-dawn darkness. The climb was actually much steeper than it appeared from the base of the rock. We walked up the side as far as we could, then debated which way to continue. I followed Fred's direction as we scaled across the face of the rock on a narrow four-inch ledge, loose pieces of shard falling with each step we took. We reached the center and had just ten feet left to climb over the top of the rock to reach the vortex, when fear overwhelmed me.

I had wanted to take the path which circled around the rock to the top, but followed Fred's lead up the path which led directly up the front. As we began the climb up the crevice, I tried to reassure myself, "Lots of other people have done this. You can do it too. Move through the fear." But with each step the loose shard beneath my feet slipped away. Then

I made a mistake. I turned my head to watch the pieces of rock falling below me. I panicked, "I can't do it!"

Fred could have climbed to the summit with ease. I didn't like being scared or holding Fred back. But he just said gently, "It's okay. We can find another way." He stepped back and down a couple of steps to the ledge, waiting for me to do the same. Then we scaled our way back across the face of the rock. We found a place to sit which was a wider shelf jutting out on the side of the rock formation. We were still quite high and facing the south side with a sheer drop-off of about 150 feet to the canyon floor below us.

I sat by Fred's side. Fears had surfaced to be released, and I allowed them to be replaced by the calm of the breaking dawn. Three crows flying in a circle broke their pattern and flew toward us. One passed directly in front of us, the other two flew below, and we looked down upon them as they glided by. We were perched in the territory of the winged ones and, in the stillness, I sensed a oneness with everything around us.

The long silent shadows of the rising sun cast themselves across the valley floor in shades of red and blue. The greens of the trees burst forth as the sun rose higher in the sky, and I saw three deer walking together on the mountain across from us. If only all of life could be this serene. I opened my journal and began to write my thoughts as they came, "Earth Mother. Sky Father. Great Spirit. Three crows. Three deer. Three points. The strongest form when joined. The connections can change and move, but the structure made of three points remains strong."

Why wouldn't I go to the top, to the greatest source of power? Am I afraid of reaching heights – the top?

Why?

And then, I wrote my own answer, "Much is expected of the one at the top. It takes much courage and confidence to get there, a trust in self and God. Know that you cannot look back. You cannot fear what is behind you or beneath you. You must keep your eyes focused on what you want to accomplish.

"Each one must choose, and each one must follow, their own path. Another's path may not be right for you. No one can reach their heights of glory on another's path. Know this for all."

What had been difficult for me was following the path which Fred had chosen, which was more direct but steeper than the one I would have walked.

"Do not choose a path for another – ever. Each will be guided. Others who share your alignment will join you in harmony. That is the way.

"Be yourself.

"Be a Light.

"Others will go their own way and will see their own missions. If all humanity shared one purpose, all could not be accomplished. Together, all is.

"Bless each one on his own way.

"How beauteous each is. How beautiful the whole. Remember this all your days. You can just be yourself and strive for the grandest flight."

I continued watching the deer on the mountain across from us. Six deer had now gathered. Then, without a sound, they all turned and ran away, disappearing quickly into the brush.

I remembered that this was Indian country. I had read that often Indian spirit guides work with people here, and I asked if I could know who was talking with me. Was there a Native American spirit giving me inspiration, challenging me and guiding me in this place?

In reply, as I listened to the wind, I heard the words, "This is Running Deer."

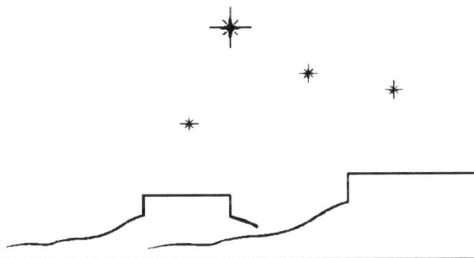

MORE CLUES

The time had come to leave Sedona, for there was a schedule to be kept. The energies we experienced here were of earth and of Spirit. We felt a shifting within us, a quickening to new awareness, the preparation of our cells to accept something new. Our agenda urged us onward to Albuquerque and to Santa Fe.

We drove around the countryside, criss-crossing the territory as though we were plotting the sections of a grid, taking in the sights, and trying not to miss a thing. The colors of the landscape were vibrant against the backdrop of the arid land which stretched for hundreds of miles. The altitude of the high desert made the blues in the sky seem bluer, the clouds reflecting light back to the ground below. Adobe buildings became more prevalent the closer we got to Santa Fe.

We went to the Indian marketplace on the Plaza to browse, arriving before the crowds which often filled the walkways. Native American craftspeople had spread their wares along the ground in front of the museum. They were bundled up in their handmade blankets and chatting over the cups of morning coffee they were drinking to counteract the morning's chill. Silver and turquoise jewelry, leather belts, and pottery were displayed along the sidewalk. Some of the jewelry depicted animals, and it occurred to me that it would be wonderful if I could find a deer to signify my experience with Running Deer in Sedona.

We didn't find anything at the Plaza, so we went to the artist's area on Canyon Road where we wandered into an Indian artifact store in an old adobe. There was a collection of animal fetishes in the display case. One in particular caught my eye. It was a silver deer – running! I held it in my hand. Its lines were soft and gentle. I was touched by its simplicity as I remembered my connection with Running Deer in Sedona.

I asked the owner, "What do you know about this piece?"

He replied, "This was a style of animal being made by the Navajos around 1945."

"Oh, my," I thought. "That was the year I was born." And then I asked, "How much do you want for it?"

"Forty-five dollars."

Its beauty and symbolism touched my heart, but it seemed extravagant. "I guess not," I said thanking the proprietor as I returned the pin.

I stepped outside to join Fred who was standing in the sun waiting for me. It was a beautiful fall day. Few people were about, and it was a relaxing stroll among the shops. We stepped down a steep set of stairs into another shop to browse. Nothing there.

I told Fred, "I'd really like to get the deer we looked at in that last shop. Do you think it would be okay?" I didn't want to leave Santa Fe without it. This was Running Deer, my totem animal running toward her spiritual destiny. The more I thought about it, the less practicality mattered.

Fred looked down at me and smiled as he put his arm around my shoulder. "Sure, let's go back and get it." He was pleased that I had found a treasure. We returned to the artifact shop to make the purchase. Fred pinned the deer over my heart as a symbol and a reminder to me about staying on my path. There was a silent understanding between us; magic was in the air.

Each evening we watched the skies for a special sunset. I was always looking for the mesa I held in my mind from the vision. There was a part of me that knew exactly where we were to go to find it, but apparently I needed to eliminate every other alternative first. My inner knowing had a subtle voice, so long ignored. I needed to test its worth.

Another last night had come – it was our last night in Santa Fe. This was the final opportunity for the sunset to appear. "If we're going to find that sunset, it has to be tonight," I told Fred. "I'd like to drive outside of town at dusk to watch. There's a little town to the east. Maybe we could head that way to find a spot with a good view." I felt that would be the place.

"It's too late."

"Phooey! We'd better try to find any place we can to watch it then," I said, glancing anxiously at the sky.

"All right," Fred replied, "We'd better hurry! The sun's already beginning to set." We got in the car and began driving, looking for an open space where we would have an unobstructed view. Would this be another disappointment?

Fred spotted a park with a baseball field, "Let's go out there to watch."

I agreed.

We walked out to the field where we sat and waited. The ground was damp and the air felt chilly as we sat together in center field, wondering and watching.

Then it began. The setting sun threw its colors across the sky, dancing brilliantly around the four corners – now South, now West, now North, now East. In each direction the sky took on a different hue. As I looked to the East, I saw what I had been looking for: The colors! The skyline! The horizon was ablaze. The sunset of my dream! It glowed a vibrant shade of pink, the color of summer geraniums. This was the direction we were to go. The sky was showing us the way.

We spent the night at an inn nearby and rose early, full of anticipation. Now was the time to call the phone number I had been shown in my mind the night I heard the voice telling me to go to the Southwest.

I closed the door to our room for privacy and dialed the number written in my journal.

The telephone rang as I planned what I would say to the person who answered. I would ask for an invitation to meet whoever it was. There would certainly be something for us to discover together.

The telephone rang a second time. I didn't care what the person thought. I would just tell them that I got this number in my dreams and was calling to find out why. Things were going smoothly. All was in order. They may think I was nuts but that would be all right. Certainly they could not refuse me. It would either seem so outlandish that their curiosity would compel them to invite me over, or they would know instantly that they had been waiting for me to contact them.

The telephone rang a third time and then it was answered. I held my breath as I waited to hear the person's voice on the other end of the line. "You have reached a number that has been disconnected or is no longer in service."

I pulled the receiver away from my ear and looked at it in dismay. I couldn't believe there was no one there to talk to! No one to give me some answers! Thoughts raced through my mind. I only knew it was a Santa Fe number.

I went back out into the living room, where Fred was talking with the inn's proprietor. "I've made my phone call to the number I was given."

"Well, what was it?" Fred attentively awaited my reply.

"Nothing."

"What do you mean – nothing?"

"No one was there. It was a disconnected number."

"Oh. You weren't supposed to talk to anyone."

"I guess not."

"Now we know we're on the right track."

"That's the only explanation I can think of. I think we may have reached our destination."

"Or, maybe someday we'll move here and that will be our number," Fred chuckled.

"Maybe. I guess we shouldn't try too hard to figure it out. It's a Santa Fe number. That's all that really counts."

I pinned the Running Deer to my sweater as I felt the breath of destiny. Fred called the number listed in the brochure to talk to the realtor for the Apache Mesa Ranch. She was a woman named Jan Gardner, who was also the owner of the land. Jan wasn't available.

We spent the morning driving around the country roadways with only the general location from the brochure. We had seen the sunset. Still, we didn't really know what we were looking for or even understand in the simplest way where these clues might lead us.

After we had been driving for a couple hours, Fred asked, "Do you want to stop and get something to eat? I'm getting hungry."

"Sure," I replied. "But there's not much out here. Any place you can find is okay with me."

Fred turned the car into the parking lot by a small adobe building, its whitewashed paint begging for attention. The red letters painted on the window read, "La Casita - Good Home Cooking."

"Does this look all right?"

I nodded. There was something we were looking for and chances were we'd have to get out of the car to find it. It would be good to talk to some of the local people. Everything about this area was so different from California. We could have been in another country. It was another culture. Another pace of life. Another set of realities. I wanted to know it and to understand it.

As Fred pulled the car around the side of the building and stopped, I saw something unexpected. "Look at that!" I exclaimed. "Look at that!"

Fred was mystified. "What?" he asked, stepping on the brakes.

I nearly jumped out of my seat, pointing in excitement at an old sign leaning against the building, its paint peeling from years of exposure to sun and wind.

"So?" he said, wondering what could be so exciting. "What about it? It's just an old sign someone threw away."

The sign was another trigger for me. I had seen this picture in a dream some time after I received the message to go to the desert. It was a man wearing a large sombrero, asleep against a saguaro cactus. A silhouetted figure was walking up to the sleeping man. I had wondered about the symbolism of this image. Was I the person asleep on the desert? Was I the person approaching? I couldn't understand and had discounted the images. The dream hadn't seemed significant enough to cause a second thought or mention. But there it was! I was seeing this same scene again, now painted on the sign. It was another clue encoded in my dreams waiting to be revealed. I began to know beyond all doubt that we were onto something. My senses became more keen and I felt that every person, every thing, I saw or touched could lead us to our destiny.

We were the only customers in the cafe. We ate chicken tacos, which were quite ordinary. But I was looking for something else – something unusual – and tried to have a conversation with the owner, hoping she would lead us to our next step. Nothing was revealed.

After lunch we continued driving, sensing we were near our destination and searching for something that would tell us we had found what we were seeking. We were thoroughly enjoying the beauty of the Sangre de Cristo mountains. We stopped the car and got out to walk, to be closer to the land, to sense its vibrations, to smell its fragrance, to listen to its voice.

But the shortness of our time pressed upon us, and we returned to the car to continue our search. We were driving down a dirt side-road on the outskirts of this little village when I saw it.

It was the mesa!

I told Fred, "That looks like it. I think this might be it." And then with more certainty, "That's it! That's what I saw." As I spoke, an eagle soared overhead across our path. I remembered the eagle soaring off a mesa in my meditation many weeks earlier.

This wasn't *deja vu*.

We had found the place!

We tried to find a way to get onto the mesa. For hours we drove around, attempting to approach it from all sides. There seemed to be no road. No entrance.

The treasure map had been revealed to us in pieces. Now we were there. We were sure we had found what we were looking for, but we were once again out of time. We needed to drive back to Albuquerque for a meeting we had scheduled at my brother's house, where we would spend the night. We would then leave on an early morning flight to Colorado Springs to visit my sister -- the "relative-visiting" part of the trip.

We asked each other: What was this all about? Why had we found what we were looking for just when it was time to go?

As we were driving back to town, I turned to look back. A large white cloud had formed over the mesa. It was unlike any of the other clouds. It was a compact pure white pillow in the sky. A shaft of brilliant white light was beaming from the cloud onto the mesa, as though the light was streaming down onto the land from the cloud itself.

"My God, Fred. Look at that!" I exclaimed. "It's a sign that we've found the place!"

He stopped the car and we both looked back in amazement. The shaft of light couldn't have been a reflection of the sun behind the cloud because we were facing east with the late afternoon sun behind our backs. We turned our heads and then, a moment later when we looked back again, we saw a second smaller cloud had appeared. It was jet black and sat directly in front of the larger white one.

Was this also a sign? Were there both positive and negative forces present? Darkness and Light? Was it being shown to us through these mysterious cloud formations? I tried to push the thoughts away. I was still trying to believe we had found the vision site from such a loosely woven set of clues. From the seed of, "Go you to the desert of the Southwest," we had found it, the one place in hundreds of miles of desert which matched the pictures in my mind. I certainly wasn't ready to deal with the notion of any forces in opposition to this quest. Our belief and trust were being kindled, but there was much we did not yet know or understand.

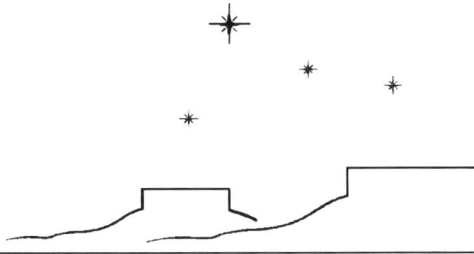

FLIGHT

We wanted to stay, to contact the owner of the mesa land and walk on it. We wanted to know more, but it was time to go – a schedule to be kept. We stopped at a gas station and tried once more to contact the realtor, Jan. This time she was in the office, and Fred spoke with her briefly about the land we had seen, describing where we had been.

When Fred got off the phone, he told me, "She said we were there!"

"At the land? The Apache Mesa Ranch?"

"Yes. She said there was no sign. That's why we couldn't find one. She said she could take us up tomorrow if we want."

"Wouldn't you know it? We have to leave in the morning. I can't believe it. We're so close." I was trying to understand what was happening. Were we really going to leave without completing what we set out to do?

Fred said, "We'll just have to make another trip back to see it."

"Did you ask her if she knew about the history of the land?"

"Yes. She said she didn't really know much. Just that the Comanches and Apaches have fought over this mesa for centuries. Many people have tried to buy it over the years but it hasn't been available. She's going to send us some information on it."

We were torn between our yearning to follow this puzzle to its completion and our need to follow through on the plans we had laid out for ourselves. I remembered a troubling dream from the night before. In it, our airplane was overloaded and flying in a snowstorm when it crashed in severe weather. But I saw that the road was lined with giant crystals and we would be protected if we drove. I was beginning to take my dreams more seriously now and, as I watched this quest unfold, I didn't want to fly. Even when we were making our reservations, this part of the trip hadn't seemed right. Going to Colorado Springs had been expensive and complicated from the very beginning. I remembered sitting in the travel agent's office saying, "Let's skip Colorado Springs," and feeling myself relax. Even then, I ignored the signals my own body had been trying to give me. Now, I wondered if we were supposed to continue.

I wanted to cancel our flight and drive to Colorado if we were still to go there. I wanted the flexibility of leaving when we were ready instead of being ruled by the airline's schedule. The tickets were, naturally, non-refundable. Reason said we shouldn't waste the money. Reason said we should stick to our schedule. Tomorrow was Fred's birthday and he didn't want to spend the day driving. But more than that, I didn't want to disappoint my sister by canceling the visit. She had moved away from California several years earlier and we had never been to see her.

For all these "logical" reasons we ignored our own desires and all the other messages we had been getting to change our plans and headed to Albuquerque where we had another business meeting scheduled, only to find when we arrived the meeting had been canceled. Another sign if we could only have understood it.

When we arrived in Albuquerque, we shared the story of the vision and discovery with my brother and his wife. It all seemed so incredible.

They asked, "Why don't you get up at 5:00 o'clock and drive back up to Santa Fe in the morning?"

"We have this flight to catch ... " I returned.

My brother shook his head in confusion, interrupting my response, "If something like that had happened to me, I wouldn't miss it. I'd be there at dawn. It's only an hour's drive – you could still be back for your flight at noon."

"I don't see how." Now I was shaking my head too. The magical feelings of being in the flow were disappearing beneath our feet and were now being replaced with a feeling of missed opportunities. The flow had attempted to take us to our destination quickly, but our course was straight and rigid; now we found ourselves scuffing along beside the river. How many of us walk our entire lives over rough terrain, persevering, struggling, never knowing that with the slightest turning we could step into the flow and have our paths become easier? But, at this time, we weren't flexible enough to change our plans or break our commitments, so we maintained our schedule.

The next morning an unexpected storm blew in. Severe weather conditions and traveler's advisories were issued on the news. Many flights between Albuquerque and Denver or Colorado Springs were being canceled. Our flight was posted with a two-hour delay. As I remembered the dream of the plane crash, I felt queasy. The significance of my dreams bore down on me, and I didn't want to go on.

The inbound flight finally arrived. I heard the pilot exclaim as he burst through the door, "It's wild out there! I'm not going back out until it calms down!" And he slammed the door to the office behind him.

The announcement was made: "Flight #62 will be delayed until 2:00 p.m."

Another hour's delay.

"Great," I thought. "Why don't they just cancel the flight if it's not safe?"

As we waited, Fred reassured me, "It's going to be okay. There's nothing to worry about. They fly in this weather all the time. We'll be perfectly safe." He must have thought I was being pretty silly, and I tried with all my might to dispel my fears. I thought, "Everyone waiting for this flight must have extremely urgent business to be traveling today." And I looked around, wondering about the story behind each person's need to get to Colorado Springs.

The voice coming over the loudspeaker brought my attention back to the terminal, "Flight 62 is now ready to board. All passengers booked on this flight may now proceed to Gate E." I took a breath and looked at Fred as the instructions continued, "This is to be a 'light load' flight. Each passenger may select one bag to take. The remaining baggage will be sent to your destination on a later flight."

"Well, at least the baggage will be safe," I grumbled as we headed to the luggage area where all the bags were queued for loading. We bent forward and clutched our jackets around our necks as we were escorted through the downpour out to the small 13-passenger, twin engine plane. I heard someone shouting to another member of the ground crew, "It'll be okay to take all the bags – another passenger just canceled."

"Great," I thought again. "They know they shouldn't carry any extra weight in this storm and they're pushing it." I wished I hadn't had that dream a couple of nights earlier. Fred seemed confident and unwavering, but the dream was playing itself out. I wished I had been strong enough to stand up for my own knowing and say I didn't want to fly. All indications were we should change our plans.

I crouched down to avoid bumping my head as I entered the plane. There was no divider between the cockpit and the passenger area, just two single rows of snugly placed seats. I chose the seat immediately behind the pilot, as though there would be some additional safety there, and secured my seatbelt as I squeezed into place.

They started the propellers. As the plane began its taxi to the runway, I closed my eyes and clutched the crystal in my hand, visualizing the plane surrounded by a white light of protection. I knew Fred was doing the same, even though he appeared calm and didn't speak.

The plane was buffeted by the wind during its ascent and visibility was obscured by clouds. The dense cloud cover would make it impossible to rise above the weather. It would be an instrument-only flight. The pilot reached behind his seat to get the airplane flight manual from the floor beneath his seat and grabbed my foot by mistake.

"This _is_ cozy," I thought.

I leaned over and whispered to Fred, "I don't care how much I've traveled, I do not like this – not one bit."

Throughout the flight I watched the radar screen over the pilot's shoulder, not fully understanding what I was looking at but knowing that the red splotches appearing here, then there, were areas we were avoiding.

"Turbulence," I thought.

I sensed the pilot's maneuvers as he watched the radar screen. It was like watching kids playing a video game with hazards popping up from out of nowhere when, suddenly, the entire screen turned red! We were in it. The copilot, who was checking the flight manual, threw the book to the floor and leaned forward in his seat at attention, every nerve and reflex on alert.

As I reached across the aisle and grabbed Fred's hand, I closed my eyes remembering my dream of crashing in a snowstorm. If this crystal in my other hand had any magic, now would be the time to have it work. Then, just as suddenly as we were in it, an area of green opened up on the screen and I could tell we were out of danger. The pilot and his co-pilot relaxed back into their seats and resumed their prior postures as they continued guiding the plane through the storm.

An hour later we landed safely in Colorado Springs. The pilot gently set the wheels of the plane to the ground as though the runway were made of fine porcelain. I was relieved that we had arrived safely. I thanked the pilots for their fine flying as we stepped out of the plane and quickly turned my attention forward.

It had been several years since I had seen my sister, and she hugged me tearfully as she handed both Fred and me winter coats. It was 17° as we walked through the gently falling snow to the car. I wanted to reconnect with Wendy. I wanted to be close to her in a way that we had never been. I was fourteen years old when she was born; our relationship had always been more like aunt and niece. I was just 19 when I married for the first time, so she was only five years old when I moved away from my parents' home and I had missed the camaraderie that sisters often share. She both revered and resented me, and I yearned to relate with her as equals. I wanted to tell her the story of our adventures and our treasure hunt. It seemed there was so much that had happened to us we couldn't explain. All of these thoughts whirled in my mind as I looked at her and her son, and I felt that the bonding that we could do would be worth the sacrifices we were making. They had no idea what it had taken for us to get there.

Before we even arrived at her house, Wendy gave us the disappointing news: "I have to work Monday. I tried to get the day off but they said 'No way.' I have to go to Denver to train a new employee. I'm sorry, but I couldn't get out of it."

Fred and I just looked at each other. All of the struggles over making the trip tumbled through our minds, and we saw clearly that this visit was somehow not supposed to have happened. In the instant of that glance, we shared our unspoken disappointment and acknowledged silently our understanding. There had been so many signs about being flexible, about changing directions as the plan revealed itself to us. So many signs we didn't heed.

We spent a pleasant weekend with my sister and nephew. But when Monday came, we wondered once again what we were doing there. My sister was at work. My nephew was at school. And Fred and I sat in the living room alone, thinking about the mesa in New Mexico. We had been guided to that spot for a reason and we wanted to complete what we had been sent to do. Time was too precious to be sitting around just waiting for it to pass. Simultaneously, we had the same idea: "Let's go back!"

We looked at each other with excitement. Maybe all was not lost!

I said, "If we could get back to Santa Fe, we could go back to the land. Maybe we could do what we really came to do."

Fred looked at the clock, "It's only 10:00 a.m. We could still do something with the day."

"Yes!" I eagerly replied.

I called the airlines. The price was double what we had already paid. It was out of the question.

Fred called Greyhound and reported his findings to me, "The bus to Santa Fe left at 9:00 a.m."

I called Amtrak and heard, "The train to Santa Fe leaves at 11:00 a.m.."

I hung up the phone and eagerly reported to Fred, "The train to Santa Fe leaves in one hour from Pueblo. Could we make it?"

"That's an hour's drive from here. And, you realize we don't have a car."

I didn't want to give up, "There must be a way! We could rent one."

Fred just shook his head, "We'd never make it in time. It looks like we're here for the day. We've exhausted every possibility."

We felt trapped by our own doing.

I said, "I guess we're just supposed to sit here and do nothing today," I pouted in disappointment. I wished we'd been more flexible.

"Well, there's nothing to do now."

"What do you think about this whole thing?"

"Do you mean today or the whole search?"

I answered, "I mean all of it. The whole business of having a vision and then actually finding the place?"

"I trusted your dreams and visions, so it was an exciting adventure to go and find the results of all the clues. It was a time when we were away from all the things which usually keep us locked in to our lives and our pasts. We were free to go exploring! We could let our logic go and follow our hunches, our intuition, and our visions. It was exciting to be able to do all that!"

I shook my head, "Spirit created such a grand construction for us and brought everything to a point where we could choose: the desire, the warning, the dream about driving under protection, the offer to go onto the land. We could have listened to all these things."

Fred replied, "Yes, I know. But finding the land was enough to establish our connection to it and to begin building our trust in the messages you were receiving. We'll just have to go back again."

The time for action had passed. We were now being given a time for rest and reflection, together and alone. It was actually quite nice once we settled into it. That afternoon we spent some time in meditation together and asked for guidance regarding our experiences in New Mexico. Our guides had been watching our activities and had seen our struggles, nudging us – now this way, now that – as our wondrous adventure unfolded. Now, at the end of the trip, they were waiting and, as we became quiet and opened our minds to hear their words, they spoke to us in channeled messages. In succession we listened to Archangel Michael, Ashtar, Sananda, and Archangel Gabriel, who all confirmed that, yes, we had found the place where they wanted to guide us.

We would be traveling all the next day on our return home, but we knew that we must one day return, for there was much in New Mexico that remained incomplete.

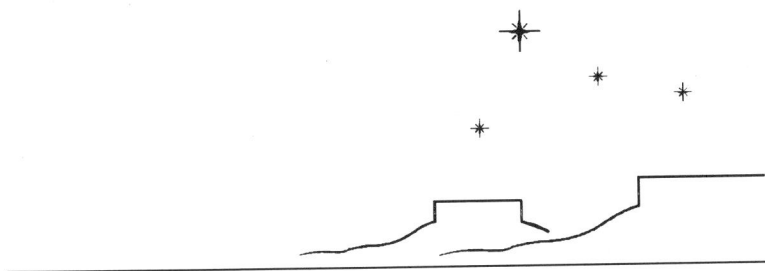

SOLTEC

On our way home we felt enlivened as we reveled in the delight of having found the mesa I had seen in my dreams. There was an exhilarating sense of freedom. We were in the flow and all was right. But once we were at home again, we wondered together: So what? What was all that about? Was it just a wonderful adventure arranged by some cosmic travel agency?

Certainly it wasn't arranged just for our entertainment! There had to be something more to it than that. We had taken a message from a dream and followed it 2800 miles. Every clue had found its place as we followed the signs to our destination. We knew there must be a reason we were guided to that spot.

We found out what happens when you follow your guidance, and we also found out what happens when you don't. We had learned many lessons about trust, about believing in ourselves and in our spiritual guidance. Wherever this guidance came from, it was real and it was to be honored.

I had brought home a token of our quest, the silver Running Deer. This would remain a symbol to each of us that we do, indeed, have a destiny waiting for us. We can run to it joyfully, as the deer, or we can ignore it and continue struggling at every turn of the road. The choice is up to each of us.

It had been difficult to see beyond our limits. What we once believed was the totality of existence was being challenged at every turn by very real experiences which were teaching us that there is more to reality than we had ever imagined. The old models of what we thought was possible were crumbling and we were trying to make sense out of the new.

I felt confused, as though I was wandering without direction. I thought I had in some way failed even though I didn't know what I was supposed to do. But I knew it was incomplete.

We told the story to a few people whom we thought would be interested. What a disappointment when they didn't understand the significance of what had happened! I told myself, "Remember Running Deer who is now with you and the importance of following your own path. Your quest doesn't need to be validated by anyone else."

Fred and I had both been greatly affected by the experiences on this trip. New possibilities were opened to us. We knew our joint missions were intricately intertwined – planned long, long, ago, perhaps even before this lifetime – and that there was a purpose beyond our understanding for having come together as a couple. We began to spend more time in meditation, expanding our ability to communicate with our guides. During the months that followed, we worked long ardent hours writing a book which delivered the message that spiritual guidance was available to all who would take the time to listen. We were becoming more aware of the importance of having this source of personal strength in our changing world, and we hoped others would benefit from the techniques we taught in our meditation classes.

In the evenings, we often sat quietly in the living room, trying to create the space for our guides to contact us. Our family was around and yet apart from our activities. One night, my son and daughter were in the kitchen, making a bedtime snack of nachos and cola, their laughter disrupting our stillness.

Fred cleared his throat in frustration, "I guess this isn't the time."

"Guess not. I'll go see what they're doing." I walked out to the kitchen and helped myself to some chips. "What are you guys up to?"

"Just getting something to eat. I had a study group after school and didn't get any dinner," Kari replied. Her long blond hair fell past her shoulders as she reached for another nacho, and she laughed as she recalled one of her day's events at the University. She was strikingly attractive, so exuberant and full of life. "What are you guys doing?" she asked.

"Just a little meditating."

"Yeah, they're talking to their unseen friends," our son, Drew, replied. I sensed his struggle. He was curious, but it all seemed too strange for him to accept.

"Do you think that's a good idea?" Kari asked.

"Oh, yes," I replied, "when we listen we can hear the answers to our questions."

"Well, I don't understand what this channeling stuff is all about. I wouldn't want to have some other entity enter MY body. Thank you, no!"

"It's not sharing your body in a real sense. Channeling is more a way of listening to information coming from other dimensions. You know, there's a lot more going on here than we can normally see. I told you about that trip we made and the land we found. That was pretty miraculous. It made me a believer in this guidance."

Both kids listened. Had their mother lost her grip on reality? I continued, "When you channel you make a connection so you can receive telepathic information. It's like listening to a radio. You have to take precautions so you don't get involved with negative influences. But we always ask for Archangel Michael and Jesus to be present with us and protect us. The psychic connections are easily severed. We're merely acting as an interpreter and speaking the words for those beings that cannot speak them directly. We do not assume their identity. When we're finished, the receiver is turned off, just as the television program stops when you change the channel."

They both looked at me incredulously. I could tell they were trying to understand what they were hearing, and I continued, "We always have our own minds and our own discretion in place to decide whether to accept or reject what we hear. It may actually be our own higher wisdom which we are bringing up to our consciousness, or it may be entities we cannot see trying to communicate with us. I don't understand everything yet, but I know it's real.

"Sometimes people attempt to take on the identity of the beings whom they are channeling, to hold it and make it their own. This is not a correct use of the energies. The beings we listen to are here to assist and guide us. They are not here to take over. We always have our own free will."

They had heard enough.

"Let's go watch TV."

They both agreed.

The dance continued between realities. There was the old way of doing things, old concepts and understandings. Then there were the new awarenesses pressing to be understood and integrated. Intellect and intuition worked together to make enough sense of our new knowingness to enable us to reasonably discuss it with others. The concern of our children challenged us to be clear and to question often enough so that we no longer had any doubts about what we were experiencing.

One evening shortly after that, the kind and loving energies of the angels descended upon us. This time, it was Archangel Raphael who reassured us, *"God has arranged all of the circumstances in your universe to be exactly the way they are at this time for a reason known only to Him. Each person will be presented a view of the choices before them as clearly and in as much detail as they are able to accept. Other choices will be presented in sequence. This is how we strike a balance between forcing your growth and allowing it to unfold without influence. We give you information and opportunities, and then we wait. You are allowed to choose based on what you understand. You will get more choices if you wish them, but the next choices will be based on the ones you are making now. We do not, indeed we cannot, choose for you. We cannot compel you. We cannot even impel you. All we can do is send our messages and illuminate you with our Light as we allow each being to make his or her own choice."*

We reflected again on the choices we had made when making the trip to the Southwest and hoped that we would have another opportunity to complete what remained undone there.

In our meditations and channeling, we had grown to trust a group of Ascended Masters. When they communicated with us, there was always a sense of loving energy and caring guidance present.

It was December 12th, 1990. Fred and I sat down in the living room for some time of quiet meditation. The world was in turmoil with threats of a world war looming as the world's leaders struggled to proclaim their power in Iraq. We closed our eyes and relaxed. I was expecting the now-familiar gentle exchange of healing energy – some words of inspiration. I was confident as we asked for the protection of the Light.

Suddenly, I felt my head rotate around in a circle and fall back. A strong energy from an unknown source had moved my body but I could not move it on my own. I could not even speak. I had been paralyzed by the power of an overwhelming forcefield, and I was swept with fear at the realization of my own vulnerability.

"What is this?" I gasped. I tried to breathe deeply and calm myself. I had never before experienced such an awesome power. I knew we had established our protection, as always, before starting. I tried to find out what was going on. I remained sitting on the sofa looking up at the ceiling, unable to raise my head. My arms lay limply at my sides as I heard a male voice speak the words, "*I am Soltec, interplanetary commander of the starfleet forces operating under the Ashtar Command.*"

Who was this? I didn't know Soltec. Were the energies that had overtaken me really those of a space commander!? My fears again rose up. I did not know I was safe.

I wanted to communicate with Fred who was sitting across from me on the other sofa. My eyes remained closed as I tried to tell him what was happening and I haltingly described the sensations I was experiencing, "My head feels so heavy. I can't lift it."

My voice trembled in terror as I whispered, "It's as though someone has unplugged me and there's no energy running through my circuits." My voice was faint and labored as I formed the words, "I can not move my arms."

Fred sat attentively by my side. After some time, I managed to raise my head briefly, but I still couldn't hold it up. The intensity of the energies continued to bear down on me and my head, like that of a rag doll, quickly fell back again. As I gently slid my body down so that my head could be supported by the sofa cushions, I heard Fred's reassuring voice trying to dispel my fear as he softly affirmed, "We are protected by the Light."

His reassuring words continued, "The Light surrounds us with a shield of invisibility and all forces not in alignment will depart. Archangel Michael stands by our side with his powerful sword and brings us his protection. Sananda is with us."

My breathing relaxed a bit as I slouched out on the sofa, and the words from Soltec resumed in my mind, *"We want you to go on a mission with us."*

What in the world was *this* about? I did not speak these words as I heard them but kept them to myself, waiting to hear more. Thoughts raced through my mind as I wondered about the possible meaning of this message, "Do they want to take me away?" Fears welled up within me as, in my mind's eye, I watched a doorway of light appear before me.

"That's it!" I exclaimed to myself. "I'm not going anywhere with a space commander!"

My Will snapped me back to consciousness and I regained control of my muscles. As I sat up, Fred and I looked at each other in confusion. I had not in any way been harmed. I was glad that I was safe – and with Fred. He came over and sat next to me, putting his arm around my shoulders, "What was that?"

"I don't know," I shakily replied. "It was the strongest energy I've ever felt. I was completely immobilized!"

I was exhausted from the experience of this unfamiliar energy, but Fred wanted to find out what it was about, "Would it be okay if we continued? I'd like to get more information about what was going on."

"It's okay if you want to, but I'm finished." I just wanted to lie down and rest.

Fred asked for reinforcement of our protection and asked that Ashtar join us to explain what had happened. Our connections were strong and Fred's request was answered immediately as he spoke the words, *"Hello. This is Ashtar speaking."*

I asked, "Ashtar, will you tell us more about yourself?"

"I am the commander of a great exercise which is about to occur on your planet and the coordinator of a host of very able assistants who serve under the name of the Ashtar Command. I come from a neighboring world which was similar to yours and went through the evolutionary processes there which your planet is about to undergo. The Ashtar Command has been serving near your planet for thousands of years. It is a vast undertaking. We have the spiritual guidance which is like a network that connects us together so we can be highly coordinated and organized with nearly no overt communication. All humans have this same potential. It is very important that you get your own agendas out of the way enough so that you can be open to all the clues and hints that we are giving."

We were glad to sense his familiar presence as he began to speak. Even though I don't remember the details of the rest of this communication, there was one sentence that stuck with me. In the middle of a long discussion, he said, *"We want you to go to Peru."*

"Peru?" I had asked in disbelief.

"Yes," was the reply. There was something they wanted us to do there and, although further details were given to Fred, the remainder of the message was overshadowed by my experience of the visit from Soltec. I hadn't shared with Fred the words which I had heard about going anywhere or doing anything. Our guides, however, were determined to get

the message across (one way or another), and now delivered it to Fred. The mission was to Peru.

The notion of going to Peru was strange to us. In fact, it seemed absurd. But now we had each received a request independently, on the same evening, to go on a mission.

After a few days to assimilate this new information, we wanted to learn more. We continued to call upon our guides. The vision and the mystery were turning into an adventure driven by a compelling unseen force. In response to our call, Ashtar's presence came into the room, "*I have been waiting to see the results from the experiment. You get a grade of B+. We're trying to widen your horizons and broaden your experiences. We are preparing you, molding you, because you have given us your permission to do this. It is true that we are using you, but you have asked us to do this so we are going ahead. We have an agenda and activities lined up for many people on the planet.*

"*Soltec is a mighty messenger. He and his workers assist us in all of our tasks. Now, it has come to the point for you to get moving. There are events in the world that are not waiting. So, we cannot wait. We cannot let you take all the time you would like to remain in your comfort zones but must push you, and those others who can accept it, faster than is completely comfortable for them. So, you will be going on a trip to the Andes.*"

"To South America?" I asked.

"*Yes. South America is correct. Can you believe it? There is a pyramid there that Soltec told you about which is an energy point on the planet. We see the fifth dimensional part of this pyramid as White Light. To you it would be gray or greenish stone. It's in a jungle.*

"*You will not stay long. You will find out some things, meet some people, then return forthwith for the next stage of your journey. The country that you will go to is Peru. It is true that they are having some political difficulties there now but you will not be involved in any of that. We will be protecting you and shielding you. It will be as though you are invisible from their governmental authorities and anyone who might wish to do* _you harm. There is an Incan connection there. This pyramid and others around it were constructed by the Incas with some direction from higher sources who had understanding of how power is handled and transmitted on the planet._

"There is an energy gridwork around Earth which is expanding. We are helping to expand it. This is the new electromagnetic body of the planet. It is like a crystal that grows to a new shape. It jumps from one stage of growth suddenly to the next. It is not a continual process, but intermittent, growing in a step-wise fashion. New facets of this crystal are coming into alignment and will soon be visible.

"You will bring back some of this energy to a new spot in your country. It is similar to lighting one candle from another. The flame is already burning in Peru. You will light the candle, which is yourselves, from the one that is burning in Peru, and you will bring this light back so that you can ignite the new crystal point in the United States. Indeed, it is in New Mexico. Have you seen anything in New Mexico that looks like a pyramid?"

I thought about our trip to New Mexico and also of the mesa where we had been guided. Was there a view of the land which revealed a pyramid? Perhaps.

Ashtar went on to explain where the pyramid was located and how it would have appeared to us on our trip. _"Inside of the energy body of the mesa that you found is a potential pyramid that needs to be lit. It may be that you will bring something back from Peru, some artifact, that will serve to anchor the Light in this pyramid. It may be that you will take this artifact and bury it on the land. This land will be available to you. You will not even have to purchase it. We have someone there now who is a placeholder for you. It is a being called Dartan. It is for you that Dartan awaits._

"Although Peru is a great distance away, it will be a great adventure. It will be something completely new for you both to do together. You may stay a week. You will not stay longer. It will not be necessary. We are doing this in other places in the world. You need not personally concern yourselves with the events in the Middle East or Europe at this time. This is not your task. However, it is the catalyzing effect of this war that is *causing us to shake as many Light Workers as we can, as many of those committed to bringing more Light onto the planet as will listen to us. This will be the most fun that you have ever had. It will be an extraordinary adventure. Do you think that you can do it?"*

This all seemed incredible to both of us. What was being asked of us was overwhelming, even in light of our recent experiences. We had come to accept the existence of other dimensions and of beings existing in them. Now the challenge would be to bring that awareness into reality in our lives in a very real way.

We would need some time to integrate this new information and to comprehend what was being asked of us. We began the process of sorting through our feelings. Hadn't we learned our lesson about trust already when we found the land which was shown to me in the vision? Still, I questioned my own ability to proceed, and responded, "Well, Ashtar, I am a bit afraid of new things."

"You're not really afraid of new things! Not really. You are afraid of the idea of new things. You are afraid of being afraid." Ashtar continued, *"Not all new things are so fearful. Just think. It will be Peru! You will have to trust this one who will come to you. Once you do this you will be on your path and on our path for you. You will go empty and you will come back full. This task will elevate you in ways that you do not think possible."*

There was something very compelling about this message which Fred had been receiving. He said, "I felt like my brain was exploding. The energy was familiar but it was more intense than it's been before. It was all I could do to allow the information to flow without stopping it."

Ashtar continued, as there were more details to impart, *"Now it is time to spread the flame. We are trying to start a fire of Light on your planet. The more places that we can make into physical Light receptors, the easier it will be for the people who are within the influence of the resonating grid that exists between the power points to come into the Light on their own. By using Earth and beaming our energies down to these power points we can recharge the battery of Earth a little bit. This battery of Earth will, in turn, charge the humans. It is a way for us to do our blasting from within. So, we get you from the top down and from the bottom up. This blasting is an electromagnetic and electrochemical blasting of the subtle energy bodies of Earth. We have done this many, many, times to readjust and calm Earth's energies in times of earthquakes and volcanoes to lessen their effects. We are not always successful in doing this as the physical Earth is not completely in alignment with this electrochemical grid. However, Earth is coming into alignment with the grid at this time. That is what Earth's ascension means.*

"The third dimensional part of the Earth will recede. It will be transformed and, as a crystal makes the jump of growth with new facets and becomes larger than it formerly was, Earth will grow new facets of its own. We are helping to select the spots that will be most efficacious when Earth is ready to pop into its new existence. This place that you know in New Mexico will be a point between several facets and you are going to light it. Then, in a sense, this place will always be a part of you. Have no doubts that you will be forever changed.

"You will try to look at this from your past perspective and say you cannot go to Peru. It is outside your experience. We have waited, though, to tell you what your mission was until such a time that you would believe us. We gave you a little scare earlier (when Soltec first came) and you feared bad things were happening. You were not sure where you were or who was communicating with you. Then, you found out it was just another good guy."

This made me angry and I retorted, "You were playing with us!"

"We are playing with you all in a certain way but our purpose for doing this is quite serious. We can't come to you and be serious, nor can we sit down and say, 'Here is our plan for the rest of your lives.' You wouldn't be able to accept it. So, we have to judge. We do have some superb guidance ourselves in Sananda and the angels. They say to us, 'Now is the time you may give them a little more communication. Now you must wait; they could not handle it yet.'

"You know that you are ready for another step now. We do not wish to traumatize you; we do not wish to shake your beliefs or even disturb your flow. These things will not happen immediately but you have already been to New Mexico. You have already made the first step, and it was fairly easy for us to arrange because you already wanted to go

there. We just arranged for you to visit a place we were particularly interested in having you see. So, now your destination will be familiar the next time you go back.

"We did not tell you about Peru before now and you can surely guess why. You will have to think it over. See if you can do it. We think you can. We will send you signs and as you gather your questions we will attempt to answer them to your satisfaction."

I told Ashtar, "I'm still having difficulty believing this information."

"There is still some leaping to be done on your parts."

"Yes. And, do you have a pogo stick for us?"

Ashtar began to laugh. *"This is why faith is important. The challenge you had when Soltec introduced himself to you was a test of faith. And, yes, you passed. It was a test of taking new and unfamiliar energy from a being whose energy you had not felt before and who came to you unannounced. It was new and scary for you; but if your faith was tuned-in to our protection, you would have known without the chills going up and down your back that we would not let anything untoward happen to you. Now it is time to say good night. We will speak again in the morning. Remember, God is with you."*

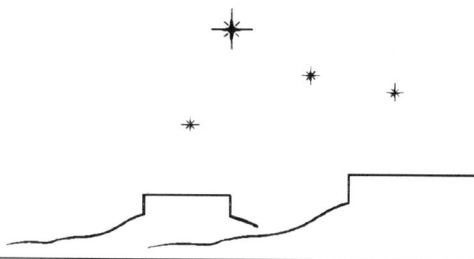

GRIDWORK

We knew from a very deep place within that we wanted to accept this assignment and sensed that we would be helping the planet and humankind by doing so. We continued to have many questions as we tried to understand more fully what it was we were a part of, and our communications with Ashtar, Sananda and Soltec increased as a result of our desire for more information.

The next night Ashtar returned. "*Hello,*" he announced his presence through Fred, "*We want to say something tonight about your paths. We want you to understand what we have been asking you to do so you can see where we all stand and what the next steps might be. As you know, we have asked you to help us establish the grid of Light that will guide planet Earth into its ascension. Some of the points of the new Light Grid are above the current surface of the globe, as the new surface of Earth will be slightly larger than the current surface. There are one or two anchors that we will have to provide, such as those anchors over oceans, but the land anchors are all being done by individuals such as yourselves.*

"Indeed, this is a very large scientific undertaking. When we say scientific, we mean something that is much broader than when humans use the same word. To us, scientific means a melding of what you call physics, chemistry, mathematics and so on, with what you call religion, or God, or metaphysical ideas. We have a scientific-spiritual undertaking to create a grid of Light that Earth will use when it forms its new body. The old body will be filled with Light of a much greater intensity than it has now. This will change its constitution. Its chemical structure will be different. Its size will be slightly different due to the tremendous influx of real light that Earth has called for herself.

"We will now talk more specifically about this grid of Light. We have spoken before about many places on the planet where Light will be received from our dimension. You can visualize these locations as places where the veil between dimensions will, for a time, be made to disappear, allowing the full intensity of the Light to come in at these points and be absorbed by Earth. It is only with a geometrically regular arrangement of such points on the surface of your globe that Earth can stay in balance during the actual infusion of Light. Were only one point chosen, Earth would suddenly become so unbalanced and unstable that it would likely explode. We do not wish this to happen.

"These points of the future Light Grid are places where the veil between dimensions is already quite thin. Earth needs some stability at these points, a way to focus the Light. This is for the benefit of Earth itself, particularly the outer layers, and the beings existing on the surface.

"It is the entire planet that will be ascending as the Light is drawn into it. This is a process you could compare to osmosis, where a fluid of one kind passes through a thin membrane and then diffuses on the other side. The membrane is this veil of perception. The fluid passing through the membrane is the Light. What we wish to do is to control it, concentrate it, and begin running this Light energy down into the Earth to distribute it to the beings who desire it: humans, animals, trees, plants, the very rocks and soil.

"The benefit for yourselves in strengthening and expanding the foundations of your Light Body are very substantial. Letting the Light pass through you and being vehicles in service of the Light is the highest calling that one may accept. Indeed, we who are assisting you have all accepted this calling unhesitatingly.

"As Light Workers begin to awaken, they too will begin to realize their nature of service. I believe that if you look at your emotions you will find the prospect of being of service is one for which you have growing enthusiasm. If this is truly your wish, Archangel Michael is indeed the Being to whom you may address your desires to loosen your limitations. We know you are endeavoring to do this. Once the first limitation is loosened and gone, its very absence creates room where more change can occur. Each time this happens, the possibility for change is increased and the realization of change becomes easier."

I asked, "Ashtar, why do you need us to make connections on the Light Grid when you are so powerful yourself?"

Ashtar responded, "You are just as powerful as we are, even though you do not know it. You have landed on this sphere to do a task. This process of strengthening must go from both sides. We cannot build a bridge to your side without using you to anchor your half. We cannot come and assist you in doing this, so you must do it on your own. This is the main advantage to you on your ascension path. You are doing this of your own free Will and this will stand you in good stead. It is about God's Will; it is about remembering what your volunteer service was in the beginning. Not many will have their beings so illuminated on such scanty evidence.

"There will come a time when we will come and do certain tasks but that time is not ordained yet, so we must wait. When it is time, permission will suddenly exist in the Light and all beings who exist here in our dimension will know it has been given instantaneously. It is much like, during a warm spell when a sudden cool breeze can be experienced at once by a family on a picnic. Everyone knows at the same time that it has just gotten much cooler. It is in this way that everyone in our dimension knows that a certain event is to occur."

"Can you give us more information on the purpose of the Grid?"

"It is plugging Earth into the celestial energy patterns. It's like a transfusion, like connecting wire from the sky to the Earth so that the kind of energy which exists here on the fifth dimension can be transferred to Earth. This will make Earth's ascension swifter and easier. The grids are to balance Earth's energy in the coming times. Instead of a local upheaval affecting one spot, the energy of that upheaval can be spread out so that its effects are less drastic.

"It is like induction. Human beings can absorb the energy when they are near the energy points. Then, as people move around on the planet, this new grid of energy transceivers will be shunting energy around from one grid point to another, making a whole that is appropriate for Earth to have. This is the only way we can assist Earth and its humans at the same time. There are places which this must be done first, such as the ancient spots where the pyramids were built in times past. After those are erected and established, it is necessary to go to the secondary spots and the tertiary spots so that energy can be distributed."

I had not yet assimilated the information which had already been given but continued with the questions, "Are the configurations of the new gridwork available to man's understanding?"

"Eventually. There will come a time when this information can be introduced, bit-by-bit, but we cannot let this knowledge out now. When the grid is completed it will make it easier to move between dimensions. Soltec is one of the primary architects of this plan for energy transfer and distribution, which is why he chose to make himself known to you in conjunction with our introduction of the plans about bringing the energy from Peru to New Mexico. Now, we would like you to do these preparations:

1) You must keep a rigorous schedule of meditating twice a day. You can keep your circuits charged with the Light by doing this.

2) We want you to write down or remember every doubt or question regarding any of this. Your conscious cooperation and understanding are required if you are going to do these active tasks that we have set for you. There is to be no more mumbo jumbo. No more doubts or second thoughts are needed.

3) We wish you to understand that we need to let you know as soon as possible what we expect of you, which is to begin the process of unhinging yourselves from those things that are holding you where you are. It may be most beneficial to call on Sananda in times of hesitation and doubt, as he can come to you on a level that we cannot due to his experience on Earth. His spiritual Light is so strong, we are aware of it constantly. As you have been growing in your own awareness, it can be a very powerful asset to you now.

"So, this is your program. Bring your concerns to the forefront. It is not good to suppress them and hide them away because that just delays your inevitable development, and it is the inevitable that we are relying on. The only things that will defeat you are your own fears. Once the seeds of fear have been planted they can grow out of proportion. The angels will help you to see that your fears are nothing more than wisps from the mind. The angels are so clustered around and happy for you. Archangel Gabriel sends his presence to you and this will continue."

This was a long communication and Fred, who was channeling, was weary from holding a focused energy. The assignment which was being asked of us was pressing. Over the months which followed we maintained our lines of communication so that we could learn more, each of us intent upon fine-tuning our skills of receiving information. We had started taking turns: one of us would receive the communication and speak the messages as the other would ask questions.

Archangel Michael told us, *"We want people to be awake and to pay attention to our messages, but it is quite difficult to get them to give us this attention without interfering with their free wills. So, we work with many people a little bit at a time. Sometimes we arrange signs for them. But this takes a great deal of time for you humans to figure out. We do not have the luxury of this any more, and we are trying to make the signs stronger to oblige those who are awake on the planet now. Small groups have been used for many years to pass these traditions forward by word of mouth, but this is quite slow and we need a faster means of communication now."*

We learned that there was a great unfolding of history occurring. We talked with many people who noticed things rapidly changing around them and within them. There was an intensity in their lives and in their relationships as the pressure from the forces of change began to cause discomfort and upheaval. Most of them had no idea what was causing their stress and couldn't understand their feelings. Almost everyone we talked to knew with certainty that something was happening. It was a time of planetary evolution.

Frequently, I had to remind myself about the lesson in trust which we received on our journey to the Southwest, and I knew that I must keep going forward in spite of the continuing intrusion of doubt. I sometimes felt confused and disoriented, like a toddler just learning to walk – trusting, stumbling, and then picking myself up to try again. We were trying to walk a path for which there were no road signs to guide the way, and we began to rely more and more on the only guidance we had – spiritual guidance from the higher dimensions.

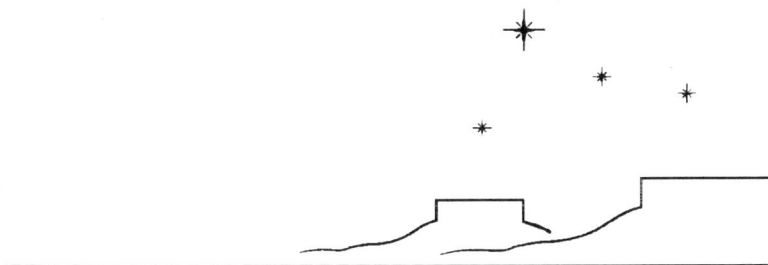

A Sign

Fred and I both felt the urgency of what was being asked of us. But there had been nothing like this in our experience, and we continued to have reservations about its validity. Sometimes I was attacked by my own disbelief. Sometimes it came like an errant vehicle racing down the highway which suddenly appears in the rear view mirror from out of nowhere. I didn't see it coming, but there it was, threatening my progress.

Each night before I went to sleep, I asked for confirmation of the nature of this guidance. "If this is not in alignment with Divine Will, please, I beg you, give me a sign. My intentions are pure and honest and I do not wish to be led astray."

None came.

Again, I asked in earnest, "I pray to you Masters that I trust, I pray to the angels, I pray to Jesus, I pray to God, I pray to anyone who has been accepted in my past understanding as providing guidance between right and wrong. Please give me a sign so that I no longer have to question! Is this work which is being asked of us in alignment with Divine Will?"

With lingering requests for guidance, I pulled the covers up around my neck and prepared to sleep. That night my dreams were vivid and detailed, a reflection of this struggle. In them, I was trying to get somewhere, although I couldn't see where I was going. I was disoriented. I knew I needed to get home and that there was nothing to do but keep going. I stopped at someone's house to tell them about my quest. It was a family, doing family stuff. The parents were preparing dinner while the children played. I tried to show them a video to explain the information that I wanted to share but the video player didn't work. "I guess I'll just have to tell them myself and see if they believe me," I thought.

I reluctantly told them about the space brotherhood and the project which was underway, thoroughly expecting them to laugh at my foolishness. They listened politely and then they told me that they already knew.

They believed me! They knew! I didn't think anyone else knew about this. Outside of the house again, I looked up at the night sky in amazement. It was full of spaceships. There were lots of them flying around. They didn't seem to be doing much except pausing to display themselves. They didn't look the way I expected. The ships were appearing and flying toward me; stopping, posing, turning. Was this an air show arranged for my benefit?

"Come out! Come out!" I called to the people in the house.

The family came outside and everyone saw the ships, but I was more surprised than anyone to see the spectacle in the sky. Then, on the horizon, a twin rainbow appeared. Its colors were almost iridescent against the black backdrop of the midnight sky. The rainbows made narrow arches which stood side by side, ending in pinwheels of turning color, sparks flying onto the horizon as they spun.

"It's true! It's true!" I shouted, "The rainbow! I have seen the sign.!"

Awaking from my dream, I sat upright in bed and turned on the light. The realization of the truth held me with vivid clarity as the words, "It's true!" repeated in my mind.

"Well, there you have it," I thought. "You asked for a sign. You asked to be shown if you were being led astray. There was nothing elusive or vague about this dream. You now know that all this is true. You <u>must</u> listen to your answer!"

So I began to develop the confidence to share our story and the new information we were receiving.

I first told our friend, Kate, who immediately sensed its importance. Kate had always believed in things which were magical and had no doubts that what we told her was real. She wanted to be a part of this adventure and began to join us whenever she came to town.

Kate had studied for years to become a minister, and at her ordination was gifted the crystal she had given us before our quest. It continued to sit on my night stand, but I had not developed a connection with it. I knew the crystal was a gift, but I didn't feel it belonged with me; I kept thinking about how much it meant to Kate, and I wanted to return it to her. The next time she came over, I placed it in her hand. "I think the crystal is supposed to be with you."

Her affection swelled as her eyes fell upon the crystal, "Oh, I was really wanting to have 'Crystal' back, but I couldn't ask because I had given her to you."

"Maybe we were just to take it on the trip," I explained. "I think it really belongs to you."

Kate rejoiced at having the crystal returned, clutching it to her heart as she confided, "I was afraid I wouldn't be safe without her because I know she has given me protection over the past several years. I knew it was time for you to have her... but I've really missed her."

She laughed a little at herself as she contemplated her attachment to this special crystal, "It felt good for me to give her to you because I knew I was following my Truth, even though my human self was lagging behind my knowing and I felt a sense of loss."

Kate continued, trying to describe her feelings, "I really like knowing that I'm following my guidance, regardless of what emotions – like separation, fear, or attachment – come up for me. I know that the emotions are just a part of my own unfolding, and have to do with things like attachment or ego; I try to put these emotions into perspective with what my inner knowing says must be done."

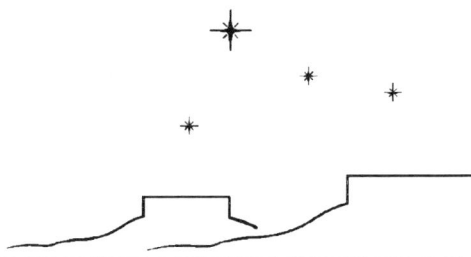

Pieces

We continued receiving more pieces of information as rapidly as we could accept them. As soon as we had almost assimilated one, another was thrown our way. We came to understand that there was much work to be done by every person for themselves, their families, and for the planet.

"*Hello. This is Ashtar.*" The words interrupted Fred's concentration on the book he was reading. He looked at me sitting across the room and said, "Ashtar wants to talk to us."

I turned my attention to Fred who had shifted his awareness and was now ready to speak Ashtar's message, "*I have been pushing you; it is true. I am generating in you a sense of duty that you committed to prior to this lifetime. It is a little scary, though, being out on the limb when you are asked to do things that are a bit uncomfortable. We are sorry about this in a way. We do not wish to traumatize you; we do not wish to shake your beliefs. We do not even wish to disturb your flow. However, there are some things you must do if you are to use your capabilities. You know, there are very few people that we can call on to be of this level of service.*

"I am referring to the things that we asked you to do the other day. We would still like to send you to Peru, if you are willing to go. I know it sounds outrageous, never having done anything like this before. If you could see all of the plans from the past into the future, it would not seem at all unusual.

"When you find that you can no longer go on and that you have doubts, you should immediately center yourselves; call on us for clarification and strength. Remember, these are missions you volunteered for – although you have naturally forgotten. You have declared it your duty to help us in these ways and you are beginning to wake up to that realization. There is much you can do. There is much you want to do. And, there is much you should do. We are just telling you what your hearts decided before you incarnated on this planet.

"The scope of your activities has been enlarged now. It's going to be easier than you think. In fact, it is as if we've been lining up logs, and all you have to do is to fall off of them, one after the other. It will be fun. The only problem now is getting you out of your familiar surroundings and letting us show you what some of the new concepts are. You can see and feel that we are trying to help you. There is nothing we have ever asked you in the past that has been against your own deepest wishes. Soltec, he was a funny one. He naturally has a very strong presence because he is very adept at tuning in to individual minds. He operates with pinpoint accuracy."

Some evenings it seemed as if the Masters were lined up waiting for us to dial them up; it was like making a conference call back home as they talked to us one after the other across the inter-dimensional communication lines which had been established. We were always ready to learn more. Another evening it was Kuthumi (another Ascended Master who has spent many lifetimes on this planet) who sent his energetic presence forth, *"Hello, this is Kuthumi. My heart is full of love for you and for your family. There is an Indian warrior who grows impatient now. There had been a promise that his land would be protected and used in accordance with the Chief in the sky, that the eagle feathers could spread and the spirits could soar on gentle breezes. The symbol made of metal gold will anchor the Light here. It will be a shrine and an anchor."*

"What kind of a message is this?" I asked. "Indian warriors? A symbol of metal gold? We've been talking with the Ascended Masters, with Sananda, and with the space brotherhood. Now, we're hearing from Kuthumi that American Indians are involved. This is even bigger than we thought!"

"The prophecies foretell of this time, you know." Fred replied. "I think we're getting another puzzle piece."

"Phew! This is incredible! No wonder they had to give it to us bit by bit."

Kuthumi left and another presence joined us. My head gently rolled around in a circle and then dropped back; I knew at once by my experience of the energy who it must be, "Hello, Soltec."

"*Hello,*" he returned. "*I, Soltec, am with you with my wings of flame, working to balance our energies and come into clear alignment. I wish to be working with you more. So, we will make short little visits and see what we can do.*"

This time I was comfortable with the presence and I raised my head to continue. "*The energy grid overlay is proceeding, but additional assistance would be greatly appreciated. We are weaving a web of Light around the planet, but the anchoring must be done by ones of the planet. We are not wishing to impose our Will, even though it is in alignment with Divine Will; it must also be in alignment with the free Will of the people.*"

Now we were beginning to understand that this was not just our own personal growth experience but a project of much greater magnitude. We were being asked to participate in something which would benefit the planet and were eager to learn more. We had already received a number of communications this evening and were ready to retire. It was 1:30 a.m. As I sat on the edge of the bed and pulled off my socks, I became aware that Soltec had returned and wished to speak again. I felt a tingling sensation raining down on me and my head rolled in a gentle circle. Although I was tired, I invited him to give us his message, "Hello, Soltec. Do you wish to speak with us again?"

We quickly turned the tape recorder on as Soltec responded, *"There is so much information to give you. You need not have any fear about what we might say. Trust that we are with you and looking after your interests from a grander perspective.*

"Now, with some haste, there's a configuration which needs to be established. It is based upon the moon, its position in relationship to Earth and the grid lines that we spoke about another evening. This gridwork which is being established is of paramount importance to your planet. Many are helping already, but additional assistance is needed at this time. Events in the higher dimensions have been accelerated by your global events and the urgency is even greater now. Hesitation and inactivity will not bring the results which are needed. In fact, you are correct in sensing that if everyone who is assisting in this plan suffered from hesitation, it would be most grave.

"I don't know how I can help you to understand, with your limited view of reality, what this is really about, but it is to be accomplished through our cooperation. I would enjoin you to continue gathering the pieces of information as rapidly as you are able to assimilate them. We understand that much of it may seem absurd. But remember that all the sides on your boxes are being blown away. You are becoming aware of new and expanded realities – you and humankind along with you. The veils are being lifted between dimensions. We are here to assist you and the planet. This project is grander than you can imagine. It is a part of the Plan for the universe. The beloved garden planet, Earth, must evolve along with the universe, and many are here to help.

"We can only give you pieces of information. That is all you can bear at a moment. It is time now to allow the teachings which you are receiving in your sleep to rise to your conscious awareness. Your intention and desire to cooperate will help this to transpire. Having your heart and your intention in alignment is the biggest step. We have gathered from many far off places to assist Earth and Earth's beings in this process of accelerated evolution. Our purpose is directed by the Source of Light.

"There are a few who are in the process of gathering power on Earth. Their purpose is to control Earth's riches and resources. But when the Mother Earth begins to exhibit her powers and accelerates her cleansing process, those men will discover the folly in their plans. They will experience, for the first time, their own fragility. They will see that this game that they are playing with your lives was like child's play. Indeed, it is. You have games you play in your living rooms for amusement much like the games that they are playing. The only thing is that they are playing the game with Earth and it is quite real. It is not pieces of plastic that they win or lose. They will eventually strangle themselves and become caught in their own web and their own schemes.

"You must know there is hope for your future. It is our understanding that you who are workers of the Light are this hope. The network of Light Workers already extends to every corner of the planet. We can, in a moment, contact each of you and transmit the same message to all of you at once. So you must maintain your receiving instruments in top working condition. When you feel that there is a transmission coming, as tonight, we would advise you to stop, quiet yourself, and listen."

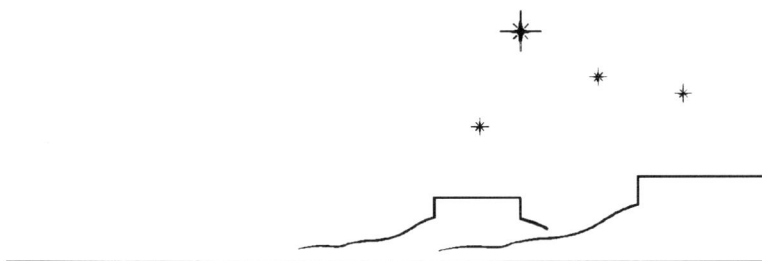

TRUST

Most of the preparations in the months that followed were internal ones, expanding our minds and increasing our abilities to have direct communications with beings in other dimensions. Sananda spoke to us many times, giving us reassurance as we continued to pray for guidance. To have this real experience of loving Christ energy allowed our hearts to open in new ways.

One night Sananda said, *"I've come to speak with you tonight about love, the kind of love which fills the heart until it would expand; love so great that it would fill the room. That is the love of the Father for his children on Earth. You know the essence of this love, but its magnitude is so vast, it is so Light, it could sustain you through trying times. There is love all around, abounding. You see it on the wings of a bird, you see it in the trees, you see it in the smile of a child. If you could let this love fill you, it would come down from above and fill your being so that what*

*shines out from your countenance is a reflection of this expanded heart.
All who come near you will be touched by this love, be attracted to this
love, and will know this love."*

I remembered the Bible said that in order to enter the kingdom of
heaven you must be innocent as a child, full of wonder and awe. It's
difficult for people to regain their childlike sense of wonder once it has
been lost. Now the information is so new, so incredible, that all will be
forced to have this childlike wonder when they hear it because these
ideas have never been heard before. I knew that many would judge these
new ideas, but I also understood that they were simply new and could not
be judged as right or wrong. Sananda reminded me, *"Once people believed the world was flat, but now we know that was wrong and people
just had a limited view of reality. Those clinging to their old beliefs were
simply unaware. Now we are in another time of new and expanded
awareness. There will be those who insist there is nothing beyond the
third dimension. But, in this lifetime, it will be proven that there is more
to reality than man believed in the past."*

New concepts are often uncomfortable when they are first introduced. The beings who were communicating with us were trying to help
us develop more trust and to gain new understandings about our definition of reality. Ashtar explained, *"There is a curtain between dimensions.
You may not think this is true on your side just because you cannot see
the whole picture. You are pointing backwards. You are looking at your
past. It had to be this way, where the present is analyzed in view of the
past, for the survival of the human race. But, now, the future must be
analyzed in view of the present and the past must be dropped. It must be
left behind because things are changing. Now it is all present and
future."*

I must have understood this at a very deep level, otherwise none of
these communications would have been possible. I knew that my experiences were real; now my challenge was having the courage to share this
new information with others. I knew there would be people who would
not understand who the Ascended Masters were, and I wondered how to
respond to them when they asked why they should want to speak with
an Ascended Master. These questions which I asked for others were,

of course, my own as well. Kuthumi responded, _"We are the instruments that God is using to communicate with you at this time. We are God's messengers, the stepping stones, to pass information to your level. We are the channels for God's desires for you and for your planet."_

I asked, "Do you mean like a radio relay?"

"Yes, just so. But it is a radio of exceptionally high fidelity, experienced in these matters. Once it was possible for you on the third dimension to perceive different dimensions, but this has not been possible for a long time. When one was said to have gone to the mountain top, it was a way to say that he had raised his vibrations to the outermost limit he was capable. The easiest way to relate this experience was to say that he had gone to the mountain. This is what happened when Moses went to the mountain and spoke to God. It was also what happened to Reverend Martin Luther King when he received his vision of all races living in harmony and told us he had been to the mountain top. It is best that you do not let your fears overwhelm you because your fear keeps your face turned away from the Light. We are protecting you and holding your hands all the time. Yes, it is unfamiliar, but it is time for faster progress."

"How can I learn to have more trust?"

Kuthumi responded, _"Go with your first impressions. It is the thinking and churning in your mind that brings up pictures of so many different kinds of denizens and bogies. This is fourth dimensional stuff creeping in. The Light will protect you. Trust and certainty also protect you. Your doubts only make you vulnerable. When the veils are lifted quickly, when they are so thin that real Light from above shines through, they are blinding and can sometimes be frightening. You are very close to us in the fifth dimension these days. The portals are beginning to open and you are beginning to get a peek, but your sight is not adjusted as yet. It is still safer to deal with your sleeping sight where the features of the third dimension fade into the background._

"You may ask the beings that come to talk to you about their purpose. You may ask them what has attracted them. It is possible that fear attracts lesser beings but you must know that no beings may approach unless invited and they must also leave when asked. There are universal *laws regarding all of this. When you maintain your focus and trust on the Light, only beings in alignment will be allowed to join you.*

"This speaking is going on even though your conscious mind is not fully aware of it. You are partly near us when you are in your bed asleep. You are a little like a mountain climber pulling himself up the mountain with a rope. The hands that hold the rope are your trust. It will help you to tell yourself what you wish to experience when you retire. State your intentions. Make a plan. You can say, 'I will remember my dreams' or 'I will sleep without interruption' or whatever you desire. This will help you and will remind you what is occurring."

It became clear that the most important thing we could do at this time was work on ourselves. We not only had to work at opening our own channels of communication but we had to work on clearing out the blocked energy which we were holding. We knew that we must be the highest and purest beings possible. This meant we would need to release any emotions which continued to bind us. We wanted to be pure spirits of Light and Love. We wanted to be understanding and compassionate. The teachings of Jesus became our example, and we understood them more clearly as we tried to become more Christ-like in our daily lives. It was a noble but difficult goal.

We became more aware of the ascension teachings and learned that the same messages we were hearing were also being received independently by other people all around the world. We understood that this was a time of great transformation and change on the planet, and that these changes would be viewed in many ways.

I looked at Fred, his brown eyes smiling kindly at me. He had fewer doubts and concerns than I from the beginning. I said, "It's strange that I was chosen to receive the vision and the initial messages about this. You accept it all without doubt, but it came to me."

He replied, "That's the way they work these things, you know. They pick the biggest skeptic in the group. When that person accepts what's happening, they're home free."

I laughed, "That's true for sure. I would never have believed it coming from anyone else. But I can't deny my own experiences."

"You know, your fears are hurting you rather than helping you." Fred's sense of connection to the Light and his trust in the Beings trying to guide us was unwavering.

I lowered my eyes, feeling ashamed for having so many doubts and reached out to take his hand, "Your certainty gives me so much encouragement. I don't think I'm being fearful so much as I'm trying to have discernment. Nothing like this has ever happened to me before. I don't want to be led astray. It's all just so new."

Fred nodded his head, "I know."

"It feels like such an honor to be asked to do these things – an honor and a responsibility – but there's still such a nagging question about whether it's truly real. I'm always glad when Soltec comes to talk with us. Let's call for him."

Fred agreed, "Okay."

And Soltec came. I spoke his words as soon as I began to hear them, _"As you wished, I have come to be with you tonight. This one is more agreeable than she was on our first meeting. There is, of course, much that you would like to know. In due time it will all become known to you. The first steps are your willingness to expand beyond what you have become accustomed to and a willingness to undertake new projects which are more strenuous and require a higher level of dedication and commitment to the work which we are overseeing on your planet. We are aware that desire and intention exist in you. We know of their great intensity._

"Third dimensional concerns have no place here so you can just allow them to go. Allow the waves of information to come to you as they will, remaining open to receive them. If you can focus on keeping your opening wide, we'll be able to work with you. The analytical parts of your mind must be set aside at these times because, indeed, we will be giving you new information. If you try to make assessments of it as it comes through, you will interfere with the reception and will be prone to interpreting it as it comes. You are not capable of doing that at this time. So, the greatest service that you can do for yourselves and for your planet is to allow us to transmit as freely and as accurately as possible. You can

expect to receive thoughts, words, and images which you do not understand. The understanding can come later. This is the only way you can
make the next leap beyond your current reality. Do you understand
clearly what I am saying to you?

Fred answered, "Yes."

"We know this is a new level but we feel you are ready to accept the
challenge. In this world of accelerated time, it is coming to you sooner
than we had expected. You had not even anticipated what is about to
begin. So, we wish you to take care of yourselves on all accounts: to
maintain your focus on the Light, to get adequate rest so that your heads
will remain clear and you will not feel drained due to fatigue or tension.
Practicing your meditations regularly will help you to remain focused.
Every meditation does not have to be a channeling. There needs to be
time for centering and focusing, as well as meditation for maintaining
and holding the Light. If you do this, you will be more prepared for the
intensive channelings which will be required for our next wave of information."

No sooner had Soltec said good-bye to me than he announced his
presence to Fred, "*Soltec here.*" It was a thought, a name spoken in his
mind. Fred began to speak the message being sent from Soltec. "*We want
you both to know that you can bring me across – one as easily as the
other. Understanding these concepts will not always be easy. As you
begin to collect the pieces of information we give, you will be able to see the
patterns and they will begin to make sense to you. But, since the band-
width of the channel is limited, it is not possible for us yet to give complete
pictures and diagrams so you can have a thorough understanding. You
will have to just take a little unedited information and wait for the next
piece. Then, there will be one session where the previous bits of data will
link together and you receive a whole concept. It will continue to become
easier for you to understand these new concepts.

"If you think things have been outrageous up to now, prepare yourselves. The work that we wish you to embark upon is special in that it is
only being performed in a very few places on your planet. We are going to
help you, as you help us, sew together parts of the fabric that is Earth's new*

Body of Light. This gridwork forms polygons, areas that are bounded by strong beams of Light, that go from one power point to the next, and eventually the entire surface of the globe will be interconnected.

"There are some types of objects that are capable of storing and retaining a special kind of light. Some humans have known this for centuries. Crystals can do it. Crystals can store energy that you may think of as light. There are some metals that can also do it, the primary one being gold. There are, of course, other kinds of objects that can store real Light. Human beings are an example, as are beings that assist on higher dimensional planes. After all repairs on your planet have been completed, transformed beings will populate it and will live in the kind of Light that exists in higher dimensions. It is in preparation for this ascension, this changeover, that we will conduct this rebuilding program.

"It is redistributing energy to different places on the planet. It will not be surprising to you that the points that will become the anchors for the new gridwork of Earth are not in populated areas. They are mostly on open land such as the land that you saw in New Mexico which has, somehow, been left strangely empty when land all around has been built upon. By not building at the wrong time, the energy is relatively intact and positive so that new constructs of reality will be able to be moved into place when it is time. So, we will be bringing you an exercise for bringing Light down and anchoring it into Earth very shortly."

Soltec then left without saying good-bye. It was late once again, well past midnight, and we were both tired and ready to sleep. I turned off the recorder as Fred finished speaking the message and we both crawled into bed. Sometimes it seemed like these nightly communications were a marvelous bedtime story that always ended "... to be continued."

Our friend, Ashtar, continued to "pop in" from time to time to encourage us, even though our main assistance was from Soltec. Ashtar told us, _"Achieving one's dreams takes courage. Your quest is a part of the grander dream. You have tapped into this on a certain level. So I encourage you to follow your dreams lest you end up old and full of regrets. There is but a moment in time, a window for each one, and you must reach through that window when it is in front of you. There is a time_ *when the preparations have been made, the groundwork has been laid, and you are prepared to achieve the dream. That time for you is now. You could not have done it before when you were younger because you were not prepared. Old attachments are falling away, old limitations are being dissolved, and it is time for you to grab your dream. There is a great Light shining on you. What more could you ask?"*

I said, "Thank you, Ashtar. Your encouragement is most appreciated."

He concluded, *"Remember that coincidence is not a part of your current reality. Everything occurring now is a part of the Plan and is happening for a reason. We are glad to be on this journey with you. You are an earnest and trusting partner and you should do well at anchoring the Light. Think upon this and you will know that it is so."*

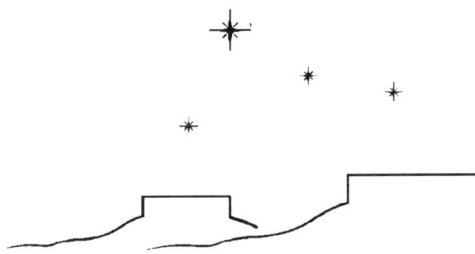

A Council Meeting

One evening later that same winter of 1991, Kate was visiting us. I knew an opportunity to gain another piece was at hand and asked, "Do you want to meditate?"

Fred waited with me for Kate's reply. She cast a glance out the window at the darkened sky, "It's about time for me to go."

Her reply came without intention and we waited for her to continue. "I guess I could stay for a little while." Heart had overruled mind, for the desire to pursue the quest at hand lay deep within her.

We went through our usual ritual of asking for the protection of Divine Light, and dimmed the electric lights in the room so they wouldn't distract us. I lit the candle which waited on the table, an outward symbol of our focus on the Light, and soon we had settled into quietness. In the stillness, unexpected laughter began to swell up, seemingly without cause, within me. As it reverberated against the inner walls of my Being, it spilled forth and I began to laugh out loud. It was the laughter of joy, deep and true, that comes when the spirit has been set free. The energy was familiar, that of an Indian spirit-guide named Wa-Tanna. This one had visited me before, often unexpectedly, and always brought a light-hearted presence that made me smile. I welcomed his "grounded" energy as I spoke his forceful greeting, "*Hello! This is Wa-Tanna.*"

There was something of importance which he wished to speak about this night and I felt his urgency. "*The Indian Spirits are coming. You can hear them if you listen.*" He spoke with seriousness now, his words unfaltering and clear, "*Many spirits are waiting. They have been held on this sphere and are waiting for their release. The Indian Spirits wish to share their knowledge with you. They can be released without being in human form and will be lifted with you. We will pass the pipe around the circle now.*" I felt his satisfaction at gaining our attention.

With that, his presence departed, and the spirit of another Indian introduced himself through Fred. His name was Chief Watanabe. "*I am in your circle in the sky. There is a wheel in the sky that Indians of old used to worship. This wheel had powers. It was a place where the bravest warriors went when they died and from which they returned when they were to be born into this life. The wheel swings across the sky, and has for hundreds of years.*

"*As you can imagine, there was much distress when the White Man came and slaughtered so many Indians, not only in the northern part of your hemisphere but in the southern part as well. True, the Indians fought back, sometimes savagely. It is also true that the Indians fought among themselves, but it was the coming of the White Man that so upset the balance that the Indians had long kept.*

"*The wheel began to turn faster as many great warriors died so rapidly. You can understand why these warriors are in this wheel since the population of the Indians was so decimated in such a short period of time. It is true that Indian souls are looking for the opportunity to get off this wheel. It is true that the wheel is not in the sky, as you understand that term third dimensionally.*

"*The Indians lived close to the land and in harmony with the Earth's vibrations and cycles. One place where this occurred very strongly was in* certain areas of New Mexico where Indians roamed across the mountains and high deserts. No roads were there to break the expanse of the land. No barriers existed. No fences. It was a free and noble life.

"The Indians left many sacred spots. Black Mesa is the most famous in these times but there are many others. Some are not so obvious. Each tribe had sacred places and they were not always burial grounds. You have been introduced to one such spot. You have seen it although you have not yet set foot upon it, as you were simply not ready to be on the part of the land that is important now, just as it was important hundreds of years ago. The Indians will come to these areas at special times of the year to commune with the Great Spirit. There is a handful who understand and appreciate the significance of this spot. But, you see, a handful is enough. It only takes one or two to preserve the traditions to be able to take correct actions at the proper times. That time is very close. The time of The People is very close._

"This is going to be a message to the White Man from a very, very, unexpected quarter. The Indians who have been so passive for the past decades will be heard from again. Attention will be focused on Indian rites. Many people will be aware of this wheel in the sky, as the veil between your world and the world of the Indian Spirit becomes thinner._

"We want this spot to be reconsecrated. This will be done by Indian and White Man together. This will be a token that will show that the White Man and the Red Man are no longer separate. It will be the most significant undertaking ever between White Man and Red Man. We are inviting you to be representatives of the White Man."_

We sat spellbound as we listened to this most unexpected message, and Chief Watanabe continued, "We are going to come together to reconsecrate this land. If you wish to participate, you must simply make your intent known to your Higher Selves. You know how to do this. If your intent is strong, the path will be opened for you. Your acquaintance of the warriors will begin. You will all recognize one another at a certain level. You have the same mission even though you have different cultural backgrounds. These differences will be set aside as they serve no purpose. You understand that this is not going to be a public display; this is to be a_ *sacred ritual and the profane will not be made aware of it. I ask you to examine your hearts and see if you are willing to embark on this task."*

I understood, at a very deep level, the importance of what was being asked, and I wanted with all my heart to help. I leaned forward as I spoke with soul-full passion, "I want to do this!"

Chief Watanabe replied, *"Yes. I know."* There was a tenderness in his voice now.

I asked, "Does this have to do with the artifact we were told to find and take to New Mexico?"

He responded, *"The artifact which you heard about from Soltec is Step Two. Step One is getting the ground reconsecrated. It is also getting yourselves reconsecrated and meeting your allies. It is like spring training where the team members are being assembled. We are the coaches. The team will get to know one another and learn to function like a unit so that when the season begins they will be aware of their capabilities and responsibilities, as well as the strengths and weaknesses of their team mates."*

"I sense an urgency about what you are asking. What can we do?"

"We are selecting the team. We are asking those who can be successful to join. As soon as the individual members are ready, the team will be formed. There will be a wonderful feeling of cooperation. Your sense of the great importance of this mission will be magnified. At times you will not be able to stand the heady, wonderful feelings of doing such a task."

Fred listened with keen attention, for it was clear that something new was being revealed. Kate sat sleeping in her chair. Chief Watanabe directed his attention toward her, *"How does Kate feel about this?"*

Jolted when she heard her name spoken, Kate opened her eyes and said, "I'm just having trouble staying conscious. I'm usually in bed by this time and the energies are so intense, I just can't seem to stay awake."

Chief Watanabe continued without responding to Kate's comment about the effect of the energies, *"Many humans are involved in time-wasting activities, from our point of view, because you are lacking direction. But as a good scout always finds the best talent, we have identified you. It is time to make the energy that you each can wield be useful and meaningful. When this happens you will not be asleep. If you accept, you will have all the motivation and dedication in the world. You will begin to feel that you have much of great importance to do. You should watch for signs in the coming weeks. They may come from the Indians; they may not. You may each get signs that you deem important, and you should pay particular attention to your enthusiasm."*

Chief Watanabe's message ended.

Wa-Tanna's presence had remained with me. He wanted Kate, who had drifted off to sleep again, to participate in this council meeting, and he spoke again with authority, *"Each in the circle must take a turn with the pipe and speak. Morning Star wishes to speak to the Princess Umchaca!"* I felt his attention directed toward Kate and knew that he was referring to her as the princess. She, too, felt the energy being directed toward her and, in a dreamy haze, Kate began to speak the words now filling her mind:

This is Morning Star.
I sing in the meadow.
I am sun light and I am star shine.
I am beyond time.
I wish you to join me in a dance. To sing. To dance.
All these things have much meaning
in the tasks you have set for yourself.
Come dance with me.
I'll see you on the mesa.
I'll have a feather for each of you, a feather dipped in blue, a feather for
each of you painted magenta.
These can be called on.
The future lies ahead.
A merry treasure hunt you have.
You have nothing to fear and everything to enjoy.
I am Morning Star.
I bid you farewell.

Wa-Tanna was delighted. The council (Pam, Fred, Kate, and their respective guides – Wa-Tanna, Chief Watanabe, and Morning Star) had been gathered. Wa-Tanna's energy was fully merged with mine; I felt unfamiliar strength and certainty coursing through my veins. I sat tall and felt my head nodding Wa-Tanna's approval as he acknowledged each one in turn. My arms were crossed to match his posture. A triumphant smile spread across my lips as I spoke Wa-Tanna's declaration, " *We shall dance tonight. We shall end this council meeting with dance!"*

Wa-Tanna then began to laugh. Uncontrollable laughter overflowed as I shared his jubilation. Kate and Fred were infected by this presence and the three of us laughed together until tears rolled down our cheeks. The joy was our own, for it came from a place within that had been touched by the awakening of that latent sense of mission, and I rose to my feet to make the triumphant pronouncement for Wa-Tanna, *"Let the dancing begin!"*

The sounds of Indians in celebration filled our heads and we began chanting and dancing around the living room. We were the living expression of what was felt but not seen as we moved with steps remembered from another place in time, stepping in a circle, each casting our commitment to be part of the Great Plan whose time had come.

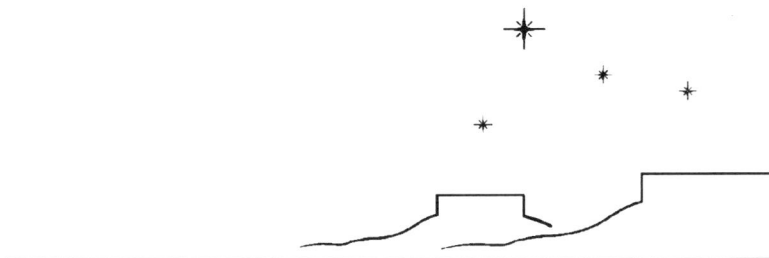

Communications

I don't know why it surprised me to receive this unexpected communication from Native American spirit guides – it had all started with a vision of an Indian standing on a mesa. But over the months our communications had been with other beings from the Galactic Brotherhood (Ashtar and Soltec) and the Ascended Masters.

We pondered what had happened, trying to grasp the scope of this project. It was a mental stretch to try to comprehend the implications of this association between Native American spirit guides and the Galactic Federation – our Star Brothers. I felt humbled by our company.

That night Soltec joined us again. *"My message to you this evening will be brief. You are flexible to be able to bring in the energies of such a variety of beings. Last night was Wa-Tanna. That was a delight for you. It was very grounding. Wa-Tanna helps us in this manner. He helps to prepare you and open you for even more lightness. As you become more grounded we can transmit ideas to many telepathically— if only the channels are open. There is a great deal of progress being made at opening the telepathic channels at this time, and soon it will become a very acceptable form of communication. There are many now who are aware of it, who receive it but do not wish to acknowledge it because they are uncomfortable with the notion. This is just a matter of growing pains."*

What a process we were in – the turning, the opening, and the integration. In time, with patience and dedication, we would understand. Soltec continued, *"There is some additional information I can impart to you. I have responsibility for establishing a communications network under my guidance. But we cannot merely blast out communications without having appropriate receptors ready so that, when we beam this information down, there is an appropriate place for it to be received. If a radio station sends out radio waves, no matter how strong the frequencies are, there must be receivers tuned in to the proper station, or nothing is heard. That is my role, to help you become tuned in, to have your channels set and your antennae pointed in the right direction so you will be able to receive these signals. Now the network is being established. The frequencies are being aligned. You may get information at unexpected times if there is an urgency. You are well aware of our signals now, so it will work out."*

We now had the *what* and the *where* pieces of the puzzle. It was to be an activation of the new energy grid around the planet; the mesa from the vision would be the place. But we still hadn't learned about the *how* or *when*. Remembering the unfolding of our magical trip, we trusted that all would be revealed to us in its proper time. We continued listening to our guides as we found ourselves shifting gears between our commitments in the business world and our growing dedication to the planetary evolution.

It was at this time that I, once again, heard a voice in the night. It came loudly enough to wake me from my sleep.

"Be there by August 25th!"

Somehow, it seemed the most important messages always came unbidden in the night when my allowing was at its maximum. I shook my head in recognition. Another piece had just revealed itself. I reached for a pencil and noted the message in my journal without turning on the light.

The next morning when I looked to see what I had written, I saw the date, *August 25th,* written above a series of symbols on the page. As my eyes fell upon the hieroglyphic circles and spirals, my hand involuntarily reached out and grabbed the page, tearing it from the book as I muttered, "That's not even English!"

This was just too much! I jumped up and headed directly to the kitchen, crumpling the page as I walked, and threw it into the trash. It was all one swift movement in an attempt to erase the memory of having written these symbols in the night – as though the symbols would cease to exist with the paper they were written upon.

I had never before torn a page out of my journal, for it was a sacred record during this time. Destroying a page of the journal was a knee-jerk reaction to something my conscious mind could not accept. What were these codes I was receiving? Surely my pen had not written an encoded message from another dimension.

With the evidence destroyed, I gathered up my things and left the house to go to the office. I would turn my attention to making a long list of sales calls. This was real. No one, especially me, could question the credibility of this activity. The new worlds pushing their way into my awareness didn't fit into any definition I knew of, and an inner tension set up a mighty resistance to their arrival. Each time I accepted a piece of new information, another was presented and, again, I was challenged to expand. I found my emotions swinging between resistance and acceptance as I continued to be driven by some powerful super-conscious force.

As the weeks passed, Soltec continued communicating with us. He encouraged us to continue regular meditations and stressed the importance of allowing our minds to be clear and uncluttered so that there would be an open space to receive their signals. It was a time of preparation.

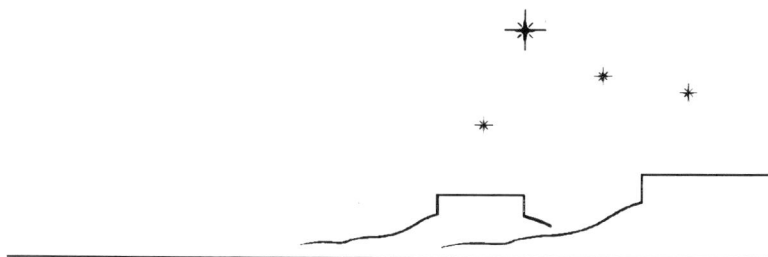

ANCIENT VOICES

Fred often stayed late at the office, engrossed in one of his computer programming projects. I spent this time alone in the silence of my own mind, making the link with my spiritual guides a nightly ritual. After the house was quiet, I would consciously focus my attention on raising my vibrations so that a communication link could be established. My confidence had been growing and I began to assume that I was under permanent protection from any lesser forces. My intentions were to be open to Spirit and, in my familiarity with the process, I gradually became less conscientious about the ritual of asking for protection.

One evening, I sensed a presence I had not experienced before. I wondered who it might be and welcomed it without hesitation. I spoke the words I heard into my tape recorder, *"Hello. This is White Cloud, Chief of the great warriors, Chief of the native rulers of this land."*

I felt the urgent energies of this entity as the connection was made, his desire to make his message known pressing down on me.

"We have been waiting for you. We are waiting for you now. The time has come when we wish you to accept the call to action.

"The spirits of the Mother Earth call forth.

"The spirits of the sky call forth.

"The spirits of the eagle soar.

"All are waiting. It is time for the ceremony of the Great Reunion.

"This message is urgent. It has been waiting for many moons. It has been waiting for the time of alignment. It has been waiting for the Chief in the sky to drop the feather. All eyes look upward and wait. We see the feather now and know that it is time. The spirits who wait, the warriors who fight for right, are ready now to proceed.

"Your assistance is welcomed. This reunion is not for Native spirits alone. This is the grand reunion of all souls who are pure of intent, of all souls who love this Earth and care beyond man's knowing, who see magic and know it is the Great Spirit moving.

"Come swiftly now along your path. Do not falter. Do not tarry. Do not go astray. Keep your focus and your eyes set on your goal of joining with us in the grand ceremony. It is promised. It is long awaited and it is a new beginning to you who will go forth from this ceremony changed, with new understandings of the meaning of all life."

Fred had arrived home as I was receiving this message. He walked into the bedroom where I was sitting in a chair with the tape recorder humming next to me as the cassette turned. He sat on the side of the bed and waited for me to continue with the message from White Cloud, *"We were speaking of the Ceremony of Great Reunion. We wish you to be a part of this and not be left out of any of the preliminaries. In this ceremony there will be a lighting of the flame. There will be a releasing and soaring of the spirits. There is nothing you will find written about the Great Ceremony, as it exists only in legend. We have been waiting for the timing and alignments to be correct."*

The communication ended and White Cloud's essence departed. What was being asked of us now? Were we being asked to release trapped souls? The door to the Indian spirit world had been opened by the council meeting with Wa-Tanna and Chief Watanabe the week before. Now, others were taking the opportunity to communicate with us.

Then Fred began to speak the telepathic thoughts which were building within him. *"This is Natachoka. I was an Indian chief many years ago. I was Nez Perce Indian. I have some understandings to give about land. Indians have always recognized the land is sacred. The land is holy. It holds the power and certainty that Indians always sought. There were teachings passed from father to son in pictures and stories. These teaching stories about the land told that different spots of land can be used for different purposes to enhance one aspect or another of the Indian's relationship to the universe. So, part of the land had special power. This sense of power made the land sacred.*

"Now many points of power land have been corrupted and nullified by non-sacred activities. Some places remain as they have been for thousands of years. The land which remains undefiled has become dormant. The power still exists but does not manifest. One could walk across the land and not be aware there was anything special about it. But, if the land is reconsecrated, this activity will draw the power out again and will reactivate it. To do this takes knowledge, certainty of purpose, absolute confidence and the right elements gathered together at the right time. Humans bring the elements and, if they are present in the right combination, the land can be reawakened.

"Sixteen people, or more, are required for this ceremony. It is called the Ceremony of the Living Heart, the ceremony of the heart of the land. To the Indians it is as if this ceremony starts the pulse of the land; it starts the energy of the land to pulsate and wake up. When the Indians put themselves close to the land, lying on the land face down, they felt the energy could be transferred from the land to themselves. This is the story of the land and the story of the celebration – the reawakening."

A couple of days later Soltec returned. Fred was eager to ask the questions he had held quietly to himself about White Cloud and Natachoka. Before Soltec could begin, Fred asked, *"Who is White Cloud and what is his connection with the Ashtar Command?"*

The response was persistent, urging me to speak, "*White Cloud was merely acting as an interpreter for the Great Spirit. He was attempting to take advantage of an opportunity now that the barriers are being lifted and channels are being opened. He is busy at work contacting about his own aims. I'm sorry if this is confusing to you.*"

Fred said, "I think this is a lesson in discernment for us. Something didn't seem right because he never mentioned any of you, and you never mentioned him. In trying to put the pieces together, I had to ask who he was. Is there anything more you wish to say on this subject?"

Soltec continued, "*You were not in particular danger with White Cloud. There will be many tests along the way. For your own growth, we cannot protect you from all such things and such forces. You can, however, protect yourselves. You can do this with a stronger intention. This one speaking, Pam, had assumed that her protection was permanent and in effect at all times. She remained open to the crosswinds. A clear and strong focus on the Light truly is essential.*"

"*When the Ascension takes place many souls will be freed and lifted. There is no particular help which you need to give. This is not your task. Your task is to help people to their own divinity. To help people seek their own spiritual guidance, to know what possibilities are available to them. It's not your task to take responsibility for anyone else on any plane. That is a personal responsibility for each being. Self-sufficiency is the key. You are each powerful. You can assist one another by working together but need not rely on each other. That is giving away your personal power. That is a travesty.*"

Fred asked, "There was another entity called Natachoka. What can you tell us about him?"

"*Natachoka was also taking a ride on the open channel which Pam was holding. He has given you some teachings about the land which you may understand more fully at another time. There is much occurring on your planet as the veil between dimensions is lifted. This was an experience of the overlapping which will become more and more prevalent as time goes on and you are more able to communicate with beings existing in other dimensions. This project which we are guiding will call forth many levels of participation. You must use your discernment, just as you would* when meeting someone new in your dimension. You must listen and you must decide what to accept and what to reject. You must decide what is founded on truth. You must decide for yourself what applies to you."

I didn't know what to think. It had been such a struggle for me to overcome my initial fears. Just when I was starting to feel comfortable, this lesson came about discretion and the need for unceasing vigilance of focus and intent.

Soltec was ready to proceed with more information about the Light Grid project. "*This transmission is about how you can use the Light for energy, for external as well as internal illumination. The Light Grid will make higher concentrations of energy available in new forms (or at least forms which are new to those of you on Earth). In other planes and other areas in the galaxy, these forms of light energy are used extensively for transportation. It would all seem quite wondrous to you to imagine yourself connecting into a gridwork of light which is available to you. You can use it to teleport your thoughts or your whole being. It is used more extensively for amplifying and teleporting thoughts.*

"The Light Grid must not be misused for purposes of ill-intent. Before it is firmly in place, there will be much purging done of ill intentions, of karma, and of lower thought forms on your plane. Being a Light Being will become much more prevalent than it is now. This is happening rapidly. The Earth must be populated by beings in harmony with the transition underway. This is why many are being called to action. The Light Grid is just one facet of the new age which is coming into fruition now. You will begin to get a better idea of the magnitude of the project as you become acquainted with individuals with various missions.

"We understand that questioning and doubt are to be expected as we allow you to go through this process of unfoldment. They do not concern us because we hold a larger vision than you are able to see just yet. We are much like a parent taking their child for their first haircut. The parent has no concern, knows that the child is perfectly safe, that the outcome will be good, and places the child in the barber's chair in spite of any level of protest which might occur. The child, who is you, is feeling some anxiety, perhaps even kicking and screaming, 'I don't want to go.' That is only the child's fears exhibiting themselves. Deep inside, the child

wants to go with the parent. He or she is curious and wants to be a part of this new thing. Once the experience is over, the child understands that there was nothing so fearful. It didn't hurt. And, now, somehow he is a little wiser because he has had a new experience and made a small step toward being grown.

"This is how it seems to us when the inevitable doubts begin to surface for those who have committed and dedicated themselves on many levels to helping with the project. You can dry any tears of apprehension and know that you are protected, you are sheltered, you are under the watchful eye of a living Father who will surely not allow any harm to come to you."

We were interrupted by a knock on the bedroom door and our daughter, Kari, called, "Can I come in?"

"Sure." I turned off the tape recorder and shook my head to bring my attention quickly back to the room.

"I need to talk to you."

"All right. What's up?" I asked.

"I've decided that I'm going to move out."

I said, "I'm not surprised. I know it's time for you to get out on your own. Is it because of all the channeling we've been doing? I know it makes you uncomfortable."

"No, I just don't understand it, that's all."

I told her, "The world is going to be changing. Each person will have to have their own direct experience regarding what's coming; each will have to go within and come to their own understanding. I'm not going to try to convince you of anything."

"I really need to be closer to school. I've been getting home so late after my study groups."

I nodded, acknowledging much that remained unspoken.

Kari began making preparations to move out. I regretted the concerns she had expressed over the weeks. I didn't want to distress her in any way, but our guidance was too compelling to deny.

We could not be deterred.

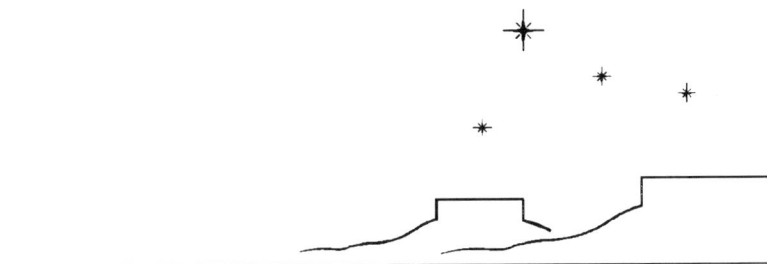

Birthday Surprises

The month of May had arrived, and summer was fast approaching. We planned a surprise birthday party in Kate's honor, looking forward to meeting some of her friends from what I affectionately referred to as "Reverend School." I was planning to share some of the information we had been receiving with them. I wondered what their reaction would be.

As the evening approached, I felt apprehensive about just what to say, but Archangel Michael encouraged us, *"You have progressed enormously. You are making these changes and this progress secretly, and there are many of your old friends who no longer know the real you. It is now time for you to begin exposing yourself a little bit more, shining that Light around in dark corners, being an example of courage, of transformation, and of becoming a master. When you begin to reveal yourself in wider circles, you will be surprised at the response. It's okay to be out there with what you think and believe. The ideas may seem new to many and their first exposure may not bring overwhelming acceptance. However, it will crack open a door. It will change a corner of their reality as they hear about new possibilities, and a seed will be planted."*

Michael was reassuring but I still wondered about just what I should say. We called on Soltec and asked for his advice. He said, *"This group that is coming over is a very close group, almost like a family. Every one, without exception, will be a Light Worker. Not every one will be awake. Some will be snoring soundly with dreams of waking. The best thing you can do for these people who dream of waking up is to shine the Light in their eyes. And, ahhh, what a wonderful feeling that is for all parties involved. All you need to do is the shining; it is the person who must do their own waking."*

I said to Michael, "I feel calm about the evening, and yet I feel a little overwhelmed because I don't know what to expect. This will be the first time we've shared this information with a group."

"You are ready for your meeting. In fact, you are more than ready. You will find it surprisingly easy. I know that you would like to have a plan, but you should consider having a little more of the commodity known as flexibility. Things will not go as you foresee them no matter what, but they will go well. Do not confuse your capabilities now with your former capabilities. You must act fully at every moment and not look back at how you used to be. You are constantly surrounded by entities on higher dimensions and you are doing a good job of filtering out those entities which are undesirable to you. You will have so much fun. This meeting will be the best thing yet, in ways that you may not know at first. It is not necessary to maintain feelings of unease or inability, as these simply serve to sabotage the efforts of the greater Self who knows that she can do something.

"We don't wish people who have gained knowledge to sit in their ivory towers and think grand thoughts about themselves. We wish for each person to be a teacher by example and by answering questions to the best of their ability. Because the boxes which determine your boundaries of what you believe is possible are constantly expanding, your understandings will be changing. So presenting yourself as you are, as a whole person in a process, is the best approach. You can say, 'This is what I've

learned,' 'This is what I'm doing,' and 'This is why.' So, be who you are. Think of where you have been and of where you are now. Think of inviting your friends to join you where you are, and be a Light. All will go exceedingly well."

Kate arrived early, as usual. Fred and I surprised her at the door, "Happy Birthday!"

"What's this?" she smiled as her eyes fell on the festive preparations. The room was decorated with yellow streamers and gifts were waiting on the table.

"Well, we thought we'd make a little fuss," I giggled.

Soon the other guests arrived. Old acquaintances were renewed and new ones made. There was enthusiastic sharing with Kate's friends from San Francisco, Stan and Syd. They were preparing to move away from California. Kate intended to join them later, and many plans needed to be made. Anticipation was in the air.

I was eager to share our story about the vision and our trip to the Southwest which led us to the sacred land. At dinner I revealed how the story began, and continued, "Then, one night, a message came to us that we're supposed to find an artifact from Peru. Can you imagine that? Peru!"

Everyone listened intently. I looked around the table at their faces, wondering what they were thinking. I couldn't tell. I took a deep breath before I continued to explain about the purpose of the artifact, "There are new energy grids being established around the planet. What we're supposed to do is find an artifact from Peru that will be used to anchor this new energy grid here in the United States."

Kate's friend, Stan, was sitting next to me. He reached into his pocket, pulled out a small piece of gold, and set it on the table in front of me, "Is this what you're looking for?"

I reached over and picked up the little piece of gold.

I asked, "Where did you get this?"

"A friend of mine who spends a lot of time in Peru gave it to me." Stan continued, "When I asked him what I was supposed to do with it, he told me, 'You will know.'" He picked up the small piece of gold and turned it in his hand. As he set it back down on the table between us, he looked back at me, "If this is what you're looking for, you can have it."

I couldn't believe it. Here was an artifact from Peru, and it was being handed to me right in my own dining room. It was all too incredible! Could this be it?

Well, I didn't know what I was looking for. I picked up the small golden object to look at its the ornate inscriptions. Dinner conversations and laughter were bouncing around the table. How could I know?

I tried to close the sound of the chatter out of my mind. This was an important decision; I couldn't make it while passing the bread and butter. I handed it back to Stan, "I'd like to look at it more closely later."

Stan and I became engrossed in conversation and, before I knew it, everyone else had left the table leaving Stan and me alone in the dining room, completely oblivious to the activity around us. Stan said, "I guess we ought to go join the others."

"I guess so. Do you think I could see the object you brought again?"

Stan pulled the gold piece out of his pocket and handed it to me. I took it in my hand and closed my fingers around it as I sat down. I was sealed in my own world; I couldn't move the hand holding the golden piece while I wondered how I would know if this was the artifact I was looking for. Conversation filled the room but the words were a blur.

After awhile I felt I *should* return the piece to Stan. I tried to give it back, but I couldn't let go of it. It was riveted in my palm, my fingers firmly fixed as I clutched it in my hand. I told myself, "You have held this long enough and you don't know anything. Now give it back." But I could not.

I thought the others in the room would want to hold it and that I should pass it around. I thought about passing it to the person sitting next to me. But I could not.

Finally, I looked at Fred across the room. He was intimately sharing this journey with me. I wanted him to be able to hold this object too. With great determination I stood up, walked over to where he was sitting, and placed it in his hand. What would his reaction be?

Fred held it for a few minutes, then said, "I think it's a battery. I felt some sort of energy, like subtle electrical currents coming from the object and running through my hand."

The air was pregnant with curiosity as each one wondered what they would experience when they held the artifact. Fred passed it around the room for each to hold. One woman said it felt like it was burning a hole in her hand and quickly passed it on. Many felt nothing.

I watched it move around the room like a puppy watching its bone when one man commented, "Cute little gadget."

I got up and left the room, too angry to sit still. Didn't they know how important this was? Inside I raged, "This is not just a party curiosity! It's an extremely important device and should not be treated with such irreverence!"

Recognizing that my reactions were the answer to my question, I returned to the room and quietly told Stan that I thought maybe this was what we were looking for. I remembered his offer to give me the piece if this was so, and thought he would understand that I hoped to keep it.

As the evening drew to a close, I wondered where the gold piece was. I didn't have it. I looked around and didn't see it sitting on any of the tables. Had it been returned to Stan? Did he have it in his pocket? The only two guests who remained were Stan and his friend, Syd. I kept thinking about the gold piece from Peru but didn't have the courage to ask him for it a second time. Instead, I asked him, "How long have you had the artifact?" attempting to remind Stan of his offer.

"For several months now. It's just been sitting in my living room with some other pieces on the mantle. People often notice it when they come over because it's so unusual. Sometimes I carry it in my pocket."

I wondered why he hadn't given it to me. Was he having difficulty releasing it? I asked, "Does it mean a great deal to you?"

"No. I have other pieces and crystals I use. I will say, though, that I began getting really clear information after getting it. It seems like my psychic abilities have increased. I've begun seeing visions about some difficult times that are coming for California which have motivated my move."

I thought he would give it to me before he left. I thought he understood my desires as well as I did. But as Stan was heading for the door, there was still no indication he would leave the object with me. I attempted to remind him once again, asking, "Did you get the gold piece back after it was passed around?"

"Yes," he said, "I have it." And then, as he turned to leave, "It was nice meeting you." He gave a wave and flashed a friendly smile as he opened the door to go.

I felt a sense of panic and wanted to scream, "Well, are you going to give it to me?"

I pinched my lips together, saying nothing.

Fred said, "Good luck on your plans."

I said, "Good-bye," filled with disappointment as I watched him walk away. The object from Peru was leaving with him.

Once he was gone, Fred asked, "What happened to the artifact?"

"I guess Stan took it with him."

"I thought you were going to keep it"

"Yeah. So did I."

"Why didn't you ask him for it?"

"Well, I did – kind of. I didn't want to be pushy about it. If it's that important to him, I shouldn't take it. You know, I'm not really sure of anything."

When I talked about all these feelings the next day with one of the other guests, she said, "From the very beginning, I thought you were going to keep it."

"So did I, but it didn't work out that way."

"Well, you just may find it returning to you. That's the way these things work. If you're supposed to have it, it will come back."

That didn't feel very reassuring. How could I have let this opportunity slip away?

Days passed and I kept thinking about the events at Kate's birthday party. How close this artifact from Peru had come. I became more and more aware of the lesson I was learning about speaking up for myself. I couldn't stop thinking about the artifact and Peru. Perhaps the mysterious ancient artifact I needed had come to me and all I had to do was ask for it.

Stan was soon to move away from California. Fred knew that it was gnawing away at me, and finally said, "Well, why don't you just call and talk to him? We can drive up to San Francisco this weekend and you can get it. Just tell him this is what you were looking for and you'd like to come and get it."

"Doesn't that sound simple. I should just call and tell this person whom I hardly know that I want him to give me his golden treasure? It seemed clear to me he didn't want to part with it."

Fred watched my inner struggle. What more could he say?

I knew I had to call Stan, but it was a difficult thing for me to do. Time was running out. I couldn't trust fate to bring the artifact back again as our friend had suggested. I would have to take some quick action to assure its return. I felt backed against a wall as the pressure mounted on me to do something about the compelling need to have this piece. I thought about it night and day, and, even though I still didn't fully under-stand why, I knew that I must retrieve it.

I scolded myself, "Speak up before it's too late!"

Finally, I called Stan and told him, "I really think I need the gold artifact."

"All right," was his reply.

How easy that was when I finally gathered the courage, "Can we plan a time to come and get it before you leave?"

"We're leaving next week. On Monday morning we pick up a van and begin loading it."

That gave us just three days. I thought about trusting its delivery to the mail and realized that I would much prefer to go pick it up and assure that it was safely in my hands.

"Maybe Kate can come along with us."

Stan was pleased with the suggestion, "That would be great! Why don't you come up late Sunday afternoon."

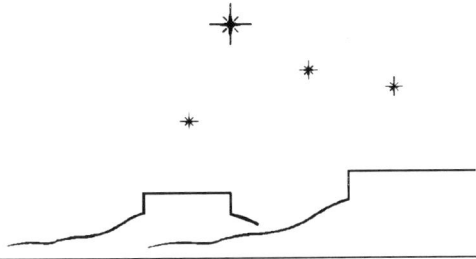

COMMITMENT

It was a mild May afternoon the day we drove up to San Francisco. Fred and Kate were in the front seat, and I sat in the back so that I could be alone with my thoughts. There was a compelling sense that I must acquire this ancient golden artifact, but still I was uncomfortable with the notion of taking it. To follow a sense of purpose which would serve the greater good of humankind overrode any lesser thoughts, those of personal gratification or self-worth. It was a heady and difficult notion for me to accept, and feelings of purpose and surrender consumed me.

Fred maneuvered our small car in and out of traffic as we drove up and down the hills crossing the city. At every intersection we had to stop and wait for traffic lights to change. The trip took a couple of hours, and yet it seemed like minutes. I was in a space of no-time.

We found Syd's address and parked the car in the closest available space, a few blocks away from the old Victorian apartment house. As we got out of the car, we looked down the hill at the marina. Sailboats peacefully glided by, their sails glistening in the sunlight as it reflected off the bay. What a beautiful day in the city!

We walked up the hill to Syd's house, then up the steep stairs to the second floor. The floorboard creaked as we walked up the dark stairway. Gaping cracks in the walls had been left unrepaired from the 1989 earthquake two years earlier. And I understood some of Stan's urgency to leave California. The building seemed to sway with each step we took. This must have remained a constant reminder of the ever-present potential of another quake.

"Do you know which one is Syd's apartment?" I asked.

Kate replied, "Up the stairs to the right."

We were greeted in the hallway by a neighbor who knew we were expected. She directed us to the apartment, which consisted of two small rooms (a kitchen and a living room), each with tall ceilings. The walls were riddled with fractured stucco and one small window in each room looked out onto an overgrown and untended courtyard. The living room was filled with boxes which were labeled and neatly stacked to be moved. The only furniture in the room were two straight-backed chairs and a bed.

Stan and Syd were looking forward to the changes in their lives, and described their eager anticipation for a new and different life-style in the country. We talked for hours about their plans, the state of the world and our own lives. Later, Syd served tea and crackers for a snack. All the while, in the back of my mind was the object of our visit – the artifact. The wanderings of our conversation seemed to carefully avoid mention of it. Finally I asked Stan, "Do you have the artifact?"

"No. I forgot to bring it over."

I could clearly see that he did not want to give it up.

"Would you like me to go get it?"

"Well, I guess so." Did he think I had changed my mind?

He said, "It won't take long; I live close by. I'll be right back."

While Stan was gone, we all noticed time stretching out as the conversation idled during his lengthy errand. He had been gone for over an hour, and I thought he must be having difficulty parting with his treasure. I kept thinking about what I would say to him. It felt as though we were approaching an important moment. And, while the conversation continued around me, I kept hearing the words in my head, "You must tell him that he may not get it back." I knew that Stan's understanding was that he would be loaning this piece to us for our quest to the mesa, but there was a strong message that this would not be the case.

Finally, Stan returned and entered the room at a rapid gait. He walked directly over to me, dropped the artifact in my hand, and then sat down in the only available spot – next to me on the edge of the bed. It was apparent that he wanted this exchange to be as casual as possible. But it was a significant moment for me and I knew there were words to speak. Something within me shifted as I rose and turned to stand in front of him. I held the artifact between my palms which were raised to my heart and said, "This is important."

Stan raised his eyes in amazement as he too felt the energies, "I know."

I lowered my hands and opened them to reveal the ancient piece of gold, then continued, "This is not about me and it's not about you." I felt myself standing taller and speaking with authority about the importance of this moment. My inner strength was activated as I performed this outward act of claiming my Truth, and I continued with power and conviction in my voice. "This is something we do together for the planet and for all humankind. We will be anchoring the Light of the heavens into the Earth in a way which has never been done before. It was your task to be the courier of this piece so that this could be completed. As you pass this on to me, you are playing a significant role in the Divine Plan for Earth."

Fred and Kate listened. Their amazement was obvious as they witnessed this blossoming of my new-found strength. Stan's face was flushed with emotion as we shared the intensity of the moment, and he stood to face me. I then voiced the words which needed to be spoken, "I have to tell you that you may not get this back."

"Wait a minute," Stan gasped. His face paled and he shook his head in disbelief, sweat beading on his forehead. This was not what he had expected. He felt out of control and didn't know what to say.

I spoke again, "I cannot promise that you will get this back. It may be that it is to be passed on to someone else or it may buried on the land. I don't know exactly how this is to be used, but I have a strong feeling that it will not be coming back to you. You have to know this."

He nodded in acknowledgment. Powerful forces were at work and any attachment to the object would have to be released.

I opened my arms to give him an embrace. He responded and we held each other. We were two strangers brought together by a piece of gold and a connection to something greater than either of us fully understood. We were, for a moment, standing together in the shaft of Light which surrounded us.

Then, the moment passed and we parted. I was grateful to have received the artifact and was full of joy as I spoke the unexpected words, "I feel like I just got married!" I could not really explain what that meant, but everyone in the room realized that something significant had happened. With these actions, I had just made a deep personal commitment to the Light. It was not consciously planned nor was it anticipated. I knew our own Higher Selves had arranged all the circumstances surrounding this day. My heart overflowed with Divine love and, as I skipped down the sidewalk returning to the car with the artifact in my pocket, I knew that I had also reclaimed a lost part of myself.

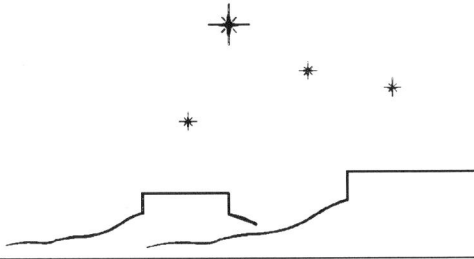

ARTIFACT

The next morning, I sat on the sofa in our living room and turned the golden artifact in my hand, examining it more closely than before. It was a piece of something, an ornate knob that had been broken, or cut off of something larger. It was small, only an inch long, yet it had the density and weight of something much larger. What were the encodements programmed into this piece? Were they, indeed, in alignment with the Light?

I pondered the ornate engravings which seemed to hold information about the mysteries of life. On one side was a kundalini spiral of creative energy coming out of an infinity symbol and running up the center in a double helix pattern. I rolled it over and examined the other side. There was another infinity symbol, above it a symbol of balancing spirals, and a pair of primitive hands. The molding of a partial creature with hands covering its face reminded me of the gargoyles standing over the doorways of cathedrals in Europe, warding off evil spirits and proclaiming their oath to keep the secrets held within.

I continued to turn the piece, its sides rubbed smooth by many hands – for how many centuries? – and I pondered my own feelings of urgency about obtaining it. Where did it come from? What was it to be used for now? I sensed its mystical power and wondered about its essence.

I asked Fred, "Will you sit with me and see if we can get any more information about this piece? Now we have it in our house and I need to know more about it."

"Sure," he responded and immediately sat down.

Soltec was there, waiting for the call, and began to speak to Fred, who relayed the message to me:

"I know that you are thinking that this object might have an alignment that goes against you. You can trust that we would not send you an object, or anything else, that was not fully in alignment with yourselves and your life's mission and purpose. This artifact is like a battery or amplifier; it's an aligner. It has an automatic on/off switch which is off for all of those that are not in alignment with their highest good and divine purpose. But for those that are, it turns on, just as it tends to turn on those that hold it. The artifact is for those who want to go spiritual surfing. It puts you up on the crest of a spiritual wave, which is where the Beings were that created it."

I said, "I would like to continue receiving the information about the Light Grid that Soltec has been sending to me. I'm also ready to make the connection that will give us the lead about our trip to Peru. Time is passing and we need to begin making plans."

Ashtar joined us as he responded with a bit of a laugh, *"Peru is a milestone for you, is it?"*

Fred replied, "Well, it sounds like it's a milestone for all of us. Yes, I think it would be a milestone for us."

"It is a milestone for all of us. The connections of the Light Grid must fully encircle the planet. There are those who must be willing to make this traverse to first connect themselves with the Light Grid physi-

_cally, mentally and spiritually, and then be willing to cross the bound-
aries of lands and make the connections. Your friend, Kate, is a person
who is doing person-to-person Light weaving at a level right on the surface
of Earth, weaving and connecting people together. She has connected
you with some others who have a role in this. Then there is another level
of Light weaving which actually weaves the energy grid, calls it down,
and anchors it. The artifact which was brought to your house assists the
one bearing it to become personally connected to the Light Grid. It is not
the anchor stone, but it does assist in the individual connection and am-
plification of the Light transmissions. That is why it is being passed from
one Light Worker to the next. It is more of the weaving."_

Fred then asked the question which burned in each of our minds,
"Who is the person that should have the gold artifact at this time?"

Ashtar replied without hesitation. It was difficult for me to speak
the words I heard. But they came with such certainty, I soon surrendered
to the reply, _"Pam should have that stone. This object goes where the Light
sends it. The Light sent it to you, and its previous owner was no longer
meant to have it, so you cannot feel there was any problem with that.
Pam should carry it to New Mexico and then she should carry it on to
Peru. As a spider spins a web, so will this leave behind it a web of silver
light. It is not to be buried. It is to be passed on again. Someone else will
come to you with a strange message they do not understand and you will
know it is time to pass it on to the next one. Do not allow yourselves to sit
in judgment of your worthiness. You surely do understand the importance of this stone. This artifact is a gold-alloy. It is of Earth and it is not
of Earth. Because you have accepted this task, you are worthy of every
aspect of it! You are working on many planes at this time._

_"Because of this, the miracles will be quite unexplainable to oth-
ers. What is visible on your Earth plane will surely be amazing to you
and to those around you. You can accept them with a knowing and an
appreciation for your own dedication to the Light, your dedication to the
good of humankind and the welfare of Mother Earth._

_"I hope you understand that spending time in doubt about your
guidance truly can no longer be a part of you. There is not time for it!
The time is now for you to move forward with love in your hearts and_

certainty in your steps. By involving yourself in this work and progressing along, all the information you need will become known to you at the proper time."

Our true Essences were being allowed to expand and we were beginning to know that we did not need to hide our truth from others. We knew that this project and this time in history would mark a new beginning for humankind. Soltec continued, *"You will need to get some facility with this stone, this artifact, in preparation for retrieving the larger artifact from Peru. Without this practice stone you would not be able to keep the larger stone in your possession for more than a few seconds. This object has many uses. One of them is strengthening the Light of the one who holds it. In fact, you need not even hold it to benefit from its effects. This is not an object of worship, so you should not concentrate on the object. It is simply a catalyst. Its markings really have no purpose or significance in this age. Its function is alignment and it is the results of the process that you are after. What is important is the energy that the object channels. If it is too strong at first you can simply place it beside you and let the object help you from a couple of feet away.*

"You will find that you will gain the strength and the facility to bear this object very quickly. If you have an intention to do healing, your ability will be intensified by this piece to the limit that you are filled with the Light. Likewise, you can use it as an intent magnifier for any intention that shares its alignment. So, it would not help you to rob a bank but it would help you with your spiritual alignment.

"You should continue to hold it if it is your desire to align your physical body with your Light Body, as changes will be taking place at an accelerated rate in your body in order to facilitate this alignment. To be a channel of the Light does not mean only that one sits in their living room and speaks words at certain times. This is step one. To own the information that is being channeled is to do the mission, as your planet is mostly a place of doing. There are other places that are a place of being. The fifth dimension is one. But, at this time, there is so much doing and so much preparing that is required that we are going to ask you more and more to get out of your chairs and do. These communications, indeed, are the preparations that fit between the intent and the action. I will now

withdraw, temporarily, and hope that I will again speak to you this evening. This is Soltec of the Circles wishing you a good morning."

It was a busy time for us. It seemed as though we were leading two separate lives: one in the spiritual world and one in the material. We were standing between two worlds, one foot planted firmly in each. There were stretches of time when we became consumed by our "regular" lives and failed to take the time to meditate. Our business had slowed down due to the state of the economy, and our own shifting focus had helped us make the decision to vacate our office in town. Our daughter had moved closer to the college she was attending, and we had turned her room into a guest room. We would once again transform the extra room, this time into an office. Our days were filled with the details of liquidating our office furnishings, sorting, packing, and transferring things to the house.

In the midst of all of this activity, Fred began talking about taking another trip to Santa Fe. Our guides had told us that we would be returning there twice: once in August to anchor the Light, and once prior to that to prepare the land. It was already the end of May, but I didn't even want to consider Fred's notion of another trip until we were settled from the move.

When we did sit down to listen for guidance again, Sananda's presence was there. The Masters encouraged us to achieve our growth as rapidly as we were able, nudging us forward with gentle hands. They were also there when we felt the pressures in our lives or bowed to our own feelings of limitation. Sananda brought us his support, reassuring us, *"I am suggesting that you take a little pause tonight. Relax. Let all your cares and concerns evaporate. You may send them to me. I'm doing some deep healing for you both right now. We would like you to not get frazzled, to not view yourselves as being incapable of doing the things that you wish to do and the things we wish for you. The relaxed approach is better. You need not worry along the way. You need not have cares about whether you are doing well or whether you are doing poorly, whether you should be doing this or that, because these worries and cares just create static. Ultimately, they just slow you down.*

"*Now, we have sent you a small artifact that was made by Beings of very high alignment. This can be your alignment stone. This artifact is a touch stone of Light and through it, truly, miracles can be created. The object can be used as a launcher. It may assist your intent on the higher dimensional levels in an accelerated fashion because it can create a very powerful bond between your conscious selves, your physical body, and your Higher Self. This strong Light connection, then, can continue beyond your Higher Self and to the Higher Selves of others. One of the uses this object can have is to help you find and create an attraction to the artifact in Peru. Simply request that you be united with it. You should not attempt to describe how this will happen; simply state the desired goal.*

"*The other feeling that I will mention briefly is enthusiasm. Enthusiasm of the heart indicates that the object of the enthusiasm is something that corresponds with your divine path at the time. It is like a game that you used to play as children where one person closed their eyes and the others would say, 'You're getting hotter,' or 'You're getting colder,' depending on how close you got to some object. Well, your enthusiasm – or lack of it – is exactly like this. Enthusiasm of the heart means you are getting warmer. If your feelings about something are lukewarm, you're not particularly close to your path as your Higher Self understands it. If something that you are feeling in the moment leaves you cold, you can be sure that you are not very close to your true path. But when you are enthusiastic, it is a good sign you are on your path.*"

Sananda's love and warmth penetrated our bodies and our minds as we sat in the presence of his energy. We were touched by his hand and felt more ready to go forward. Still I voiced my concerns, "I'm afraid we won't be prepared."

Sananda asked softly, "*In what way?*"

"We are failing at our task of meditating twice a day. I'm afraid the Ascended Masters must be disappointed in us. Your coming tonight was just what I needed."

Sananda reassured us, "*Your days are full now and will be for a time as you take care of the endings and start new beginnings. It is sort of double trouble. You are not doing one thing. You are doing two different things. There is a winding down, a closing. At the same time there*

*is a building up, a beginning. These things do not usually happen simul-
taneously in your world but we have doubled you up. Things will fit
together. You will see. We have folded time together for you and many
others. This is why you are advised about being flexible.*

*"Remain flexible. Remain positive. Be joyful. Things will get done
in spite of you. The wheels are in motion. You do not know it yet, but
often you will only have to show up. We can see your progress from a
broader vantage point. Your fears and frustrations will not make any
difference – so, why have them?"*

I was having such difficulty with the notion of going to Peru that it
was preying on my mind almost constantly. My vision of landing in a
third world country, unable to speak the language, and searching for an
"artifact" which we knew very little about, was overwhelming. We didn't
seem to be getting any clues about its location. I said emphatically to our
trusted guide, "Sananda, I really don't want to go to Peru! I don't know
why going to Peru seems so formidable to me, but it is."

"Well, suppose we sent you to Peru, Ohio, instead?"

"Oh, that sounds easier. Yes. I could handle that one."

*"Unfortunately, the artifact is not in Ohio. I suggest that you both
try some exercises of attraction. And I suggest that you put off thinking
about a second trip until after you have taken the first trip. Let things
unfold for you in the proper time. I would prefer not to tell you too much
more at this time. The experiences you will be having in New Mexico may
throw a completely different light on things Peruvian. So, if we could
leave that for a time and speak of it again in a week or two ... I would just
counsel you that this is something that need not prey on your mind. It is
not time for such a trip. It is now time for other things which will lead to
other things yet. By the time the first trip is over you may be interested to
look back on the past couple of months and see if your attitudes have
changed. Will you agree to let the Peru concerns be released for a time?"*

We both agreed. I was, frankly, beginning to feel foolish at my
concerns and was relieved at the advice to take one step at a time. Being
in the flow meant being in the moment. We needed to make another trip
to New Mexico before going to Peru. I imagined the Masters looking at

the probabilities of all our actions here on Earth. (If she does this, then Plan A goes into effect; if she does that, we go to Plan B.) I remembered about individual free will and choice, knowing that I had the ability to say what I would ultimately do. But, deep within my being, I knew that what was being asked of us was of tremendous importance. I felt a deep yearning to respond. What a different perspective this was. Peru was just another place!

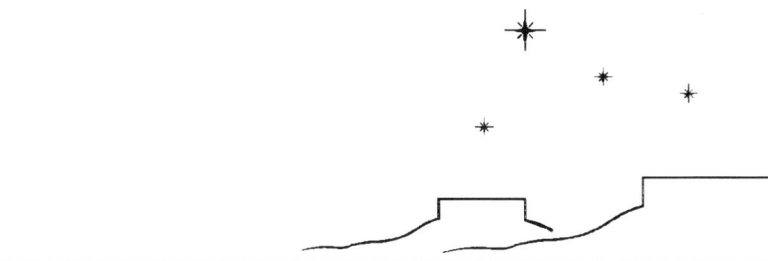

DARTAN

Weeks passed without further communication. A part of us knew this was all real, but another part of us wanted to dispel the notions that these voices in our heads came from anywhere except our own daydreams. Could there really be multiple coexisting dimensions? Right here? Could we actually communicate between them? These were new concepts, and we needed time to integrate them into our lives.

Then, one night, I received an energetic signal that an entity wanted to communicate. It felt like gentle drops of energy raining down and then coursing through my body. Together, Fred and I sat down to listen as I brought through the message.

"This is Dartan. I am the courier of the message for you tonight. I have been waiting for you to make your decisions about whether or not you are going to accept the invitation to participate in the project which is now underway for establishing, balancing, fixing and maintaining the

Planetary Light Grid. As you have been informed previously, it is my assignment to oversee the activities on the Crystal Mesa at the Apache Ranch.

"*Now, for your part, there are things to be done. But the first issue is your willingness to cooperate. This assignment does not necessarily require you to abandon your lives. It is not necessary for you to walk out the gang plank and jump into an abyss. Whether you are aware of it or not, you are already, in effect, participating. The work and the sharing you are doing with others is helping to reinforce the Light connections on your dimension. As those who are receiving the messages communicate with each other, they are affirming the validity of the messages they have received. And, you know, this seems so preposterous that all of you do benefit by getting validation from others who are receiving these same messages and putting the pieces together. Bit by bit, it will help you to understand more.*

"*Your presence here in Santa Fe would be appreciated. We acknowledge your other obligations but we would like you to come. <u>Plan on being here by August 25th.</u> This is a time of great joy for all of us who are here to assist planet Earth and her peoples. As we see the lights of your beings shining more brightly, as we see more lights becoming lit, and we begin to see migrations and gatherings of workers of the Light who are coming together to fulfill their purposes, we know that the calling is being understood deeply on the inner levels. You are beginning to respond to this calling and know that the time of momentous changes and events upon Earth is near.*

"*Your hearts can be filled with joy, as are ours. You have waited for lifetime upon lifetime for that which is coming. The sharing which you are doing is of great importance. It is a spreading of potential, of possibility thinking, kindling of fires, lighting of flames and you are supported on many levels for the tasks which you have undertaken.*

"*You know that when you are moving on purpose there are no questions or doubts. There is sureness in every step. Such certainty will spin the heads of those around you and cause them to stop and think, to ponder upon their own directions. That is also a service. As Earth moves forward in the planetary grid into higher vibrational frequencies, so each of you are making this shift along with the planet. Those who cannot make the shift will not move forward with the planet. This is a time of choices and movement and growth.*

"This is Dartan of the Lightship protecting the land near Santa Fe. We are waiting for you to return. We are waiting for you to bring your light and your love to join others here. They are waiting for the instruction you will bring. So plan your trip. Drive your car so that you will have flexibility in going and coming. Put your house in order. Handle the affairs of your business so that you can be gone. Bring with you the artifact as a symbol that will welcome you into the secret community. Bring your moccasins to tread lightly upon the Earth. And bring your love to share."

"That was a new energy," I told Fred, "this one who calls himself Dartan."

"Yes. But we've heard that name before."

"Uh-huh. Do you remember Soltec told us, some time ago, that Dartan was the placeholder on the mesa? It's great to hear from him. But that in itself is not the only exciting thing – I was given that date weeks ago by the same compelling voice that first told us to go to the southwest! I didn't know what it meant and I never mentioned it. August 25th. That's the date! It has been confirmed by the one who waits for us!" It was the signal pulling our attention back to the project we had, together, agreed upon. We knew our time of quiet was now over, the next phase to begin.

We moved our office furnishings to the house. The phone continued to ring with questions from our customers, none of our computers were hooked up so answering any unusual questions was difficult; all of our files were in boxes in the garage, and we were trying to squeeze a three-room office into one small bedroom. Amid this chaos, Fred came in and announced, "I think we should go to New Mexico this weekend."

I could hardly believe my ears. What was he thinking? Couldn't he see that we were in the middle of moving? How could we take a vacation NOW? I thought, "Give me a break!" but instead I just said, "Oh, Fred."

The exasperated tone of my voice revealed my feelings. "We can't just drop everything and take a trip."

Fred persisted, "We're supposed to go again. You know, we're supposed to make a second trip to Santa Fe and a trip to Peru before we return to Santa Fe again by August 25th. That's less than three month's time. It's already the 1st of June!"

"Yes, but we can go later," I responded. "I don't think it needs to be right now."

Fred turned and walked out of the room, disappointment on his face. And I continued with the task of getting the business settled in its new location at home. We each continued with our own tasks and didn't speak of the trip again until that evening, when Fred said, "Let's sit down and see if anyone wants to talk to us. I think we need to get some guidance here."

"All right," I agreed. We sat down in the living room, and Fred turned on the tape recorder to capture any messages which might come. Dartan was waiting for us to put our "antennas" up and, immediately, Fred began to sense the words forming in his mind, "*I bid you greetings, Earthlings. This is Dartan. I am the keeper of the gate over the land you know in New Mexico as Santa Fe. But, more specifically, of a particular point of power which you became aware of when once before you ventured out on a quest. This power point is now being activated and ones of your plane are invited to assist and to be a part of, and witness to, this process.*

"*The work to be done on your part is minimal as the majority of the work is being performed by those of us on the other side of the door of dimensions. This power point is to be activated with a great ceremony. Those seekers who are invited will be there to participate in the ceremony of awakening. It will be a celebration of love and Light. It will be a celebration, a verification to those who have been receptive to our calls.*

"*You are among the chosen few who have been invited to participate. You will show up at the appointed time and place. Your commitment to the work of the Light Grid will bring you there. Your desire to be there will be so compelling that nothing will stop you from arriving at the proper* time. If you are stopped from trekking, do not fret. This only means that the timing is not correct. We will not let you miss this major event that you have been working toward.

"You are doing a good job of following your instincts, so be sensitive to your feelings. They will be your verification when the time to come is right. Our preparations are nearly ready. Your preparations on yourselves, on raising the vibrational frequencies of your body, on releasing your fears and limitations, on becoming more Christ-like, are nearly completed. That is good, for there can be no darkness and no doubt in the circle. You can make an arrangement with the owner of the land so that you will have access to it."

I heard only: "If something stops you, do not fret – the timing isn't right."

We said good night without discussing the messages we had heard, each believing we shared the answer to our questions.

MESA

112

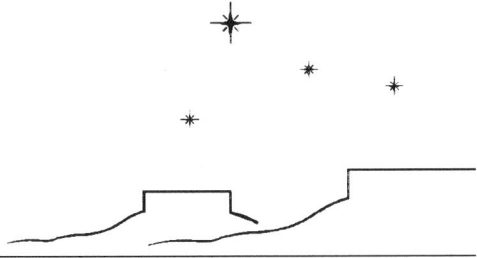

INTENTION

Fred woke early the next morning and began packing the car; I got up and began organizing our office. Around mid-morning, Fred came in and, when he saw me at the computer, he asked, "What are you doing?"

"I'm working."

"I don't understand. I thought it was clear that we were leaving today."

"I have to get these orders shipped out. I have to get these letters sent and the bills paid. I can't leave with all these things undone. We are still in business, you know."

Fred appeared stunned. He turned and left the room without speaking. He stepped into the living room and looked at the pile of cassette tapes he had been making so we could have some music on the trip. They were all ready to go.

A few minutes later, Fred came back into the office and said to me, "Were you listening to Dartan's message last night?"

"Yes, of course I was. He said that if something stops you, it's just because the time isn't right. We have obligations and commitments here which need to be handled. We can go later."

Fred shook his head as he watched me continuing to put some software manuals together to be shipped out. "That's not what I heard."

"Well, then, what did you hear?"

"Dartan said, 'Your commitment to the work of the Light Grid will bring you there at the proper time. Your desire to be there will be so compelling that nothing will stop you.' Aren't you listening to our guides?"

"Of course, I am. This work is stopping me from leaving now, and it's okay. I don't feel anything compelling about going right now."

Fred said, "I think we should sit down and channel again. Maybe we can get some more clarity on this."

I sighed, "Okay." I put the half-filled orders aside and joined Fred who had gone ahead of me to the living room. His glasses were already lying on the table next to him, and I could see he was prepared to channel.

"Hello. This is Soltec, Mighty Messenger of the Circles. I bid you welcome and thank you for coming to your place of meditation. Now, I will tell you a little bit about the coming events. New Mexico is a very good idea at this time. You should not miss it. You can still make the necessary preparations as this trip is part of your service. You are both in alignment for leadership roles if you are only willing to accept them. They are like garments that you can put on. The more you wear them, the more comfortable they become. You can make yourselves tools of service by being examples for others. This lies in our design for you. The people that you meet will all be looking for something that you can deliver ... understandings and experiences. You can also deliver a context in which yourselves and others can practice Light alignment techniques. As you are doing this, all the resources you require will come to you. Finances will not be a problem.

"So, act on your heart's knowing. Ignore and squash those creations of the mind which embody fear. You may use the technique of saying, 'Yes, I know this fearful thing might occur, but I will not spend any time worrying about it. Instead, I will simply push it aside and proceed down the path of No Fear.'

"This is intent working. When your intent is strong, your doubts and fears get pushed aside. You know that the things you fear could happen, but they don't bother you. You know that Earth could start spinning the other way around. It might be possible. But it is not going to happen and you don't worry about it. There is a possibility that you will get hit by a drunk driver or another car near you on the road, but these are not realistic concerns and you don't worry about them. The secret is to allow the possibility that something untoward or undesirable may happen, but not worry about it. Simply concentrate on the road that is taking you to your desired destination. The other fears need not bother you.

"Human beings are so powerful. For you two, the awareness of this power has been increased. So, practice in the Light, practice in the sunshine, and let your doubts and fears be off to the side. Eventually there will be no room for them as the strength of your intent becomes stronger and creates a glow around you. We give you the understandings and show you the steps, but you are the ones who must take them. Go forth and make the preparations that are dictated by your intentions. Perform the actions and then the results will be as you desire. That is truly the way that Light works."

As soon as the message was completed, I got up and returned to the office to resume my tasks while Fred, who had brought the message through, remained sitting on the sofa. Shortly, Fred came into the office and saw that I was, once again, sitting at the computer. "What are you doing?"

"There's no one else to do this work. I'm so frustrated! Everything seems so difficult today. Most of the boxes aren't unpacked yet and I'm trying to rush. Each thing I try to do seems to take twice as long as it should."

"Can't you just let it go?"

"But what about our customers? What about these orders?"

"I've tried everything I can to get through to you but you just seem to ignore the messages we receive."

His patience had reached its limit, and he spun around on his heels and headed outside at the speed of a full balloon with its pressure suddenly released. He sat in the front seat of his truck and lit a cigarette, thinking about what he should do.

After awhile, Fred came back into the office where I was frantically trying to take care of the business details. It was already noon.

He announced, "I'm going to Santa Fe without you!"

I couldn't believe the words I was hearing. I dropped the papers onto the desk and looked at him in dismay.

He continued relaying his decision, "I'll take my truck so you can keep the car."

He had made a plan.

Shocked by his resolve, I began to protest, "I *will* go with you, but I just can't go this morning!"

"I'm going alone!"

"But your truck gets lousy gas mileage," again I protested.

Fred turned and walked out of the room again without responding, leaving me sitting alone, stunned at his determination.

Well, I didn't want him to go without me. I knew that for sure. I didn't want to miss out on anything and I certainly didn't want to be left behind! I went to find Fred to tell him how I felt.

The telephone rang as I was passing through the kitchen, and I stopped to answer it.

"Don't go!" There was urgency in the voice on the other end of the line. She didn't give her name, but I recognized her voice. It was Glenda, a friend who knew we had been discussing the trip. She was aware of the pressure I was feeling about it. This woman was a psychic and I respected her ability to "see," which was both a blessing and a curse to her. She could see into the future and she could see into people's physical bodies.

If there was disease, she saw its ravage; if there was danger, she saw its warnings.

She repeated the warning with even greater intensity, "Pam, please don't go!" I could almost see the determination on her face.

"Well, it looks like we're going," I replied.

"Listen to me, Pam!"

I had never heard her sound this way before. And she pleaded with me again, "Please don't go!"

"Why not?"

"I just don't think you should go. I don't know when I've felt anything so strongly. You've been on my mind all day, and when I think about this trip, I feel almost a sense of panic."

My mind filled with the thundering of missiles coming at me from all directions. I didn't share Fred's yearning to make this trip right now; I felt obligated to fulfill the commitments to our customers. Now there was a warning which came from out of nowhere. I struggled to balance all of these conflicting messages and make a decision. I wondered if there would really be danger if we went. Unseen forces were at work, pulling me first this way and then that, and I knew the only answer lay within. Should I pay attention to this warning?

I understood we were to return to Santa Fe as well as Fred did. How could we balance the various aspects of our lives? I went outside to talk to Fred. When I found him he was loading his old pickup truck, making preparations to leave. "Please sit down and talk to me," I pleaded.

"That's all I've been doing for days. There's no use in talking."

"Please!"

He obliged me with his expression and I proceeded, "I want to go with you."

He just returned a blank stare.

"I really do. I just couldn't leave town without taking care of these things. With the move, I'm already behind on everything."

Again, he said nothing.

I tried to share my dilemma with him. "I just had a most unsettling phone call from Glenda."

"Oh, yeah? What did she want?"

"It was a warning, Fred. She said 'Don't go.' She was pretty insistent about it. It seemed like she thought there was some danger if we went." I waited for Fred's response.

"What kind of danger?"

"I don't know. She couldn't really say. She got into a whole thing about when she was a little girl and got locked in a car in the heat near Phoenix. It might've been her stuff even though she's usually pretty clear about what she sees."

"I don't think it means anything."

"Well, I don't know." I noticed my own body to see what it would tell me. There was no anxiety. "She does like drama. You're right, it probably doesn't mean anything. Fred, I've looked at it. If I do just the very minimum, I think I can be done in another hour. Then I'll need an hour to pack and we can leave by 3:00 o'clock this afternoon."

He just kept staring at me.

"Is that too unreasonable?" I raised my voice. I tried to calm myself and reason with him, "It really might be better leaving later in the day. We can get started this afternoon and drive to the edge of the desert to sleep. Then we can get up early and drive across the Mojave before it gets too hot."

Fred said nothing.

I wondered why I hadn't shared his urgency about going. "Fred, we have to work this out! I don't know what's so important about going right now."

"I don't either, but it seems very important to me. You know, sometimes we just have to act on our trust. I agree with you, it's sometimes hard to do, but when new things start to come into your life, maybe you just have to let go of some of the old things in order to make room for them."

"Well, can we agree on this compromise?" I begged.

Fred lit another cigarette, staring at the ground in silence.

I was crushed to see his disappointment as he exhaled slowly. I wanted desperately to do what we were supposed to do, and I couldn't understand why there was such conflict over this trip. We usually got the same information about things.

Finally he replied, "All right."

"Okay. I'll just finish what I'm doing as fast as I can and then I'll pack." I gave him a kiss on the cheek, which wasn't returned, and quickly dashed back into the house.

I finished the necessary work and went to our room to pack a bag. I pulled out some clothes. I didn't know why we were going or what we would be doing in Santa Fe. Tomorrow would be the first of June and it was bound to be warm. Nothing special was needed. In a matter of minutes I had packed some comfortable clothes and was ready.

Fred had been silently preparing for this trip all week and had made twenty-three hours of music cassettes for the drive. Our son, Drew, would stay at home and take care of the place. The prospect of a week of independence delighted him. The answering machine was connected to the business phone and we would check each day for messages. Our clients didn't even need to know we were gone.

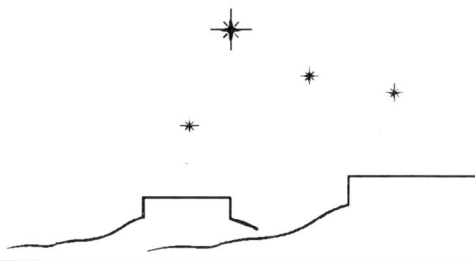

JOURNEY

It was four o'clock in the afternoon when we finally drove out of the driveway. I slipped a cassette into the tape player and the sound of the Beach Boys singing "Good Vibrations" filled the car. It was a relief to have extricated ourselves from our life. We drove for three hours and stopped at a restaurant along the highway in Paso Robles to meet Kate and her friend Mary for dinner. They were already waiting at the table when we arrived. Kate's face was full of anticipation as she raised her shoulders and clasped her hands together, "You're here!"

"Yeah, we made it," I replied.

Kate motioned to her companion and said, "This is Mary." They looked at each other and giggled like two schoolgirls with a secret.

Fred allowed his enthusiasm to swell as he responded to their excitement by greeting them, "We're on a mission from God."

Everyone laughed.

Kate said again, "This is Mary. She's the one who gave me 'Crystal'."

I acknowledged the connection, "I didn't understand it when Kate gave the crystal to us but I knew it must be very special. It didn't seem right for me to keep the crystal once the trip was over, so I gave it back to her when we returned."

Kate interrupted, "I've given it back to Mary now."

"You have?"

"Yes. Once I had 'Crystal' back, I realized she no longer held the same power for me. I didn't need to hold her at night anymore but started leaving her on my night stand. I began to realize that my strength was within me so I gave 'Crystal' back to Mary." She paused, "It was given to her when she was ordained too."

"You've been ordained as a minister too?"

"Yes, I completed my schooling about five years ago, but I clean houses and am a massage therapist these days to make a living. I'd like to be part of a school so I could share my real talents more, but this is what I'm having to do right now."

Now, the crystal was Mary's once again. It had been years since she and her friend "Crystal" had been together, and Mary giggled with delight as they told the story about its return. "'Crystal' does have a mind of her own. She decides when it's time for her to move on."

Kate changed the subject, "Did you bring the artifact with you?"

"Well, of course. We are on a mission from God, you know." We were intoxicated with enthusiasm, and our raucous laughter bubbled forth. I pulled the artifact out of my pocket and handed it to Mary, asking, "What do you think it is?"

Mary's eyes closed as she clasped the artifact in her hand. Kate had told me that Mary had psychic training, and I hoped she could give us more information about it. I leaned forward, "What can you tell us about it?"

"I don't know. It's some kind of an activator."

"What kind of an activator?"

Mary shook her head and her eyes remained closed as she responded, "I just feel this pulsation in my head. I don't know. It's a very powerful piece."

I wanted her to say more. Perhaps she couldn't.

We enjoyed our visit, laughing and talking with Kate and Mary about the trip, even though I was still a little cranky. We all laughed at my silliness as I grumbled, " ... and we _had_ to leave today."

"I'll go for you!" Kate chimed in.

"Me too," Mary's mischievous laughter bubbled up again. "You can clean the houses I have scheduled tomorrow."

"Well, that puts things into perspective." I could see the irony of the situation. These two were aching to share in the quest. It was such an honor to be called upon in this way, and I had only felt inconvenienced.

Mary gave us the phone number of a friend of hers, Annie, who lived in Santa Fe. "I told her you'd be calling; she's looking forward to hearing from you."

"Thank you very much. It'll be good to have a contact when we arrive."

Now it was Mary who pulled the crystal out of her purse as she said, " 'Crystal' wants to go with you again."

I gasped and my head swirled as I recognized that Mary was about to give us her treasure to carry along. I said, "I'll take good care of it," as I extended my hand to accept the crystal once again. Mary's eyes welled with tears as she accepted the direction of her own guidance and released the beloved "Crystal" to my care. I was touched and humbled by the crystal's return, not understanding the strange workings of Spirit which caused the crystal to continue being passed to me each time we ventured out.

By the time dinner was completed we had shared much laughter and the story of our adventure. It was now time to embark on the next leg of our journey and to see where the road might lead us. I shook my head as we headed off into the night.

Fred asked, "Why are you shaking your head?"

"I was thinking about the day. We've been given this crystal again. It's a reminder about what has happened already – finding the mesa. Kate and Mary would give anything to be going, and I was fussing about it! I can hardly believe myself! It seems so ironic. I had so much resistance to leaving, and then that phone call came to test me. I had to really go within to see what felt right in spite of all the conflicting outside pressure."

Fred smiled, "I guess it was all right to come after all."

"Oh, yes. I always knew it was. It's just so difficult to shift back and forth, to integrate the two different parts of our life. It's difficult trying to keep a balance between two worlds. I'm really grateful that we can do this. We're a little like Bilbo Baggins as he headed off on his quest in the *Trilogy of the Rings*. We've been given just the things we need for our journey – a crystal wand, a piece of gold, a set of clues. It's amazing!"

Fred nodded in agreement.

We drove until midnight and stopped at a budget roadside motel in Bakersfield. A woman who was obviously intoxicated walked past us as we were heading up the stairs to our room. As we passed, she shouted over her shoulder at Fred who was walking ahead of me, "Well, you're not very friendly!"

I gave a little shudder at the clientele as I stepped around a barbecue, hot with glowing embers, which remained at the edge of the balcony from the late-night supper of the guests in the next room. The air was hot, even at this hour, and the room did not appear to have been cleaned after the last tenants. There were crumbs on the table and residue littered the basin. I shuddered as I looked at the grimy carpet and grumbled silently, once again, about the trip.

I didn't sleep that night. The air conditioning whirred but didn't cool the air, and I lay awake in the stuffy room wondering about the warning that I received on the telephone, dreading the next day's drive across the desert.

❖   ❖   ❖

We traveled across the desert with all the windows down in our little Nissan 280ZX. Fred's music blasted and the hot wind blew. We stopped in Flagstaff for the night, exhausted from the drive. This time the motel air conditioning brought welcome relief and I collapsed on the bed. I didn't care about dinner, or whatever was holding me back at home, or what might lay ahead. I knew only my exhaustion.

The next morning the world looked different. The heat, the physical stress of the drive, the wind, had all purged my psyche of its attachments. By the time we arrived in Santa Fe, we were both focused on the unfoldment of our charge. We wanted to stay as close to the mesa as we could, and stopped for lunch at the same cafe where we had seen the sign on our first visit.

I asked the waitress, "We'd like to stay around here tonight. Do you know of any place close by?"

Her English wasn't very good, and my Spanish was even worse. I wondered if she understood me. "No," she replied in a heavy Spanish accent. "There's no place here."

Well, I couldn't accept that for an answer! There had to be a place. After we finished our meal, I got up from the table and went back to the kitchen to talk with the owner. I had spoken with her on our last trip and thought she might remember.

"Hi, Elena," I said, standing in the kitchen doorway.

She looked up from the stove where she was preparing tacos and gave me a questioning look, "Hi."

I could tell she didn't remember me and explained, "We came here for lunch the last time we were visiting and came back all the way from California to have a couple of your tacos again."

She smiled at the somewhat pretentious compliment, "Oh, thank you."

"We were hoping we could stay in town tonight. Do you know of any place?"

She thought for a moment, searching her memory. "Well, there is one place. It's just across the river. There's kind of a campground with some rustic cabins. It's pretty primitive but people say it's nice."

I thanked her and headed back to the table to tell Fred. "Elena knew of a place for us to stay. I knew we'd find something. Let's go check it out."

We paid the check, jumped into the car and followed her directions across the river to the camp. The sign was overgrown with bushes and, if we hadn't known exactly where the turnoff was, we wouldn't have seen it. The campground was lush and green, and we heard the sound of a rushing river nearby. There was a peaceful energy which we sensed the moment we stepped out of the car. We knocked at the door of the manager's cabin.

The screen door opened with a squeak. The woman standing there said, "Hello. Can I help you?"

I looked past her and peeked inside the cabin. It was a small scantily furnished room with a table and two chairs, a faded sofa, and a wood stove. On her table was a notebook. Soft music was playing on the tape player.

Fred extended his hand to her, "We're Fred and Pam Cameron."

"I'm Claire."

"Do you have any cabins available for tonight?"

"Yes," she replied with hesitation.

I wondered what seemed to be the problem about our staying. She explained, "I'm having a gathering here tonight and we're going to have a bonfire and do a medicine wheel. It's a graduation, of sorts, for my group." To our questioning looks she continued, "I'm a psychotherapist in Santa Fe. I'll have to put you in the cabin at the end so we don't bother you with our drumming and singing."

She explained the layout of the campground, "The cabins have no running water but there's a central bathhouse right across the way. There's a woodpile next to the bathhouse where you can get the wood for your wood stove."

We wondered if this was more rustic than we were prepared for, and Fred told her we'd like to check it out.

"Go on and have a look. Then you can come back and let me know what you decide."

We agreed and drove to the end of the grassy road which ran between two rows of small log cabins along the riverbank. Each cabin had a hand carved name plaque hanging over the door. There were "Raven," "Meadowlark," "Sparrow," and "Thyme." When we reached our cabin at the end of the road, we stopped the car and got out. Together we looked at the sign hanging above its door – "Spirit."

"Fred," I said, "look at that! Can you believe it?"

Fred smiled in return. "Of course." Surely this was no coincidence.

It was a rustic log cabin. Flypaper hung from the kitchen light, and the moths began fluttering around it as soon as we switched it on. The kitchen had an antique wood burning stove in the corner and a 50's vintage chrome table and chairs under the small window. The second room was a bedroom with two double beds, each topped with handmade quilts and woolen blankets. We smiled and hugged each other. "Let's stay," we both said at once and agreed without discussion that we would stay two nights instead of one.

We walked back to the manager's cabin, named "Hobbit," and made the required arrangements. We stopped by the woodshed and each picked up an arm load of wood to carry back to our "Spirit" cabin for a fire.

We hadn't anticipated camping and needed to go back to town to get provisions and make some phone calls. We drove back to the hotel where we had spent a night on our first trip to Santa Fe. We knew it would be warm and cozy in the lobby, and we could do all of our calling comfortably there.

I called Mary's friend, Annie, "We were given your name by our friend, Mary."

"Oh, yes. I've been expecting you. We're having a gathering tomorrow night to watch one of our friend's videos of her trip to Peru. Can you come?"

Peru! Was this another amazing coincidence? I got the directions to the house where the gathering would occur and hung up the phone, pacing as I waited for Fred to complete his business calls. He had also called Jan Gardner, the owner of the mesa land. When he was finished he asked, "Are we going to see Annie?"

"Oh, yes. You're not going to believe it," I replied. "She's invited us to a gathering tomorrow night to watch someone's video of a trip to Peru!"

A smile broke across his face, "Naturally," he grinned.

And I asked him, "Can we see the land?"

"Of course. First thing tomorrow."

Things were beginning to seem magical: we had landed mysteriously at a wonderful cabin named "Spirit" and were invited to a gathering about Peru. The difficulty we had launching this trip now seemed far away, and we felt the sense of moving into the flow. Now we had only to let go and see where the river would carry us.

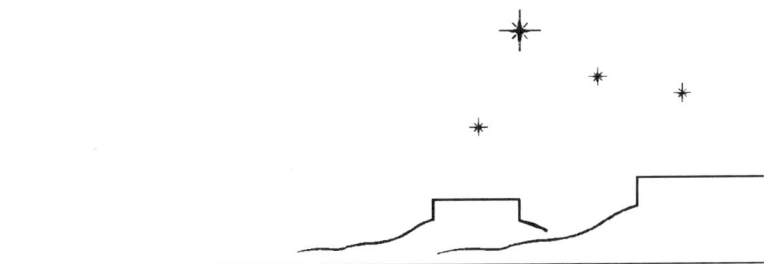

SPIRIT

It was dusk when we returned to our "Spirit" cabin. Just a week earlier the river had flooded and it now rushed by, pushing at its banks as the rain continued falling. I opened the window in the bedroom a few inches to hear the sound of the water, then placed the artifact next to the crystal on the dresser. As I went through the motions of unpacking, I reflected on the nature of this trip. It was the first of two we had been asked to make. We were supposed to prepare the land. What did that mean? How would it be done? Our sense of curiosity was keen.

Being the only ones at the campground made it feel like our very own spiritual retreat. The cabin was soon warm and cozy from the fire burning in the wood stove, and the smell of pinion pine filled the air with its unique spicy fragrance. We sat by the fire in the kitchen and asked for our bridge across dimensions to be extended. Archangel Michael greeted us, *"Greetings! There are some things we have not stressed up until now which we would like to impart to you tonight. We want you to know that the more you follow your own alignment and your own paths, the more protected you will be. You have, indeed, walked squarely into our area of protection in your spiritual cabin.*

"*Your tasks are primarily with people, so the meeting you will have tomorrow night will be very important for introducing people to some of your ideas. You will find them very interested, rapt, and eager to participate in activities that you may facilitate. Tomorrow you have arranged your first entrance onto the land that we have reserved and dedicated to a formation of a new node of the Light Grid. This will be very exciting for you.*

"*It would be good if you could arrange to visit the land from time to time. You will need to reveal as much of your situation and your understandings as you feel are necessary to let Jan know why you are interested in the land. We suggest you try to answer her questions fully, but you do not need to volunteer information that she isn't ready to hear. Although the function of the land has been dormant for centuries, it has been activated in the past two years. She does know something because she has owned the land for some time.*

"*There are to be gatherings of people who wish to strengthen their connection in spirit from time to time and from place to place, starting now and proceeding for as many years as possible. This gathering of people tomorrow will hear from you whatever their level of preparedness will allow them to hear. You can help them by listening to what their enthusiasm is saying. This is the key. This is the way the Higher Self manifests desires in your plane – by enthusiasm. You might give some thought as to how one detects true enthusiasm as opposed to the mass consciousness focus of your society, for the ideas of mass consciousness are simply not appropriate any longer. They have been sold to everyone like a false message. Sooner or later the bottom is going to drop out. The false front is going to fall down and people will see what is behind it. Then, there will be some tough going. But, if some people have banded together and strengthened their own understanding and their own practices, they will be largely immune from the trials and tribulations happening in society.*

"You are getting quite good at discriminating between those people that have enthusiasm for these ideas and those who do not. Your practice period for this has been completed, and you are now full fledged field operatives in discrimination testing and Light Worker detection. You will now have some practice in helping others see how their enthusiasm can be directed toward a group goal. It may not necessarily be your group – it may be another group – but this is the time that ones who are Light Workers must band together and support one another.

"I trust you are getting the idea from my remarks that you can be beacons. To light up Light Workers is one of the reasons you are in New Mexico now. You can be positive sources of Light. You need only be clear and share your understanding in your own words. They will jump at the chance to participate with you.

"You see, you do not need to buy this land (which you really have not sufficient means to buy), but you understand now that the land will remain as we intend it. We are taking care of it. Indeed, in the year that it has been available, no one has bought it.

"The owner of this land is quite closely aligned to Dartan. Even though she does not consciously know why, she wishes to preserve this land. This is precisely what we have described to you and that will remain so. She does not know the particulars, but she has unconsciously developed her ideas of the land in alignment with your understandings.

"No one need stay on this land. Humans may find, at least at first, that the energy generated by the anchor stone is quite strong and is uncomfortable for day-to-day activities. If people are doing spiritual activities that will bring them into alignment with the Light, they will understand that alignment and want to have more of it. Think about being near the energy on this land as standing under a waterfall. What you want to do is to get as many people soaking wet with these ideas as possible. Their enthusiasm will orient you to their desires, and they will be more willing to listen to the whole understanding if you will tap into this as an entry point."

"There is no need to worry about your trip here or your trip home. Simply stay in close touch with your enthusiasm level and communicate it. Being in the moment is a good way for your Higher Self to

communicate with you. Listen to your enthusiasm. I will help you. Thank you for coming this far with your enthusiasm, your empowerment, your faith, and your trust in us as your guides. You have a very exciting day lined up for tomorrow, so I will bid you good night."

It was late and we were tired when Michael departed. We crawled into bed full of our own enthusiasm for the next day, and snuggled up close to each other listening to the soothing sounds of the rain, the river, and the crackling fire as we drifted off to a most deep and peaceful sleep.

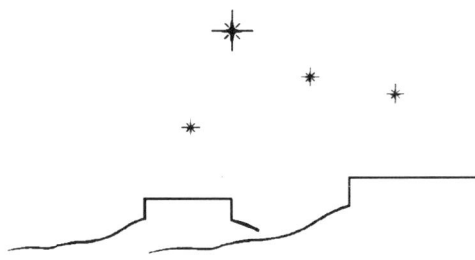

SANTA FE

The next morning we were full of anticipation. The sun was shining brightly and the world glistened with water droplets clinging to the leaves and grasses from the night's rain. We met Jan at her ranch early in the morning to avoid the usual afternoon thunderstorms while we were out.

Fred had held a long-time dream of creating a center, or retreat, which began to come to life as he described its requirements to Jan. This was our ostensible goal and we spent the morning looking at other properties. However, our real desire was to see the sacred land and, somehow, to prepare it for the activation. We knew what we must do, but had little idea of how it was to happen.

As we drove around with Jan, I shared the vision of the mesa which had begun our quest. Her response surprised me, "You know, when something like that happens, you have to follow it. I once had a premonition in a dream, and it came to pass. I trust in these things now."

Finally, the formality of looking at other properties was out of the way and we headed up to the mesa.

At last! My heart surged with anticipation as we turned up the dirt road which had been hidden from us on our first trip. Once again I recognized the mesa of my dreams. The road was rutted and steep. As Jan maneuvered the Jeep around a sharp turn, it lost its traction and began to slip. "This is the worst part of the road," she called over her shoulder, "Hang on! We're almost there." I grasped the grip-bar over the door to stop myself from sliding off the seat. We edged our way up the side of the mesa; with a bump, the car lurched forward and came to a stop at a padlocked gate. Jan unlocked the gate, and we drove through.

Wildflowers bloomed everywhere on this pristine land. We zig-zagged our way carefully to the top of the mesa, weaving between the plants growing on the roughly cut road to avoid crushing any wildflowers or seedlings in our path.

It seemed we could see forever from the top of the mesa. There were meadows and forests, arroyos and magnificent rock formations. We spent hours exploring the land, and stopped frequently to get out of the car and walk around. Neither Fred nor I knew what we were looking for but carried a strong yearning to know the touch of Dartan. And we daydreamed of living on the mesa.

Jan told us, "We've decided to protect part of the mesa by placing it in a land conservancy."

I agreed, "I know this land is very special."

Jan continued, telling us more about its history, "Many people have tried to buy this over the years, but it hasn't been for sale. We could make more money by developing all of it, but I feel it needs to be preserved."

Fred and I cast a knowing smile at each other; we understood that some unseen force was working to protect this sacred land.

Then our introduction to the land was complete, and it was time to leave. We had recognized our own deep connection there and, even though we had received guidance that we needn't buy the land, we tried to figure out some way we could make it ours to continue in its guardianship.

❖   ❖   ❖

We made a quick change of clothes then went to meet Annie at the gathering. We arrived easily at the apartment of Annie's friend, Jo, and parked the car by the open patio gate. The apartment was full of people (women actually), and cigarette smoke hung heavy in the air. A tall, slender woman emerged from out of the chatter and walked over to us. She smiled a warming smile which spread from ear to ear as she reached out her hand. "Hi," she said, "I'm Annie. You must be Pam and Fred." Her southern drawl and engaging smile made me feel instantly at ease. She introduced us to some of the others, "This is Pam and Fred – they're Mary's friends." The room was filled with lively conversation and talk of summer travel. Annie introduced us to a woman who was standing near the kitchen by the breakfast bar watching the gathering, "This is Krista Sanders. Tonight she's going to be sharing films of her trip to Peru."

She greeted us with an agitated hello, and continued, "I think we should watch the video now. I work at the hospital and I have to get up early for the 5:00 a.m. shift."

Krista walked over to the television and picked up a video tape, announcing, "I think we should get started now." Two or three women sat down, but the rest continued with their animated conversations, oblivious to Krista's requests.

She raised her voice and tried again to get their attention, "I think we should start the video now!"

Finally she was heard and everyone seated themselves around the room. Krista's short blond hair cast a glow that looked like a halo around her face. As she narrated the video she said, "This trip to Peru was truly one of the high points of my life."

She shared her experiences of trekking to the top of the ancient ruins of Macchu Picchu, being honored by the villagers with native celebration and dance, and shopping in the marketplace in Cuzco on her guided tour, while the wistful sounds of Peruvian flute music played in the background.

Fred and I both continued to be amazed at the seeming coincidences surrounding us; here she was, sharing the films of her trip to Peru on the very night that we were there to see them! Here was someone who had gone to Peru – and returned. I whispered to Fred, "She looks pretty normal. She's even a nurse! Perhaps traveling to Peru isn't so strange after all."

After the video was shown, conversations and activity resumed. I slipped my hand into my pocket and curled my fingers around the ancient artifact from Peru as I walked over to show it to Krista and find out what she thought about it. Perhaps it would remind her of something she had seen in Peru and she could give us more insight about it. I pulled the artifact out and placed it in Krista's hand, "This came from Peru. Do you have any idea what it is?"

"No," she shook her head as she looked at it, "I don't."

Without further comment, she turned and carried the artifact outside to the patio where Fred was talking with a group of women. After he briefly told them the story about the artifact, word spread around the room like wildfire that we had an ancient artifact from Peru which was to be part of a sacred ceremony. This sudden stirring of curiosity surprised me, and I asked Fred, "Where's the artifact?" Neither one of us had it now, as it was being passed from hand to eager hand.

It was returned it to me, and I took it inside to mingle with the others when another woman rushed up to me. Her name was Dove. She had long brown hair streaked with silver which she wore braided at her ears; I wondered if she could have been Native American. There was an urgency in her voice, "May I see the artifact?"

I reached out my hand.

Dove gasped as she looked at the artifact. Her face paled and her knees weakened as she took it into her hands. Before her legs gave out, she quickly sat down on the sofa and put her head between her knees. Then, sitting up, she exclaimed, "I don't believe it!" as she showed it to her friend. "This is it!"

"What?" I asked.

"I had a dream about this just two days ago."

"Go on," I urged.

"I dreamt that I had a piece of metal stuck in my arm. In my dream, I pulled it out and looked at it." She paused, shaking her head in disbelief as she looked at the gold piece she was now holding, "This is exactly what I saw!" Dove was overcome with amazement as she tried to understand the meaning of her dream two days earlier. And now two strangers from California had arrived with the object of her dream.

Dove and I sat looking at each other, intrigued by the portent of this coincidence, when our silence was broken by a shrill voice rising above the others in the room, "Let's channel."

It was Jo. It seemed like she was the "ringleader" of this group. She was wide-eyed with excitement, her energy darting about the room like a hummingbird.

"All right!" They all quickly agreed. Everything seemed to be an adventure for these enthusiastic women. (We were accustomed to much more spiritual seriousness in Santa Cruz.) The lights were dimmed and we all sat down – this time we closed our eyes. Everyone became quiet as a stillness filled the air.

The first voice to break the silence was Fred's, *"Hello, this is Ashtar."*

My goodness, I thought. Just jump right in! We don't even know these people or their customs.

The women cheered with delight, "All right, Ashtar!" The room quieted again as we all prepared to listen to his words.

He said, *"The one who is new shall become the leader."* He also warned them to keep their protection up, telling them, *"Light Workers are tasty morsels. Negative beings are attracted to the Light (which you are), like iron filings to a magnet. This is because they desire your energy. Light Workers are like flowers growing toward the light. The more light there is, the grander the blossom. You are being fertilized by spirit. So, be prepared for some wondrous growth and blossoming!"*

After Fred finished delivering Ashtar's message, one of the women said, "I'm getting another message. Would it be all right for me to speak it?" It was Sara. We both felt we must have known her from another time and place, for there was something innately familiar about her. Sara had only recently moved to Santa Fe from Cape Cod. She had come in trust and was there waiting to understand her mission. Was she the one Ashtar said would become the leader? Sara spoke Sananda's loving message and the room became more subdued as we all experienced the healing energies of the One.

When the message being spoken by Sara was finished, I felt my head beginning to fill with energy. I knew it was the presence of Spirit asking to be heard. Jo was sitting on the floor next to me and saw what was happening. She put her hand on my knee, "Are you going to channel?"

I shook my head, "No."

She knew, or thought, I would. She sensed the energies that were with me as she continued to focus her attention on me. Jo whispered in my ear, "You know, if you hold on to the energy, it'll back up on you and you'll get a headache."

"Oh, all right."

It would take a lot of courage for me to do this. I was used to channeling with Fred and sometimes with our friend Kate. I never knew what message was going to be spoken as I began, and was reluctant to start in front of this roomful of strangers. I swallowed my apprehension, took a deep breath, and began, "*This is Dartan.*"

"What?" I thought. "Why is Dartan talking to this group?"

"*There is going to be a major event occurring near here. We will be activating the new energy grid of the planet and anchoring Light energy into the Earth. The invitations have already been sent, and many of you in this room will be invited to participate; you will know if you are to be there.*"

I heard my own words in disbelief. I certainly didn't expect to be extending an invitation to this group, but I continued to allow the words to flow, "*There is no one person at this time who has all of the pieces to the puzzle, who sees the whole picture. You each bring with you a piece, and as you are able to assemble your pieces together, you receive new insights and a greater knowing. Many of you will be traveling soon. As you scatter on your own separate missions, you take with you an imprint of the new combination of pieces you have seen. As you travel around the world, you will join this knowledge with the pieces of others you encounter. Then, when this group reconvenes, the puzzle will be reassembled*

with the many new pieces which you have gathered. Once again, each of
you will secure a new imprint and your own piece will be expanded. The
gathering, imprinting, and dispersing will continue. This process will
allow exponential learning at this time of accelerated transition in Earth's
ascension process."

After the channeling there was a flood of questions from these eager women. They had been waiting. They were spiritual warriors, gathered
together at the precise time of our visit for a purpose. This was _assign-
ment time_ and we all knew it! Some asked about the activation specifics,
and we told them what we could. There was still much that we didn't
understand ourselves; there was much that they would have to discover
on their own.

Then the flurry of activity calmed down, and we all became quiet
again. Now, Dove had a message and was ready to channel. Dove's
guide was a space being she called Merc, who confirmed for the group
that the information from Dartan was "absolutely correct."

There was a question from the group for Merc, "What is the nature
of this new vortex near Santa Fe?"

"It is the new heart chakra of the planet!"

Could this be?

Dove had been channeling for only a couple of weeks; however,
skills to communicate with guides can develop instantly now that the
dimensions are coming closer together. She was trusted by her friends,
and this confirmation from "one of their own" validated the messages
Fred and I had delivered.

The hour was late after all of the channeling so we said our good-
byes, which we knew were only "see you later's." We would be leaving
Santa Fe in the morning to head back to California. We had come. We
had delivered an invitation and a call to action to any who were ready.
Now we would be on our way.

"Can you imagine what they must be thinking?" I asked as Fred
turned the car out of the parking lot and onto the road. He just smiled.

We both knew that we were absolutely in the center of our path.
We were honored to be a part of the divine plan unfolding. There was a

thread of magic in the air and we were turning the wheel which would weave a beautiful cloth of this thread.

The next morning we supposed that we had done what we came to do. We had a chance to become more familiar with things Peruvian, we had been able to gain access to the mesa land, and we had introduced the idea of the Light Grid project along with an invitation to participate.

We didn't have a plan for the day, which was unusual for us. Was our work here complete? As we ate a breakfast of fruit and granola, we opened the maps and discussed various options for our route back to California. Somehow we couldn't agree – or decide – on what we were going to do. I thought, "It took us a long time to get here. Let's just take the shortest route home."

Fred didn't want our adventure to end, "Why don't we drive up through Colorado on our way home?"

"Maybe we should just get back home and not take any side trips this time," I replied.

"Well, that would be all right too."

I thought about it and decided that if Fred really wanted to take this detour it would be all right with me. So I said, "It would probably be nice to see a little more of the country. It's okay with me."

"Well, we don't have to," Fred responded.

It was a dance – each of us wanting to please the other. And, so our plan for the day's drive remained uncertain as we prepared to leave. The route we would take home wasn't critical to either of us.

I wanted to make some tea to carry with us in our thermos. I looked in the cabin and through the half-packed car trunk. "Fred, I can't find the thermos. I think I must have left it at Jo's last night."

"Why don't you call her and ask?"

"Well, there's no telephone here at the campground. We can't even call to see if she's at home."

"We'll just have to stop by on our way out of town and check."

I shook my head, "Oh, we have to go back to Jo's again. That's probably no accident!"

"Right. No accidents."

We continued packing the car, but it felt as if something was still left undone. I didn't believe that we had begun the preparation of the land which we had been asked to do. We had walked on it; you could hardly call that a preparation. There was so much about this assignment that I didn't yet understand. Had we done what we were supposed to do without realizing it?

It felt incomplete.

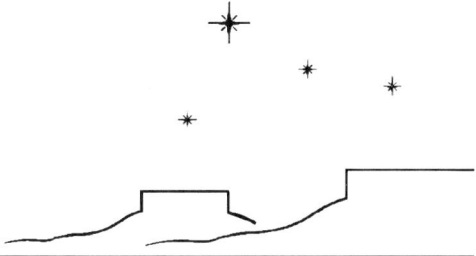

ASSIGNMENTS

We turned the car into the driveway at Jo's apartment complex and parked in the same spot as the night before, wondering if she would be at home. We peeked over the wooden fence and into the apartment. Several people were moving about the living room. Even though it was eleven o'clock in the morning, it looked like they were just starting their day. Dove had a steaming cup of coffee in her hand, and a dark haired woman was sitting at the dining table. I felt like an intruder as we knocked on the patio door, "Hello!"

Dove came over and slid the glass door open.

"Hi, Dove. How are you today?"

She gestured for us to come in and returned to her place on the sofa.

Jo came out of the bedroom, "Hello!" she said with a twinkle in her eye. "Sit down. I'll make us some tea."

Jo introduced us to the woman drinking coffee at the table, "This is Rita Farnsworth. She's from Rochester, New York."

I remembered Rita from the night before. She had sat quietly in the background, almost like a shadow in the corner. I don't think I heard her speak at all. There was an agelessness about her. She looked like a little girl, curled up with her feet on the seat of her chair, and at the same time she looked like a wise old woman.

"Hello," I said.

Rita was sitting at the dining room table, lost in her own thoughts, smoking a cigarette. "Hi," she returned, glancing up at us and then back down again.

"Rita just flew in this weekend from Las Vegas for a little rest and relaxation." Jo explained, "She's been through some tough shit there with a guy and came here to recover." It seemed by her expression that Rita would have preferred Jo keep her mouth shut. She looked like she just wanted to be left alone.

We had exchanged idle conversation for awhile when two other women who were there the night before arrived. It was Sara and her friend Margo. Sara said, "Hi! We just thought we'd drop by. I got up this morning to go out to the flea market to try to sell some jewelry I made. I'm trying to earn a little more money for my trip to Cape Cod. I don't know why, but I couldn't get a space. I was there really early too, but they were all gone. So I decided to get Margo to go out for breakfast. We just felt an urge to come over here after we ate."

Jo's eyes widened. "Okaaay," she stretched out the word as she looked around the room at the group assembling. "We were going to get together later in the day to channel. But it looks like this is it, now. I'll call Iona and tell her to get right over here."

She dialed the phone, "Iona, come right over. I think something's happening."

There was a pause as Jo listened to Iona's response.

"I think you'd better come over right now." There was excitement in Jo's voice, "Well, can't you clean the house later? Something's happening here. Something very unusual."

We could tell that Jo didn't want Iona to miss out on anything and sensed the synchronicity of something unusual coming together. Jo, a wise sprite, was now nearly hopping around the room with enthusiasm. Fred and I looked at each other, trying to figure out what was happening.

A few minutes later, another woman dropped by. It was Sheila. "I have this crystal wand that I found out in Apache Canyon when I was hiking there with a shaman from Peru last summer. I wanted to show it to you after hearing about the artifact last night. Maybe this is important too."

Just then, Iona arrived, "What's going on?" she asked as she walked in, a little out of breath. Her short hair was cut in a style that stood up straight on top, echoing the look of uncertainty in her eyes. She had only recently met Jo and the rest of the group. The many new metaphysical ideas she was hearing mystified her. "Just sit down and wait," Jo directed. The room was full of people once again. Nine of us had gathered mysteriously on that Saturday morning.

Jo said, "Why don't you show Rita the artifact? She didn't get to see it last night because she went to bed early." She had a twinkle in her eye, as if she were up to something, as she curled her wiry body into a cross-legged position on the floor.

Fred pulled the artifact from his pocket where he had been carrying it and handed it to Rita. She held it for a moment, then quickly put it down on the table. "Whoa! That is too intense! I can't even hold onto it. It has such a powerful energy! Phew!" She sat quietly for a few moments, as she looked from Fred to me and back again to Fred. Rita said, "This is mostly for her," and she motioned over to where I was sitting.

Fred nodded his head in acknowledgment, "I know."

There was nothing mysterious about what Rita did. She just started talking to us. She told us a story about the artifact, as though she knew its complete history. She verified everything that we had been told about the piece, much information which we had not shared with anyone, and gave some additional details about its origin. For four hours she talked, channeling non-stop information about the artifact and our mission in conjunction with it.

"This is very old," Rita said. "I think it's pre-Atlantean. It's a piece of something larger." She rolled her eyes back, trying to connect with the history of the artifact, and said, "I can see it. It's a sphere made of gold. It has a handle on it." She paused a moment and then continued relating the description of what she was seeing, "It looks like a scepter from a pre-Incan civilization. The globe is gold with twelve spikes, or knobs, protruding out. This is one of those knobs. The wand holding the globe is made of silver. The total size of the device is about a foot across. It was some sort of power device. It was misused." She paused again, "Pam, you were a part of this."

She looked at me, sensing my alarm, and said, "It was not your fault! You were a young man in your early twenties – around 24 years old. You knew what could happen if this device was used improperly and you tried to tell the elders. But the older men wouldn't listen to you. No one would believe you because you were so young. The scepter's power was abused, and a great tragedy occurred. It was a great cataclysm. It is your task now to right the wrong which was done so many centuries ago."

The story might have seemed absurd, but something about it seemed true to me. I didn't know about other lifetimes, what some call karma reaching from one lifetime to another as the soul learns its lessons. But why was I picked for this assignment? It made sense to me in a way I cannot explain. The responsibility felt enormous. I wanted to do what was right and to correct what had gone awry so long ago. The notion that I could serve humankind was compelling.

As Rita continued, my dedication grew. "The trip to Peru is for you. When you go to retrieve the other artifact, many memories will be awakened. You're going to go through some stuff that will be clearing and healing the pain for many."

Somehow, I understood.

A picture of Fred and me walking up endless stairways flashed into my mind. I saw myself overwrought with grief, unable to continue, sitting down on some stairs, crying. Fred was standing by my side comforting me and encouraging me to go on.

Rita continued, "Fred, you're going to need to be there to support her through this." Then she looked at me and repeated, "Pam, it was not your fault! You have to know this. You tried to tell them. You were wise way beyond your years." And, then, she continued, "The artifact you are to find is a silver alloy. It's the female and balancing component to this one. "

"Can you tell us what the symbols on the artifact mean?" I asked.

"I can read them but I can't translate them for you," Rita replied offhandedly.

Was this just an excuse for not knowing? I checked in with my own sense of discernment and asked her, "Who's giving you this information?"

She replied lightly, "Oh, I don't bother with names," as she waved her hand as if to brush away the question.

I wanted to know and insisted that she try to find out. Rita closed her eyes for a few moments and we waited for her to give us a name. Then she told us, "It's a long Indian name. I can't pronounce it." My request to verify her source remained unanswered, and she continued, "The female counterpart is located high in the mountains ... far away from here."

I tried to envision what she was seeing and asked, "Is it in Peru?"

"It could be. I just see where it is. I'm looking at a time before there was a country called Peru. I can just describe it to you. It's very high in the mountains and very far away from here."

I asked, "Is the piece in Santa Fe now?" hoping we might find what we were searching for on this trip.

"No. It's far away. Pam must make the trip to Peru to retrieve this piece. It's not located in Santa Fe. This trip will be for Pam's own healing. When the pain is released for her it will be done for many, and there will be a major healing. This is a service Pam must perform. She will be able to right this past wrong as she also reconnects Earth to the new energy grid and anchors the light of Heart into the planet. This is a connection which was lost when the object was used improperly so long ago."

Rita continued with the instructions, "There are to be three ceremonies. Two of them will be to prepare Earth for the new Light node. The first will be at the new moon in July; the second will follow two weeks later. There will be seven people participating; it looks like six women and one man. It will be done in a circle. The women will be standing in partners with the lone man in the center of the circle. This is the preparation."

Everyone in the room was spellbound. I could see Fred admired her casual style by the way he looked at her, and I watched her playing with the energies in the room. How effortless it seemed for her to do this. I looked around and counted nine people – Fred, myself, and seven others. I knew beyond any doubt that we were all gathered that day to receive these assignments. Each person in the room could be a part of this, in spite of any personal doubts or questions which may have been silently clamoring in their minds.

Without stopping, Rita continued delivering information about the ceremony for anchoring the Light. "Now about the ceremony: The last ceremony on the mesa will occur at the full moon in August. There will be a three-day window of time when this could occur. It must be done on schedule!"

"I see myself standing in the center of the circle." Rita closed her eyes again briefly and laughed in disbelief. She kind of shook her head as she laughed again, "Phew! This is really going to be a big deal! Ha! I'm wearing a white robe and am bringing down the Light; it looks like I'm the anchor." She seemed amazed at seeing herself in this role and surprised at the importance she was sensing about this project.

Rita continued describing to us what she saw, "The location of the ceremony will be on a high, flat area with small trees, or bushes, sparsely dotted around. I see a large single rock almost like a pulpit standing there. There will be a circle of red dirt, different from the dirt around it. That is where you are to perform the ceremony. When you dig down a few inches with your hands, you will find the original configuration of the scepter there. When the two artifacts which you will bring are placed into position, the grid will be activated. The point for anchoring the Light will be that energy field which is created between the two stones."

I may have doubted her information, except that she verified so much of what we had already been told by our own guides. She was describing the same ceremony we had been told so much about by Soltec, Ashtar and Dartan, as well as Native American spirit guides. Her words validated our own information which we were still learning to trust, and I believed she must have had some supernatural powers, even though there had been several questions she couldn't answer to my satisfaction.

"Don't worry about who should be there and who shouldn't. Their 'people' will let them know. Anyone who tries to come up to the mesa who's not ready to be there will be stopped. They'll get sick or have a flat tire, or in some way be stopped from participating."

Someone eagerly suggested, "Let's get out the calendar and find the date for the full moon in August!" Jo jumped up and dashed into the next room to get a calendar. There was a scramble of activity as she returned with it, and we all gathered around to see.

"August 25th!"

Yes. There was certainty in that date. I could no longer assume anything related to this was coincidental. The people in this room were the group which was invited to participate in preparation of the land for the ceremony of anchoring the Light. Rita looked exhausted. We had not stopped to eat, or to go to the bathroom, or to stand and stretch our legs, for the entire afternoon. There were more questions from the others about their own concerns. Some related to the artifact and some did not.

I had Mary's crystal in my purse. I wanted to have Rita hold it, for I was curious if she could give me some information about it. But she looked too tired to continue. It didn't seem right to get it out, and I left it in its place, wondering about its purpose.

Sara seemed agitated, "We only have a couple hours left before it gets dark. Can you take us to the mesa before you leave?"

We were on our feet before we could answer, "Absolutely!" I wanted to show them the land, and Fred seemed just as eager. We walked out to the parking lot to Margo's car. She had a four-wheel-drive Jeep Cherokee. "Isn't it great when Spirit is working with you?" I whispered to Fred when I saw the car. "We couldn't have made it in our little sports car, and the perfect vehicle has been provided."

The four of us (myself, Sara, Margo, and Fred) drove out to the mesa. Part of Jan's property was down near the road and part was on top of the mesa. Sara and Margo wanted to know the general vicinity of the land so they could go back later to explore on their own. I wanted to take them to the place where I thought the ceremony was to be done – on top of the mesa. Both Sara and Margo said "Let's drive to the lower land, that'll be easier." I knew that wasn't the place for the ceremony, but reluctantly went along with the plan. The day was quickly fading, and there wasn't time for lengthy exploration, nor was our assistance in locating a particular spot wanted by these two.

We drove as far as we could and tried to find the gate. The red earth was still gooey from the prior night's rain. The car couldn't make it all the way, so we decided to get out and walk. It would be impossible to get even a four-wheel-drive vehicle out of the clay if the rain started again. Gray thunder clouds were forming in the East, and Margo looked anxiously from the muddy earth to the clouds and back again. I could tell she didn't want to stay at all.

Sara said, "Okay. Thank you for showing us. We can go back now."

"Can we stay and walk for just a few minutes?" I asked, thinking I had to help them find the spot. This was our first chance to walk on the land on our own, and I desperately wanted to help find the location. In fact, I thought I *had* to help them find it. After all, I did have the vision. Wasn't this my assignment?

"All right," Margo agreed, even though it was apparent she was uneasy about staying longer. We had walked a distance of only 50 yards from the car when the thunder clapped and a bolt of lightening snapped the distance from sky to Earth.

"All right, all right," I shouted to the sky. "I give up! I hear you! I'll let them do it!" As much as I wanted to stay, the nature spirits were sending a clear message. I understood then that it was not our task to take them to the spot for the land to be prepared. Ours was to carry the assignment to these ones. This was how we were to begin the preparation! The baton had been passed.

"All right," I said to Margo. "I guess we'd better go. You guys can come back another day when the weather is better and you can spend more time."

"We can bring a picnic and spend the afternoon," Sara said eagerly.

Margo agreed and turned toward the car, her keys already clutched in her hand. "I got stuck in the mud just a couple weeks ago. It really messed up the axle of my car. It was a real mess. I don't want to go through that again!"

Sara and Margo were quiet as we drove back to Jo's. I asked, "Do you guys think you want to be a part of this?"

"Oh, yes!" Margo was quick to reply, "As soon as I walked on the land, I knew it."

Sara said, "Absolutely. I knew from the moment you started talking about all this that it was why I moved here. I've just been waiting to find out why I came."

Before we knew it, we were back at the apartment. Margo turned off the engine and turned to tell us good bye, "Thank you for taking us to the mesa."

"It was our pleasure," we both replied. "Be sure to let us know what you find."

"Oh, we will!" they both chimed in.

We wished them luck, then waved goodbye as they drove away. We walked up to Jo's once again, and I poked my head in the door, calling out, "Mission accomplished. We can be on our way now."

"Don't forget your thermos this time!"

I laughed, "Thanks for the reminder. That was a pretty good way for Spirit to get us back here, don't you think?"

Jo grinned, "There are no accidents."

I smiled in return and shook my head in agreement, "No accidents."

We gave each of our new friends a farewell hug and wished them luck on their assignments. We knew that each person who wished to help would have an important contribution to make.

When Fred and I were alone again, we talked about the day. I said, "Now we know why we didn't know where we were going this morning."

Fred nodded his head in agreement, "You know, this project isn't only about us. Just think, we've activated a whole team! They were just waiting for us to come."

"Yeah," I responded. "I guess we were just the messengers."

"Oh, we're much more than that!"

"Well, there's no turning back now. Just think about what we've started."

"It looks like we're involved in something a lot bigger than we thought."

"Now there's a whole group of people involved – and they're all counting on us!"

"Right. And now we'll have to walk our talk."

I sighed, "We have a great distance yet to go, but we could celebrate a little for what has happened here. Let's go out to dinner."

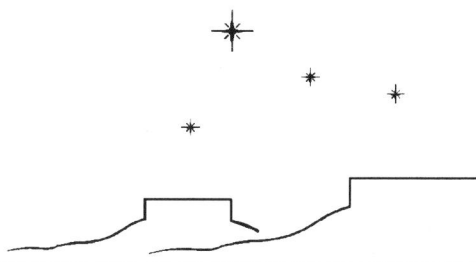

INVITATIONS

Our minds were filled with new possibilities. We were lightened with an emerging sense of purpose, and the drive back to California seemed to take no time. We chattered about our adventure as the wheels of our car spun across the miles of desert, and neither one of us noticed the heat even though the thermometer read 117° at the California border.

"Let's make a list of all that we've learned," I suggested to Fred.

"All right."

I quickly pulled out my notebook and began writing down the revelations that were bursting forth:

* *This is for real.*
* *The activation is now.*
* *Trust and allow.*
* *This is easier than we thought.*

* *We can develop our skills instantaneously.*

* *Maintaining protection is increasingly important.*

* *Every person that wants to help will have an important contribution to make.*

* *This feels right.*

* *Groups are important to support Light Workers and assist with activation.*

* *We are each more than we ever suspected.*

* *Our limits are not real. We have only limited perceptions.*

* *This project is much bigger than we are.*

* *We can accept the responsibilities that are ours and we can release those which are for others.*

* *There is a team, and it includes all the correct talents and tools.*

* *We have been too serious. We need to lighten up!*

* *There is a sense of great importance to this work. There is so much to do, and so few to do it.*

* *We had to venture out in order to grow.*

* *If you're not moving when the train comes by, you're gonna' get left behind.*

* *We all need to follow our enthusiasm.*

* *WE are the masters of the third dimension!*

As we retraced our route back home we were aware that the threads which had been unraveled just a few days earlier as we took this journey were now being rewound onto a new core. We were elated at the events which had unfolded on this trip. We had a new awareness of a larger picture, and still the images and dreams continued to expand our understandings of how it would all unfold.

The plan was to stop at Mary's house on our way back to return the crystal which had come along for a reason still unknown to me. Our journey had been safeguarded and the forces to ensure its success had been magnetized to us. Could this piece of quartz have had something to do with the magic?

The drive had been long and hot. We were dripping with perspiration as we pulled up in front of Mary's cottage. Her cat, Fletch, was sleeping on the front porch and he opened his eyes as he stretched to greet us. We unfolded our bodies from our small car and stood up. As we got out, we heard a voice from inside call out, "Here they are!"

We opened the screen door and walked in. We knew that Kate and Mary would want to hear about our adventures. But, to our surprise, there was half a dozen women waiting, their faces eager with anticipation. Kate had been at work, doing her Light weaving again, sharing her enthusiasm with anyone who would listen. She had gathered a group together to greet us and to hear our story.

So, with tall glasses of ice water in our hands, we sat down and began to tell our tale. Our trip had been magical and we were delighted to share about it. The first thing I did was return the crystal to Mary. She squealed with delight as she took the crystal back and immediately dropped it down inside the front of her tank top where it snuggled between her breasts. "Oh, good," she said. "She's back!" as she clutched her friend, "Crystal," to her heart.

As I watched Mary's reaction, I remembered a dream from the night we left Santa Fe. I told her, "I had a dream about the crystal. I saw that it was a great connector and activator, and it was placed between two other pieces (I think it was the two artifacts). This placement was the ignition switch, and the configuration was buried and left intact."

Mary clutched the crystal peeking out of her tank top once again, "Oh, no. I don't think so." She shook her head, "I don't think she's supposed to be buried ..." The words "and left behind!" remained unspoken.

I shrugged my shoulders. It wasn't for either of us to say. We would know the right thing to do when the time came. Somehow, I spent each moment as both observer and player in this unfolding drama. I struggled with my lines. Yet, it was as though it was all planned out before and I was but an actor on the stage, moving through the scene as it had been set out long ago by someone else – or by a part of ourselves hidden from our consciousness.

We told our story in great detail to this group of women who somehow seemed already connected to it – and to us – even though this was only our first meeting. We passed the artifact around the room as we told about our discoveries, the new connections we had made with people in Santa Fe, and about the ceremony for anchoring the Light.

"The group in Santa Fe is to do preparations on the land in two preliminary ceremonies; then there will be a group assembled to return to the mesa at the full moon in August to perform a ceremony for anchoring the Light."

One of the women, Aya, said, "I want to go!" Aya told us later that, at that moment, she knew she wanted to be a part of the project. She asked, leaning forward as she waited for our response, "How do we know who's supposed to be there?"

I understood that the invitations to participate were being extended by Spirit, and responded, "You have to be invited."

Aya looked crestfallen, as if she wondered who was supposed to invite her. It was not my place to say who could or would be included and I wouldn't presume to make such decisions. Only Spirit knew of the design in place for each one.

Mary saw the disappointment on Aya's face and began to giggle. "You don't think Pam is supposed to invite you, do you?"

Aya thought that she was going to be left out of something that had pierced her heart with purpose. She knew that in times past she had been given direction from her soul, but still she couldn't seem to comprehend what Mary was saying.

I watched the thoughts jumping from one side of the room to the other. I knew that Aya would have to figure it out on her own and continued with my explanation. "The invitations have already been extended from a higher source. The right people will know that they are to be there."

She reached out her hand to take the artifact which was being passed to her. "It's heavy for something so small." She closed her fingers around it to hold it tighter, and tears came to her eyes. She would one day soon realize that Spirit had already invited her. The lacy web was being spun, the encodements of the grand design were being opened, and another soul awakened to its part of the Plan.

We were weary from the long drive and were ready to be home again. So, as soon as we finished relating the events of our trip, we bade our friends goodbye with an invitation for them to visit us in Santa Cruz.

Shortly after we were on the highway, Fred said, "I don't understand it. I'm suddenly very tired. I feel like a dead battery, as though all of my energy has been drained away."

I knew this group of thirsty seekers had put their straws into his cup and sucked up every tasty morsel of his energy. It hit him like a lightning bolt. As he described to me how he was feeling, I imagined a hunk of Swiss cheese. "The mice have come and nibbled," I said, "and they've left you feeling full of holes. Let's do some energy work for you – a little exercise of separation. We can visualize drawing our own energy back to ourselves and filling up the empty spaces again with Light."

We visualized ourselves as magnets, pulling all of our own energy back to us while still leaving those whom we had visited with all of their own. Instantly, Fred felt his energy renewed and, as we looked up into the sky ahead of us, we saw a rainbow twisted into the shape of a figure eight on its side – the infinity symbol.

"Fred, look at the sky ahead! Do you see it?"

"Uhum. Maybe it's an aurora borealis."

"Not in California! I think it's confirmation of a successful journey."

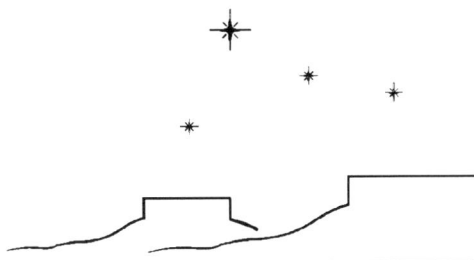

INTEGRATION

Home again, we tried to get our bearings and to comprehend all the glorious coincidences surrounding the destiny that was unfolding around us. I thought back to the difficulty I had leaving. My concerns seemed so insignificant now. All of the paperwork was still there, waiting. None of our customers had called for help. And the warning which had come to challenge me hadn't amounted to anything.

We were humbled by the understanding that this task was, indeed, bigger than either of us. Yet, at the same time, we were relieved to know that it wasn't completely up to us. We were beginning to get glimpses (which could have been staggering) of the magnitude of the project. But the adrenaline was flowing now. We had jumped into the water with both feet, and there was nothing to do but keep stroking. We knew that we were squarely in the flow.

"How do you think we're going to find the group of people who are to go back in August?" I asked Fred.

"I'm not at all worried about it. Look at how everything has gone so far. We found a piece of land 1400 miles away guided by a vision; the artifact showed up in our dining room, and we've activated a whole team to begin preparation of the land. Why should this next part be difficult?"

"Well, I wish I didn't still have doubts."

"What is it that you're doubting?"

"Look around you. Everything seems the same. I'm sure glad I wasn't doing all of this alone. I might have thought I was crazy. But we've experienced all these things together, so I know it's not my imagination. My body feels like surges of low-voltage electrical energy are running through it most of the time; every time I turn around, I'm being made aware that there is another message ready to come through. There's just so much I don't understand."

Fred said, "You know, the things we've been experiencing can't be easily explained, but that doesn't make them any less real."

"I know, I guess we just need to relax and allow things to continue unfolding at their own pace. This must be what integration is all about, taking our new experiences, accepting the changes in our bodies, and continuing on with our lives with the new understandings. It's certainly mind-blowing."

Fred chuckled, "Yes. It certainly is!"

"Shall we see if we can get any help from the higher dimensions in dealing with this?"

Fred agreed, "All right," and we sat down and closed our eyes. He began, "Let's reaffirm our connection to the Light. We are protected from all negative or lesser influences and we are completely aligned with the Light of the Divine Source. We ask Archangel Michael, Sananda, or any of the Ascended Masters to join us and share their guidance with us."

Our request was answered immediately, as the Masters were ever-present and our connection remained strong. Kuthumi announced his presence, *"Hello. This is Kuthumi. You may feel some disorientation as you attempt to continue with your old styles and habits. You are both* _transmigrating to higher dimensions. The glue and the habits that have kept you cemented to the third dimension are coming unstuck. The new reality that is brought about by the new levels of Light you are carrying will be most comfortable if you are in the place that is closest to that Light. It is attracting you as you naturally continue down your path to Source._

"_You will find a few people who are being infused with the same or greater amounts of Light, and you will find yourselves attracted more and more to these people. They are not going to be necessarily the ones you would have thought, but this should not discourage you. This can sometimes feel disconcerting. Your comfort zones have moved into the realm of increased Real Light and Spiritual presence; you've moved out of the materialistic third dimension. It is as if your feet are not always touching the ground any longer as your head and your heart are touching new things._

"_The grounding that you need to accomplish means coming back to the center of your path, so that you are going right down the middle of the route you have planned all along. Grounding no longer means grounding to the physical Earth. Indeed, you are beginning to ground to the non-physical Earth at the juncture of the Light and Earth._

"_The deep sleep of unawareness that is comfortable for many beings on your planet is no longer comfortable for you. When you begin to awaken, you are drawn up out of the denseness to areas where there is much more Light. It is as if a hollow device that was comfortably left resting on the bottom of the ocean slowly started filling with air. Eventually, the air will displace the water and, at some point, this vessel will start to rise toward the surface. You are at that stage now. You are starting to rise toward the surface. When the rising is complete, which will happen in August, you will be bobbing on the surface. You will be interfaces between our dimension and the third dimensional plane. But you will be so attracted to the part that is above the surface of the water that you will never want to go back to the bottom again. People often float to the surface and bring part of their vessel to the fifth dimension when they sleep. The waking process is when they sink back again. Your position is now that you are not sinking back as far and you are remaining closer to the surface all the time._"

We thanked Kuthumi and bade him goodbye, still desiring more information. If this was, indeed, a time of integration, we wanted all the data we could get. We both understood that we would have to begin talking about this project, even more now, in order to gather a team together. We wanted our foundations to be strong before we proceeded. As I look back through my journal now, it appears I must have been dense, asking the same questions over and over again. But these were still new concepts to us. We had never heard or read about anything like this before. There was nowhere to go for guidance. We knew of no books to read. We were forging new pathways, and we yearned for more certainty.

The next morning, when we rose, we wanted to communicate with our guides again and asked that they join us. Instantly I heard the words, *"Hello. This is Dartan. I'm so glad that you have carved out a piece of time and made yourselves available for us. We are trying to communicate with you almost constantly. So, when you pause for a moment or two, you are finding yourselves instantly aware of one of us.*

"You are going through changes at a molecular and cellular level in your bodies to be more able to withstand the Light energies, to be more able to bear them and transmit them yourselves. These changes in vibration are a part of the discomfort that you're feeling. It would be difficult for a medical doctor (or almost anyone) to help you understand what's going on, but these changes in your physical bodies are a requirement as you move forward along your path. It is the next step for you.

"You will soon become accustomed to these surges of power you are feeling. As you begin to accept a more powerful way of being, you will look back at the old you and shake your head in wonder at how you were ever comfortable with the feelings of lack and limitation you once had. You are truly moving into your power. And you thought moving into your power only had to do with changing a mental or emotional attitude! It also has to do with changing your wiring. It is like rewiring your house for 220 volts so that the new equipment and machinery will get enough power to operate properly. You are definitely at a time of transition on many levels."

Fred asked, "Can you tell us a little about yourself, Dartan?"

"I come from the planet Arcturus in a constellation far, far away. I come to help the Earth in her transition and have a specific assignment, an area which I am keeping watch over, to balance the negative or unbalanced energy changing the rates of vibrational levels in the land. After your activities and your ceremony are complete, I will remain over the land and maintain the focus of Light in that place to hold fixed what you set into motion.

"You know, there are a number of points at which the Light is going to be fixed on the planet. We would not want all the Light Workers living at these specific points. You have been told that the Light will be anchored at these points but then will radiate out from them. We would like you to be freer for new concepts and new opportunities. So, your stretch of trust at this time is requiring enormous flexibility from you. Even though you may be feeling flexible (in the flow and following Spirit), you have to explain this to others, and that's where the greatest discomfort seems to arise – when you're trying to speak in concrete terms about what you're doing because these concepts are all so new to you. You should find that everything will fall into place for you without a great deal of effort. The plan is set into motion already. So, you will merely need to walk along the path and everything will be there waiting for you at the time it is needed. We could not let this fail at this time!"

Fred said, "Well, we don't want to fail either because we are beginning to see how important this may be." Then, instead of jumping right up and continuing on with our day's activities, we remained silent. As we sat together on the living room sofa, a smile spread across Fred's face. I knew that he had linked with the energies of Sananda, as the love which overflows from Fred's heart whenever he makes this connection is always reflected in his countenance. He then spoke, _"Hello. This is Sananda. I'm just going to let our union BE at this moment while we share our love with you. When you begin to take your steps across your bridge which is still under construction, you are not exactly sure where it will lead. This requires a great deal of trust and faith. You are now standing out on the end of your bridges, adding to them stone by stone. What's on the other side is the bridge which we are building toward you. We can call across the gap, which is certainly much easier to do now than it was at any time_ *before. This is not only due to our efforts of sending the energy to your plane, but it is also due to your efforts and your willingness to extend your bridge in our direction. The two components of the bridge will eventually meet in the middle of the span. Your acceptance of the unseen, your acceptance of that which you cannot fully understand yet, is critical for the bridge to be completed.*

"As the bridge rises toward the middle, you find that you must gain some facility with stones and building materials that are not the same as the materials you could use at the beginning of the task. This facility comes automatically as you progress toward your fifth dimensional self and increase your ability to contain greater quantities of Light. So, keep working on your bridges. Place your attention on completing your half of the bridge and, before you know it, we will be joined in the middle."

"Is that what Ascension means?"

"Yes. We are able to build our half of the bridge in these times of the new dispensation from Source, much farther out than we were in times past. You need not build the entire bridge yourselves. There are many Beings who are assisting you. All that's needed, really, is the desire and the intent to extend yourselves in our direction, then you will automatically be building the bridge. There are different roles for different people. Those who can be of assistance to us and who are aligned with our intentions will indeed be given all of the powers, all of the facilities, and all of the Light they are able to wield. To become a facilitator you need only complete your bridge. Now, you both are getting quite close to the centers of your bridges."

I asked "Sananda, we all feel an opening of heart energy when your energy comes to us. We've been told that this land on the mesa is going to be an opening of the heart chakra of Earth. Will you tell us about this?"

"Yes. The anchoring of the new Light Nodes will inadvertently anchor, once and for all, the fifth dimensional frequency of Unconditional Love and Light on and in your planet. It is only reasonable that the ray of Unconditional Love starts its emanation from near Santa Fe, which is the heart chakra of your country. We have been encouraging all of our beloved Workers of Light to start first within their own heart centers by

developing unconditional self-love, for this is the seat of the soul – your Christ Consciousness."

"We're going to sock it to everybody on the planet. Some won't feel a thing. Some won't respond – they are not ready or they have made the choice that this Light Path is not for them at this time so they will remain unaffected. But many, many, others will feel something. They will remember something. A certain longing may erupt in them. They will open their eyes and look around and see a new world. They will be able to approach the world in ways they didn't know possible. We will get them right between the eyes with this infusion of new energy. Then we will need a lot of teachers! We will need a lot of information about the Light. There will certainly be some gnashing of teeth. There will be some consternation as some don't understand exactly what's going on, although they know something is different.

"The process of anchoring the nodes of Light around the planet will also sock it to those people following lesser energies. Some of them may see some Light. Some of them may be confounded. Some may know what is happening and will reject it, but these will be few. What we hope is that the momentum (the movement) will swell. You will begin to see many people coming to the same end from quite diverse beginnings.

"There will be a great deal of: 'Oh, you know that too?' 'How about this?' 'I've heard about that.' This will be a great opening of the heart because these changes will be something that people feel. There is a feeling about these ideas that precedes thinking about them – a feeling that says these ideas are okay. It's okay for me to be thinking about these ideas and to be interested in them. It's a feeling that allows you to contemplate. The feeling opens the place where such considering can occur. If that place is not opened, there is no possibility for considering because the containers existing now are already filled with other, lesser, considerations."

"What do you know of one named Dartan?" I wanted confirmation of what Dartan had told us about himself.

Ashtar responded, "He's been of service in the Ashtar Command for a long time. He has not incarnated in a physical world for some time and does not plan to do so at this time. He can spread out over the land in his present higher dimensional state and maintain his awareness across the breadth of this land (which is not bounded by the property markers but extends out for miles in every direction – including above the ground, in the sky, down into the very rocks). He is providing a matrix of balance in which the ceremony can safely occur. He is a centering and balancing energy. Over his energy, we will superimpose Light which will be fused with Earth inside the body in your ceremony. He is a guardian, a facilitator, an energy balancer, as well as a protector for your ceremony. He will continue in that role for some time afterwards."

"This is not to be a public event, but it is also not a local event. Being physically present is not important. Those who will be physically present have balancing and Light channeling tasks to perform. There may be others, however, who will wish to tune-in to this ceremony from a distance. Anyone who is so tuned-in will get a direct pulse of energy. It will be like catching a bit of this fire of depolarization simply by being aware of what's going on – even from a long distance – and attracting the Light. So, it's all right to talk to people who can be either physically or spiritually present. Outsiders, though, people who wish to play neither type of role, don't need any particulars about what is happening."

"Well," I said to Fred, "it looks like it's time to start telling people about all of this. Why don't I call a few people and invite them over to hear about our adventure tomorrow night."

"That's fine with me," Fred replied.

"We'll just call those who we think might understand what we're talking about and who might be interested. They can decide for themselves if they want to be a part of it."

And so the people came. The first night, a few friends came to hear about our travels. We were animated and excited as we spun our tale. Our enthusiasm acted like a magnet and they brought more friends. Every day someone new came over to our house to hear our story. Some left shaking their heads muttering, "This all sounds pretty unbelievable." Others returned and brought their friends. And we began to repeat the story, again and again, of how we were being guided on a project which would be anchoring more of heaven's Light into the planet, about the time of depolarization and harmony which was coming for humankind, about the time of ancient prophecies when humankind would return to oneness. Each time we shared the artifact, it was a third dimensional confirmation of the mystery and power of the task.

Kate brought her friend Rachel. As we shared our story, tears rolled down Rachel's cheeks. Something in our words struck a chord of knowing within her that it was all true. "I've been waiting to know why I'm here," she told us. "I think this is it!"

Rachel asked, "May I see the artifact?"

"Certainly," I replied and walked into the living room to retrieve it from its place on our fireplace mantle. As I handed it to her, she closed her eyes to feel more keenly its vibration and to shut out the surroundings of the room. She seemed to be, for a moment, lost in her own cocoon of time and space. When she opened her eyes and put the artifact down on the table, she did not speak. She seemed somehow altered by having held the piece, and I asked her, "We received a video today from a woman we met in Santa Fe who recently made a trip to Peru. Would you like to watch it with us?"

"Oh, yes!" Rachel was delighted to share in any way she could.

I watched intently as the scenes unfolded on our television screen. I was looking for something that I might know from an old memory or intuitive recognition of the place where we might find the artifact. Where were we to go in such a large country to look for a trinket? We needed some guidance on this. We couldn't just land in Peru and say "Here we are. Where's the treasure?"

Could we?

Was there a building, a mountain, a person that would tap into my consciousness to let me know where we were to go? I watched transfixed, hoping for a clue. Something stirred in me each time the footage of Macchu Picchu played, and I felt my blood pressure rise when the green terraces reaching toward the sky came into view. Was there something there for me? Were these feelings because this was one of Earth's power spots? I wondered about it all.

Rachel shortly became restless, "I'm sorry, but it seems like there is some information about this that must be spoken." Rachel had not experienced the channeling process before, but Fred and Kate and I all sensed that the energy stirring in her was a message that yearned to be released. We turned off the video and encircled her with our love to support her, calling on the presence and protection of the Divine Light. Rachel took the artifact in her hands. Emotion welled up in her as she spoke the words, "Silver she be. The sister she is activated tonight!"

And that was it.

Was the sister the ancient artifact, calling to its companion because now the long-awaited time of reunion had arrived? Or was the dear sister, Rachel, being activated herself? None of us knew for certain, but all of us felt the quickening which had occurred.

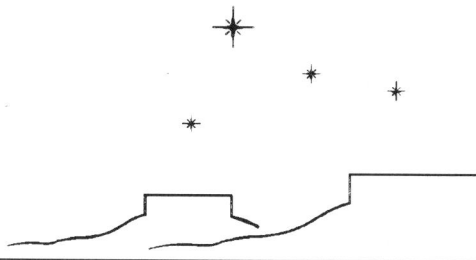

Circles of Light

The group in Santa Fe had sprung into action. All of the women who had come together for an unexpected gathering on that Saturday morning of discovery had met again the very next day, and continued meeting almost daily. Most of them were experiencing thoughts of, "No, not me." In their minds they heard, "Pam and Fred couldn't have been talking to me!" But in their hearts they knew, beyond all doubt, if they were to be a part of this undertaking. They quickly formed into a group of seven – six women and one man – and they plunged headlong into their preparations. This was a task which they had come to Earth to perform and there was a kernel of certainty within each of them, just as there had been with us, that they had been waiting and preparing for this assignment for a very long time.

We telephoned Santa Fe to see how they were doing, wondering what impact our visit had on them. Jo's house was the meeting place, and other than our communication with Sara, would be our point of contact. Rita answered the phone, "Hello."

"Hi!" we both returned. "How are you guys doing?"

"We have our seven people already!" Rita announced. She was pulling the pieces together and had quickly stepped into position as coordinator of this group. She continued, "There may still be some changes, but it looks like we have the team. Everybody is working really hard already at clearing their stuff so they'll be ready, and they're already beginning to braid their energy! We've started putting in the Light Grids for some of them already. How are you guys doing?"

Fred answered, "We're both fine. We hardly have our feet on the ground here."

I interrupted, "What do you mean, putting in Light Grids? Braiding their energy?"

"Oh, its all preparation for this thing. When people get their Light Grids activated, their vibrations get jumped up to a higher frequency."

"And braiding their energy? What's that about?"

"Oh, geez. I have to explain everything to you people!"

Her impatience made me want to hide, but it sounded important. "Humor me, Rita."

"When people want to do this powerful energy work, they have to join together into one unit. That's the only way they could be powerful enough to accomplish the big stuff. When they have blended their energy into one cohesive unit, everything becomes magnified. Then, wham! It happens. I'd like to come stay with you for a week or two in July, if that's all right."

Of course it would be all right. We were delighted to have her come. We both felt there was a lot we could learn from her.

"Sure. Just let us know when."

"I'll let you know the schedule for sure when it gets closer," Rita replied. Then, "Margo and Sara went out to the land yesterday."

"They did?! Can we talk to them?"

"Yeah. Margo's here. Just a minute – I'll get her. Talk to you soon." With that brisk goodbye, Rita was gone and we waited for Margo to come to the telephone.

"Hello," Margo greeted us.

"Hello," we returned. "How's it going?"

"Well, Sara and I went out to the mesa before she left for New England and we had quite an adventure."

"What happened?"

"Well, when you and Fred first told us about this, I must admit that I wondered, 'Am I really a part of this?' But once you took us out to show us the land and I was on it, I knew I had to be there! It felt like I had been there before. It was definitely a confirmation and I didn't care what I had to do to be a part of it. I couldn't wait from that point on. The more we talked about it, the more excited I got.

"Sara and I decided that we needed to be on the land before she made her trip to the East Coast. We had planned to spend some time together before she went. We talked about the possibility of going up to the mesa afterwards to see what it was like. Ashtar suggested that we go onto the mesa that day and told us there were two ways to get there. He told us not to stop along the way and not to cross any fences which had any restrictions on trespassing."

Margo told us how excited they had been to go, about how the animals along the way had guided them, about seeing the ancient one who guards the land, about finding three stones which Ashtar had told them to look for, and about being guided off the land by Dartan just before a sudden downpour of rain. The stones they found bore a symbol of two circles connected by a line. Ashtar had told Sara that this engraving represented the merging of third and fifth dimensions. The line between the circles represented the crystal bridge connecting the visible and invisible realms.

Margo continued with her story, "My biggest joy was being on the land. The following Saturday I went up again and spent five hours alone. I did a whole ceremony there by myself, lighting incense and smudging.

I did a prayer and offered fruit and tobacco to the four directions and to the Earth; then I went into meditation.

"The energy was very strong when, all of a sudden, I heard a sound like wind rushing toward me. It was barely perceptible when it started and seemed far, far, away. The closer it got, the louder it got. Yet there was no wind moving around me. I kept maintaining my point of focus while thinking this must be some kind of test. The wind came up from behind me and then split as the wind circled me with the stroke of a gentle breeze on my cheeks. Then it rose straight up. The leaves in the trees rustled a little, but not enough to create the sound of rushing wind. I think I was hearing the sound of energy. This sequence happened three times. The third time it stopped behind me and went into a spiral. Then, it disappeared.

"When I came out of the meditation I thought, 'Wow. This is incredible!' I turned around and looked, expecting to see something. Nothing was there. I wondered if this was a test, or an initiation. Through it all, I held my focus and didn't become frightened. I was very proud of myself."

She told us that Sara had revealed to the group that a Master had been assigned to walk with each one; six male and one female to balance the seven embodied beings. The Masters overseeing the assignment were: Sananda, Hilarion, Wa-Tanna, Commander Ashtar, Soltec, Archangel Michael representing the angelic realms, and the blended energies of Mother Mary/Kuan Yin as a perfect blend of multi-dimensional support working in cooperation with human beings.

We congratulated Margo for her sincerity and dedication. And our own conviction grew.

"Oh, Fred!" I said after we had hung up. "Look what has begun. There's no stopping any of this now." I thought for a minute and then asked, "What are we to do about Peru?"

"Well, I guess we'll have to go."

I felt an obligation now, in a very real way, to all those who were counting on us, but there were still concerns about the unknown nagging at me.

I felt a presence approach, my head circled gently, and I spoke the words coming to me, "*This is Soltec of the White Brotherhood, of the Ashtar Command, bringing you guidance from the Circles of Light which are now clustered around your planet.*

"*Would you like more information about anchoring the Light Grid? I know we've spoken of it many times, but there is still much information to impart to you. As you look around, you will find many sources giving you the validation which you desire for your quest. It should be strikingly apparent to you on a daily basis how well things are lining up. I'm glad to see that you're not distressed about the details of your trip, although you are both curious. You have established a level of trust which is great enough now for you to have a knowing that it will unfold in its most advantageous manner.*

"*You will fly to Peru (to Lima) and you will make a trek to Yachipuqui. You will have a guide so that your trek will be supported by the Light in a physical embodiment as well as supported by the unseen Light. Your physical maneuvering will be guided so that the details of transportation will not be a distress or concern for you. There are natives who will welcome you. You will be somewhat of a curiosity to the villagers, as you will not be on the well-worn tourist track. Kindnesses will be exchanged. You will feel quite comfortable.*"

Fred continued seeking the details of our mission, "Is there a name for this stone we are seeking?"

"*The name of the stone you are seeking is Magua, a pillow for the gods.*

"Does the artifact that we have now also have a name?"

"*This little one is Pita. The piece you will be finding is larger than you anticipate; it is larger than the piece you have. It, indeed, is silver and you will see the Light in it when your eyes fall upon it. It is located in a place of honor in an earthen house. Once you have possession of it, you will not wish to discuss it. You will wish to go to your destination as quickly as possible. Well, can you do this?*" Soltec asked. "*Can you make an airplane trip and meet a guide and go out into the villages?*"

Fred replied with certainty, "Yes. But, I do have a couple more questions about the details. How will we connect with the guide?"

"It will be prearranged. A man named Christo will meet you at the airport."

Fred thought for a moment and then asked, "Then, we need to make these arrangements before we leave?"

"Yes. You need to do this soon."

Fred thought for a moment about his lingering questions. He remembered that Rita had told us that we would bring the artifact back in some silver space blanket type of insulation material and asked, "Is this space blanket material the proper way to insulate and protect these artifacts?"

"Yes. They should be wrapped in it."

"Is this to allow us to easily take these artifacts out of the country?

"Yes, and to not interfere with the electronic equipment on the airplane. Before boarding you may wish, with clear intent, to deactivate them. You know they have on/off switches and you get a charge out of having them turned on. But before the trip it would be best to have them deactivated. Then they will simply be stones."

"My only concern about this part of the trip is comfortably getting them out of Peru."

"They can be in your bag with other things. They'll be looked at, I expect. They won't be recognized. You can carry them with you without difficulty. You remember, most people did not recognize anything in particular that was special about the stone as you passed it around the night it came into your house. People bring all sorts of souvenirs back from their travels – pots and trinkets and scarves. You may have a few trinkets as well, if you will allow yourself the time to gather a few things. I think you will want to do that. It's a long way to go, after all. So, it's a business trip, but you can set your briefcases aside for a time as all businessmen do."

"I've noticed how the two of you work. You play and leave completion of your assignment until the very last minute. In fact, you often begin to head home wondering why you haven't done what you set out to do and, practically on the way to the airport, you manage to complete the

task. You seem to enjoy taking the long way around to do things. That doesn't matter, of course. It does make it a little harder on you. But you know and we know that you always accomplish what needs to be done, even if it is just under the wire, so to speak. I expect that this trip will be no different. You may do a bit of sight-seeing before you reach your destination. And, then, of course, you will be anxious to return and release the responsibility that you are carrying. Know that you will be absolutely protected on this trip with a strong armada of Light surrounding you. Discretion and caution are advised, but worry and concern are un-necessary."

My imagination was running wild. The images which were drawn during this communication were as vivid in my mind as a memory. I could begin to see us there. I could feel our footsteps on the stone pathways. I could hear the sounds in Cuzco. I could smell the air at Macchu Picchu. And a sense of the importance of the trip grew within me. Our attention turned to the details: maps, schedules, passports, guide.

The quest progressed with balanced support from other dimensions, our own inner wisdom always keen as we talked with the angelic host, our Native American guides, and the space brotherhood. The forces teamed up on this project were awesome.

The next communication we had was with St. Germain. I asked, "Where should we should be placing our energies at this time?"

His reply came quickly and certainly, _"For you, it is Peru. You have not fully come to terms with going there. It is too unfamiliar. It seems too far. Yet, in your day and age it is not really that far."_

I couldn't help it. I had to ask in the most straightforward manner I could, "Tell me, is this assignment real?"

St. Germain chuckled as he replied, _"Oh, Yes! We're not fooling on this one, kids. There are others in your country doing just what you`re doing. The only difference is that they're going to Mexico, to the Yucatan. You see, what you are doing is spreading the Light around the planet. There are many others being guided to do their parts just as you are being guided to do yours. Be assured that the people who know the history of this piece you seek also know its future. They are preparing the way for you in Peru. They are preparing the others to release the artifact to you_ *and their work will be done. In fact, the final proof that they have been correct will be when you walk into their village. The ones who know will say, 'See, we told you,' to the ones who were not sure. Every aspect of this adventure has been prepared. We are as careful about your safety as Walt Disney is for every girl and boy who visits his theme parks."*

I laughed as I replied, "Oh. Security in disguise?"

"Yes. There is security in disguise and all the rides are safe. Although there may be some ups and downs, the rides are designed to be thrilling, and this adventure will be perfectly safe. Not to worry about that."

Taking this information into my mind, I began to think about the ceremony in August and Rita's direction that we were to gather a group together. I asked, "Does the group simply show up at our house one day like the gold artifact did? How actively do we need to recruit?"

St. Germain's answer was swift and clear, *"WE are doing the recruiting."*

I understood what he was saying to me. I acknowledged the enormous level of spiritual support behind the transition which was underway. Still, I tried to understand more clearly what I must do.

"How do we meet these people?"

"Do you know how your television set works? No, you don't. But when you turn it on, you expect the picture and the sound to come on. This is the same deal. Many ones whom you have not yet met have volunteered. There will be friends of yours, friends of these friends, people who phone you and write you. Things will just naturally fall into place. You are not responsible for recruiting, but only getting the people headed in the right direction at the right time." Then, before we could ask another question, St. Germain continued, *"In order to be able to perform this ceremony (this act) you will both need to be purified to a greater extent than you are now."*

"Why?"

"Because there is a minimum intensity of Light that must be brought through you during the ceremony. Due to the nature of Light, insofar as it doesn't respect shielding, you will need to be strong enough to remain

*consciously present during the whole ceremony. It would be inconve-
nient for the process of the ceremony if you were not able to handle the
energies and we had to intervene. We would like you to be able to be an
integral part of it. You see, this is going to be a meeting. We will meet you
and you will meet us. All the doubts and reservations that you are currently having would make the meeting awkward. So you must each decide
to plunge ahead. Just do it to the best of your abilities and let go of any
remaining doubts which will only serve to weaken you. We are practically by your sides all of the time. We are trying to prepare your bodies,
but this is not something that we can do by ourselves. It requires conscious agreement from each of you. Mind you, the ceremony will still take
place, but it will go more smoothly, and you will be able to take more
active parts, if you are a little more prepared.*

*"You should go back to basics: learning and doing the exercises on
Lightening yourselves. These exercises will help define your intent to manifest the Light, to prepare yourselves to be Lighter, and to become strong
enough to perform the ceremonies. This is a different approach than the
ones in Santa Fe are taking. The processing that they speak of is a going
back, reviewing, clearing, and solving. What I'm suggesting for you two
is a much more direct approach, which is simply to dump as much Light
into yourselves as you can handle, because this is what will happen to you
during the ceremony. You will be near more Light than you have ever
experienced before.*

*"I am sure you are aware that we have been stepping up the energy
the last several months. Now you are more sensitive to hearing our call.
As you grow into your Light Bodies and discard doubts and limitations,
your ability to hold Light will naturally increase. You will be preparing
yourselves to grow into the Light.*

*"In the days to come there will be fewer fence sitters. As a result of
the intensified energies, there will be more people who are pro or con and
fewer who are undecided. Right now you are both shifting in and out. It's
like you are going through a revolving dimensional door. Although it is
one thing to visit our dimension during sleep, it is another to visit it while
awake. It is like we come and get you in a wheel chair and push it
through the dimension door – that's the sleeping part. The waking part is*

when you stand up and don't need the wheelchair to get through the door; you come voluntarily using your own skills and are moving under your own steam.

"*You will be performing your ceremony in the doorway to higher dimensions. The ceremony will be one of nailing the door open so that the full intensity of the Light can come through that doorway unobstructed. You will be able to stand in the doorway unaided and awake. It's unfamiliar because it's not something that you remember having done in the past, but it is something that you can do if you will just let the Light pull you up and support you. So, do your Lightening exercises, both of you, and I will speak to you again in the near future.*"

We thanked St. Germain for the guidance, and his presence left. Then Ashtar spoke to us further about our conditioning. "*This ceremony will mark a change in yourselves and all who participate in it. This is the first thing that will happen. The energies will shift mightily on this land. It will not be a physical shifting as much as an electrical, energetic, and ethereal shifting. It will be a readjustment and rebalancing – a realigning. There will be a great infusion of Light into all those who attend. You will not be able to escape it. Your physical presence, your intent and sense of purpose, will draw the Light into each of you. This is why we are asking you to go on a crash program of preparing yourselves for the Light.*

"*At this point, you need to enter into a training program and accept a dedication to your task equal to that of Olympic athletes. Allow yourself to be all that you can be. This will help you to go forward. You are in the leagues now which demand you dedicate yourself to your preparation and training. You must get adequate rest. You must get a proper diet and adequate exercise for your spiritual, mental and emotional bodies. You will have some physical activities to perform and it will be easier for you if you exercise on a daily basis. As you walk, be aware of the energies running through you and into the Earth. Do this as a gift to Earth and as training for yourselves. You must exercise your spiritual body by continuing your meditations and channeling on a daily basis. The exercise for your mental bodies is to unlock the doors so that new concepts can come to you freely and without judgment. Things will be changing in an ever more rapid manner.*

"We will be sending you far more energy of alignment than you have ever received before. To accept this and bring it into yourselves, you need only turn your attention to it and to us. When you are completed with the ceremony there will be many changes in you. There will be changes of empowerment and enlightenment. Emotionally, you will be cleaned, straightened and developed. As St. Germain said earlier, there's no fooling on this one!

"This will be one of the first major events to overtly occur on your planet to bring in and fasten Earth's new Light Grid into place. Other events are scheduled around the globe as this gradual sewing, stitching, and balancing of the new energy grid is completed. As this weaving of the Light Grid proceeds, we must take care to keep the energy balanced. There will be ceremonies for each of the new points, although those for subsequent points will not be as grand as this one. What you don't realize is that the anchoring of the Light Grid nodes to the Earth will actually be anchoring the third dimension to the fifth. It will be a mutual drawing together and thinning of the veil.

"The first few of these really call for celebration and acknowledgment to the Earth Mother that humans, the Ascended Masters, angelic beings and, above all, Sananda Himself, are at last making the overt physical preparations. This is why physical objects are required. This is a physical statement and physical movement, unlike other attempts in the past which were simply energetic.

"The physical part of consecration, which is the purpose of this ceremony to anchor the Light, will be to bolt it down so that it directly touches the Earth. So, we have Earth which is physical and we have Light, which is spiritual. The artifact which you have is uncountable eons old. It contains a part of the Real Light that was used to make it and will be used as a guide piece to bring the Light and the Earth together."

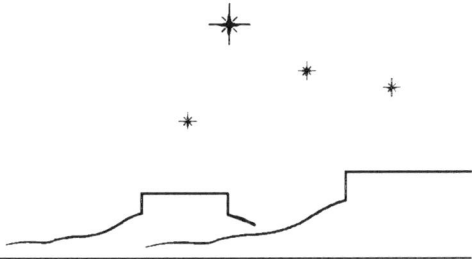

GATHERING

Fred and I were eager to have Rita visit us. We had both been impressed with her keen vision when we met her in Santa Fe. She had greatly assisted the team there with their preparations, so we looked forward to having her join us and introducing her to our friends. I thought, "If she could tell us in a couple of hours what it took us six months to discover on our own, she could surely be of value to the group forming here."

We scheduled a gathering and invited everyone we thought may be interested. Each could decide of their own accord if they were to be involved. There was one more couple that I wanted to invite. They were dear friends who lived near Lake Tahoe. I thought they would surely understand the importance of what was happening. It would be a full day's drive, but the message had to be delivered in person. I would take the time. I would make the trek so we could sit together as I delivered the invitation.

And so we met. We sat in a pizza parlor surrounded with activity and clatter. I held the artifact in my hand as I struggled with the words which would most accurately express the importance of my message. The incongruity of our surroundings made me more aware of the sacred nature of what I felt and knew must be shared. It was difficult to begin, but this was the time and this was the place. I tightened my grasp on the artifact. I took a deep breath. And I began. I told the story I had told so many times before to casual acquaintances and to strangers. But, now, the words choked in my throat. I wanted these two, more than anyone, to understand.

I told them of the vision, of finding the land, the guidance to go to Peru, and the activation of the Light Grids. They sat and listened without a word. I gave Ken the artifact to hold and he closed his eyes as he connected with its energies without saying anything.

I wondered what they were thinking. They could be a part of this if they chose, for I knew their alignment was correct. In my impatience for their reaction, I blurted out, "I am not crazy! I have questioned. I have doubted. And I know that these things which I tell you are real! I have a strong sense of discernment, and it has been on a 'Class A' alert. I'm not making this up!" Ken continued to look at me without showing any reaction.

Finally he spoke, "Oh, I know this is for real. They've tried this before, you know, and it has never worked. It's always failed in the end because the people they were working with became unbalanced and flipped out. You and Fred are grounded. You have the ability to maintain your centers." He paused a moment before continuing, "They can't let it fail this time. That's why they've chosen you!"

His response was a surprise. I thought he was judging me as so many others had. I didn't know what to say. They understood. They were not unsettled by my message, for it was known to them already – even though we had never spoken of these things. My heart filled with gratitude that I had found someone who understood so completely. I invited them to the upcoming gathering of those interested in participating in the anchoring. They could not come.

On the long drive home, Ken's response remained at the forefront of my thoughts. I wondered how many others knew. There is so much unsaid and unseen. The things which really matter, those which are closest to one's soul, so often remain unspoken. And we fill our hours with idle conversation about the things of this world, the things whose existence no one can dispute.

The next day would be the first gathering in Santa Cruz of those who had resonated with the call, their curiosity triggered by an internal encodement that they had come to Earth to serve in this way. Step by step, the Plan would unfold to us as we grew in our faith and dedication to serve the force of Spirit and the calling of our souls.

When we talked to Rita on the phone the night before the planned gathering, she said, "I won't be coming out this week. I'll be staying here a while longer and working some more with this group."

I said, "Oh, we're all looking forward to you being here. People will be coming over in the morning to meet you."

"I know but it's just not time to come yet."

We were disappointed. Everything was arranged. The group would be coming, some of them driving for quite a distance. But there was something unspoken behind Rita's change in plans. Had she sensed something was amiss? Several of those who planned to join us had expressed reluctance about inviting Rita. Had our enthusiasm about Rita unwittingly alienated those who felt our recognition of her capabilities somehow undermined their own?

I told Fred, "I don't think we should tell anyone Rita isn't coming."

"You're right," he agreed. "Meeting her is the reason some of them are coming, but we have work to do with or without her. We'll just let them find out when they get here."

"I don't understand what's going on. Some of them seem to think Rita is going to decide who's included. That's not right. That might be what happened in Santa Fe, but we know better. That decision is made within each individual's soul."

"I'm going to kick butt," Fred scowled. "All of this animosity toward Rita has got to be put to a stop. We've got important work to do and they need to find out that there's no room for a bunch of egos to be interfering."

The ones who came were directed by their own Higher Selves to be there. There were new faces, there were very close friends, and there were friends of friends. I looked around the room at this gathering of souls being activated for their Earth missions. I didn't know how this day would unfold, but I did know that it would be a beginning. I saw the emotions bubbling to the surface: anticipation, fear, judgment, resentment, anger, love, joy, purpose, and adventure. All these feelings were swirling around the room as we took our seats. My heart filled with love. It was a reunion by the design of the higher parts of each of us. We were together again – this soul group which had come to Earth to serve, and to remember.

My attention was brought back to the room as a latecomer burst through the front door in a flurry. Everyone rose to greet her. It was Aya whom we had met at Mary's house on our return from our last trip to Santa Fe. She explained her late arrival, "Well, I took a wrong turn, so I ended up driving through Monterey and along the coast. It took an hour longer than I expected to get here."

The Plan was to unfold of its own accord; individual struggles were but a part of the journey. Aya's detour must have been created from some subconscious resistance or fear which had detained her.

"Well," I said. "Let's begin."

Because there were some new people, we started by telling the story of our journey. I told of the visions and the artifact. Fred spoke, matter-of-factly, about the ceremony coming up for the anchoring of the Light and about the activation of the group in Santa Fe. He announced, "Rita didn't come this week."

Aya's arms were crossed. Like an angry and defiant child, her face reddened at the mention of Rita's name. "Well, good!" she blurted out.

I knew there were some concerns about Rita, but what was this?

Aya proclaimed, "What gives her the right to tell me if I can be involved in this or not!" Aya's fear that she might not be judged worthy by

Rita had festered into a state of rage. "Why do I have to pay someone to put in my Light Grids? I don't even know what that means!"

I hardly knew how to respond. Where did these notions come from?

Mary chimed in, "I don't need to pay her $75 to get me ready!"

Kate also spoke up, "Who ever made her in charge?!"

"What!?" My mind was swirling.

Fred was ready to blast them. "This is nonsense!" he muttered half under his breath and half aloud.

Mary seethed at the perceived injustice, and insisted, "But we have to pay Rita $75 if we want to be a part of this!"

I interceded, asking as gently as I could, "Who told you that?"

The three from out of town (Mary, Kate, and Aya) abruptly stopped their protest. None of them wanted to say where the information came from. But I remembered that the link to the people in Santa Fe had come through Annie and this group from Atascadero; I thought I knew what happened. It was a presumption which had traveled over the telephone lines as these three had fed each other's fears.

I sighed and understood why Rita had not come. This one _did_ have the ability to see, and she saw this confrontation. She understood that she would not be welcomed by some of the members of the group and didn't want to walk into a hostile situation, so she opted to wait until the well-spring of antagonism had abated.

Fred and I both knew that the situation was ours to handle. We had been asked to take leadership roles in this affair and knew we must rise to the occasion. He spoke, "Rita is not in charge here! If you want to know who's in charge – we are."

I could see it. More buttons were getting pushed. These women did not want anyone to be in charge. But we had been asked by Soltec and Ashtar to take charge. We had been asked to be leaders of this group and had been given the Earth details of the project. "God, this is hard," I thought. "I don't want them resenting me."

I wanted to make everyone happy. But we both knew we must stand fast; we must remain detached from the anger surfacing to be re-leased. Fred understood in a masculine way that we were to be the leaders of this group. We were not to be the rulers; but to lead was an assignment which we had accepted and for which we had prepared. Neither of us was comfortable in this role. It was a stretch for us, but the current situation was not about us. The process of preparation of the participants was beginning with this opportunity to feel and understand the issues which drove our lives – each one.

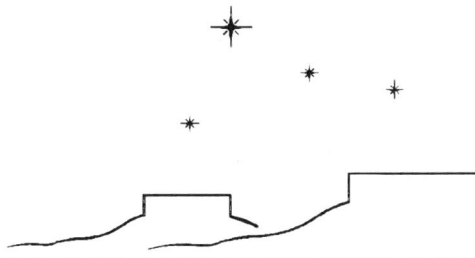

INTRODUCTIONS

When the hostility had been somewhat diffused, I wanted to move forward, to shift the energy of the group, so I asked each one to introduce themselves. The introductions made a circle around the room:

    – There was Kate: "I knew instantly when Pam and Fred told me about some exciting information which had come through in dreams that I wanted to be a part of it. It all seemed magical. It struck a chord in me, and a part of me that was sleeping began to come alive. I didn't want to miss anything, and I had no doubts that any of it was real."

    – There was Rachel: "When Kate told me about this I had an instant sense of knowing that this was what I came to Earth to do, that I needed to be a part of it. And when Pam and Fred showed me the pictures of the mesa, I began to cry. I knew I had been there before. I knew that it was home!"

– There was Mary: "I've been drawn to the Southwest for some time and I know that I'm to be a part of this. I've been working with energy and healing for some time. I know that the power of harmony on Earth must start in the ethers and that doing energy work as a group with focused intention is where I need to be placing my abilities now."

– There was Aya: "I've come up from Atascadero. Kate and Mary are friends of mine. I was pretty upset when I heard about this and Pam said we had to be invited. I knew I was supposed to be a part of this adventure as soon as I held the artifact; I wanted to be included and she didn't invite me. I know I'm supposed to be a part of this but I'd like to know more about what it's going to entail. How much is this going to cost? I'm an art teacher and I'll have to schedule any time I need to take off work as soon as I can."

– There was Beth: "I really don't understand what all the commotion is about. I just came because Rachel and Kate asked me. I really don't think I'm a part of it." I hadn't seen Beth for 20 years when she was the director of my daughter's preschool, and I remembered the tenderness and compassion she had shown when caring for my children so many years earlier. What a small world it was to have her turn up in our living room now.

– There was Allison: "Well, I don't know why I'm here. I don't think I'm a part of this. I love Rachel and I know that she has somehow connected with this. Beth told me she was coming over today too but that she didn't really know what it was about – something about ascension stuff. I'm pretty busy. I'm a nurse at Mercy Hospital and have my own acupuncture practice. I usually have to work on Saturdays, but somehow I had the day free and my husband was willing to stay with our children; so I just said 'okay' on the spur of the moment and came over. I'm pretty skeptical."

– There was Casey: "I just read Pam and Fred's book, *Bridge into Light*, recently. When Pam called me this morning and said she thought I might like to know about the gathering, I knew instantly that I had to be here. I just dropped everything and came right over. I don't know what it's all about yet."

Now we were beginning to place our attention on the present. We could move forward. When the introductions were complete, Fred introduced the group to a couple of the concepts we had been working with. Still, negative emotions lingered in the air, so I suggested we move the gathering outside to shift the energy. We walked down the stairs and along the graveled pathway to an area encircled by tall redwood and sycamore trees. It was a sacred place of mine. The sunlight danced among the trees and filtered its way down through the glen to where we stood in a circle. The birds chattered overhead, and a gentle breeze filled our senses with smells of summer.

I played a tape by Sophia called "Sacred Ground." As we listened to the words of gratitude to our Earth, the Mother, there was a recognition of our connection to our planet and to all our relations. The beating of the drums and the harmonies of music seemed to match the heartbeat of the Earth and, as our feet moved in a circle, the group began to reach a space of unity. As ego-centered issues faded, the focus began to shift to the greater purpose of our joint destiny. The Great ReUnion.

I noticed that Beth, one of the skeptics, was starting to shake. As we did our singing, as we did our chanting, and as we did our sharing, Beth continued to tremble. I sensed she was all right, but I knew something significant was occurring. I suggested, "Why don't we sit down." And we all sat in a circle on a blanket on the ground.

Beth could no longer resist the forces quickening within her and she said, "I think I have to channel. There is a message which will not be kept silent." Her voice, as always, had a quality of sweetness about it, yet now there was also a compelling sense of urgency. "It's been a long time since I've done this, so I hope you'll be patient with me."

I reached out and held her hand to try to calm her, and we all extended our love and support to her. In her mind's eye, she saw the mesa land and described the energy rising up from within it. Tears rolled down her cheeks as she described a spiral of silver light coming down and hovering just above the earth.

I knew that Beth was describing the anchoring of Light which would occur on that mesa near Santa Fe. The images she described brought life to the concepts we had been given to understand. I knew I was witness to another activation, and my commitment deepened. I sensed our connection to each other and to the whole. I saw that as each of us is reawakened and senses more clearly our oneness with Source, all of humankind takes another step closer to realizing its divinity.

Beth's awakening drew me into the vortex of a cosmic heartbeat. My own tears swelled. Belief and trust in a concept now shifted into a new level of realization, anchored by a covenant with my soul. Would Beth now be able to claim her part in this? Would she accept her role? We all sat quietly, wrapped in the healing energies of transformation.

Finally, the time came for the group to part. One by one the women left in silence, each alone to search the quiet spaces of their own heart.

Only Fred and I remained sitting in the glen, weary and filled with our own thoughts, when Ashtar spoke to us, *"You are to be commended for accepting the next phase of your assignments in an admirable manner today. You each claimed your roles. Everyone in the group experienced a major shift in their consciousness and will experience significant growth as the result of today's events. You need not concern yourselves about judging who is qualified and who is not. Some who are not qualified now will become qualified in the final moments. You know this is a time of great dispensation and Divine Grace. Major shifts can be made in but a moment. Allow the group to unfold and grow in its most natural manner. The activations are still continuing and there is still time for new ones to occur. When you finally weave your energies together, you will create a most wondrous monument as each one brings their own Light to the party of divine ecstasy. I thank you for your dedication. You are finding it rather thrilling to be a part of it all, and I acknowledge you for the great service which you perform. It is far greater than you can comprehend at this time."*

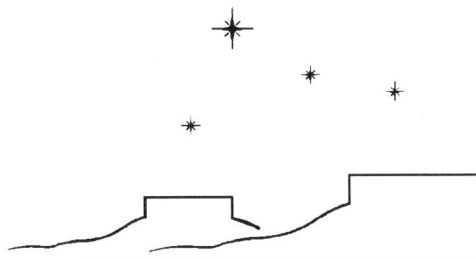

Macchu Picchu

Rachel returned the next day. The awakening within her could not be stilled. There was no peace in her dream-time, and new revelations were with her constantly. The memories poured forth like an underground stream that had just been tapped. Her voice trembled as she told us, "Last night, the image of a man came to me in my dreams. I felt such a heart connection. He gave me a message about the artifact."

I urged her, "Please go on."

"The artifact is being called here to us just as we are being called to it."

Fred and I listened to Rachel's message. We metaphorically threw this new information into the box with the other puzzle pieces, knowing that one day it would all fit together. Rachel asked, "Could we sit together and try to reconnect with whomever that was?" So much pressed on her, begging to be released. The ever-present cloak of White Light draped around our small circle as visions began to come to Rachel, and she spoke to us of Macchu Picchu . . .

"There. Standing on the hillside," Rachel's words were deliberate and measured as this birthing of an ancient connection began to take form. *"There is a Being who guards the place.*

"We fly, float over the city.

"He points to me. Here. There. The sacred places that are still hidden.

"Guards the city. Protects the sacred places.

"Shows me an entrance. Small. Rectangular. Dark.

"Now as we stand before it, we see it is very tall. Taller than a tall man. Very thin. You have to walk sideways and inch your way through.

"Sacred places deep in the Earth. Sacred places for all time.

"There's movement here, as if there have been many dancers. Still dancing. Movement. Circling. Circles within circles. The rituals of dancing. Circles within circles. Circles spinning.

"I see two disks spinning in opposite directions. Yet, when they come together, their edges spinning together, the spin can be turned inward. It can be spun outward.

"To the mind's eye they become one."

She paused as the vision continued unfolding. The memories of a time past choked her words, and my own remembrance brought tears as she continued,

"There is a breaking here. There is a tearing asunder. A shaking. A force. People falling. Things are broken. Entrances sealed off. Sacred places hidden for all time.

"No way out!

"No way in!"

This vision tapped into my own soul's memory, and I felt as though I was suffocating, trapped in the shifting rubble caused by these devices. Misused. Was this a picture of what I was involved in so long ago?

Incredible feelings of sadness and regret were emerging. There was an awareness, a recognition of my responsibility and my purpose at this time. Was this what Rita had described to us in Santa Fe as she looked backwards in time? I thought so.

Meanwhile, Rachel's words continued in the background of my thoughts,

"Now, there is a possibility, a glimmering, that this one will open. The dancers are still dancing.

"You must tell them.

"You must tell them they must stop dancing!

"Endless circles, endless circles, endless circles. Stuck. Like a record playing over and over.

"I can feel it."

Rachel gave a sigh. *"Something is trying to emerge. It keeps using old patterns. Old circles. Banging up against a wall. Not knowing what to do but trying to emerge.*

"We need to bring healing here. Let us focus.

"Imagine a room that is all stone. In the center of the room there is a beam of Light from above. We need to ground it."

We each envisioned sending our energies to assist bringing down the Light as the Guardian of Macchu Picchu had asked. Rachel sensed our energies arrive at the far distant point of her attention and said, *"We are there. What's needed is for us to allow Earth energy to flow up through us to meet the Light energy. That's what the endless circles are. Those feet aren't touching the Earth."*

There was silence as Rachel focused on the shifting energy. And as she sensed its movement, she again spoke,

"Good.

"The Light moves down. Joins. I see the energies shifting now.

"Good.

"It channels through us ... meets the Earth.

> *The dancers' feet*
>> *touch*
>>> *touch*
>>>> *touch*
>>>>> *... the ground.*

"The dancing stops."

Rachel sighed again. It was a relief, yet it was not done.

"There is still a feeling of 'No way out!' " Her voice continued to deepen and we all felt a pressure building – the weight of Rachel's words, the swell of memory's return.

"There is a rumble and a shifting. A doorway opens – slightly. We make our way out that doorway and are standing in a city – a live city. There is someone else there with us. I see you walking with him. There is much hustle and bustle. The spirit of this place will be with you. It goes before you, pulls you. Yes, this way. Yes, that way. Walking down the street. White buildings. Turning left. A gateway. Stone. People on the other side working. It looks like they are restoring something. The sun is hot."

I sensed this would be a chance to get more information and asked, "Is there a name for this place?"

Rachel's voice was halting as she searched for an answer, *"Cruzco."* She paused to confirm what she had said, *"Yes. Cruzco."*

She continued describing the scene being shown in her mind's eye, *"It's an old church that's being restored, but below it is sacred ground that was sacred before the church was there. There is something important here. I see someone handing you something."*

Rachel breathed deeply. She was strained from the unfamiliar sensations of channeling these vibrations through her body as she viewed the pictures and relayed them on to us, *"This is a big ancient power spot. Here you will know what to do next.*

"Fred, I see you standing in an adobe building, with arched windows – no glass. I see Pam standing beside you looking out the window over the city. Her eyes catch something, and you know it's a sign. It's like

_an old adobe building. White walls and high arched windows. It might
be an old church."_

I remembered the Peruvian travel video. I thought she must have
been describing the Temple of the Sun in Cuzco. We had stopped the
video the night that Rachel came to watch before it played the Cuzco
footage; she hadn't seen this scene. The church now standing there was
currently undergoing construction, and I could clearly see the scene she
was describing from the video.

Rachel continued,

_"It feels like a treasure hunt. Go to this place. Get a message. Go to
that place. Get a message._

"Your guide says, 'We must go now.'

_"You walk down the stairs – down and down and down. Turn
right, walk down the street, going to where Pam saw the sign. It's a tall
building with a stained glass window._

"There is something about focusing Light.

_"You go inside the building, a church. The light focuses on some-
thing wooden – a box with a lid that opens."_ Rachel breathed deeply
once again, trying to stay in sync with the energy she had tapped into.
_"Someone walks in the door. Nods his head. It's a priest. He walks toward
the altar. There's another sign on the altar:_

'You must not touch it.'

'You must not touch it.'

"A gleaming sword that says 'You must not touch it.'"

With that, Rachel rubbed her face, bringing her awareness back to the
room. We waited for her to regain her composure and fully return from
the altered state which had allowed her to experience this vision. Were
these clues to help us find the artifact? This message was coming from
one who was new to all of this, yet it meshed so clearly with what we had
already been shown and told.

She said, "Twice I saw the same image of something wrapped in
gray cloth. Once was in the building being restored when somebody was

passing something. Then, in the church up at the altar I saw the light and the sword. The words were, 'Don't touch it!' There, again, I saw something wrapped in cloth."

Fred said, "I had a good feeling of where we were and of being there with you. I saw the stone wall and the people working. Then it jumped to the scene of Pam looking out the window. She was just looking out over the city and saying, 'Oh, I see that over there.'"

Rachel had a distant look in her eyes and smiled as she said, "I can feel the presence of the Guardian at Macchu Picchu; he's glad he finally got the message across." Rachel smiled, "He's at peace."

It was compelling to hear the sincere messages which came through in such a pure and unaffected form. Once again, someone was speaking messages directly from her heart, sharing what she was being shown.

The veils of separation were being lifted all around us.

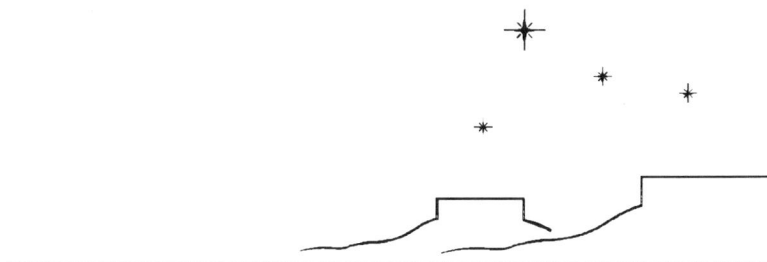

PREPARATION

Now our days and nights were full. Each person drawn to be in the circle had their own personal process of awakening and discovery, each equally significant. The group in Santa Fe worked with great intensity. They struggled as a group to merge their energies into a cohesive unit. Personalities clashed, egos were bruised, and through it all they each grew more into their potential as expanded Beings of Light.

It was July, the time of the new moon and the first ritual to reconsecrate the land. The merging which would take place during the anchoring of Light in August could not be done without a gradual awakening of the latent energies lying deep within Earth, and within each of us. The successful completion of the three preliminary activations would serve to draw these energies to the surface.

Rita was still with the group in Santa Fe. She had quickly taken charge there, giving them guidance and support. The group wondered what they should do during the ritual. At their meetings they discussed the details of what to wear, how long to fast, how they would stand, who would say what. Personal concerns, quiet doubts about personal preparation, loomed before each member of the group like giant phantoms ready to attack.

There were moments of insight for each one as they went through this process of discovery and enlightenment together. Ultimately, each came to understand that the most important preparation was their own inner work. As they succeeded at releasing their own denser energies and raising their vibrations, they were able to blend their energy into a circle of braided Light. It was an amazing process of level-upon-level of initiation into higher vibrations and greater intensities of Light.

We had arranged to have Jan, the owner of the land, take the group from Santa Fe onto the land to begin the preparations. The scheduled day was a solar eclipse, and the activities were timed to coincide with the eclipse for maximum benefit from the planetary energies.

As Fred and I went about our day's activities that day, we wondered how things were going in Santa Fe.

We heard nothing.

Did they do it?

We were surprised that no one called us to report. The next day we called to see what had happened. Jo answered the telephone, "Hello," her voice lilted the words.

"Hi, Jo!" I said. "How did the ceremony go yesterday?"

"It went great! We went up there and Iona took us right to the spot. She's a map maker, you know! I don't know what really happened; we all just kind of stood around and wondered what to do, but I guess it all got done." Her laughter was always ready, and it bubbled up, "The most important thing was our presence anyway. I'll have Iona tell you about finding the spot." And she was gone.

The next thing I heard was, "This is Iona." Jo had passed her the phone.

"Well, how did the ceremony go?"

"It was nice."

Nice? Surely there was more to tell than "nice."

"Jo says you're the map maker and it's your job to locate the place for each of the rituals. How did you do?"

"Oh," she replied, realizing what I wanted her to tell me. Her laughter was timid, "Oh, yes. I had a dream about it the night before the ritual."

"Well, tell us what happened," I prodded her on.

"We went up to the mesa in two cars. Sara and Margo were in the lead car with Jan; I was in the second car with some others. We drove up through the gates to an open meadow. There I recognized the skyline from my dream. There was no way to communicate with the women in the other car, and we didn't know where they were headed. I was so excited! The car began to slow down and I opened my door. I was ready to jump out before the car even stopped! I was thrilled that we had driven right to this place and that I recognized it. I've never had anything like this happen to me before! I jumped out of the car shouting, 'This is it! This is it!'

"Jan had led us right to the spot. When Sara and Margo gave her the description of what it was supposed to look like, Jan said, 'I think I know where you need to be.' And, there we were. Jan had driven us right to the place for the first ceremony. I knew without a doubt this was right!"

I wanted every detail, "What did you do?"

"It's hard to remember, really. Jan had brought a device made of cardboard so we could watch the eclipse. We were watching the shadow of the eclipse through the cardboard filter to determine when we should begin so that we could time it precisely to coincide with the eclipse. I could feel the energy running and my presence was there 'in channel,' so to speak. I don't know. We each stood focused and everybody did a little invocation. Then there was a silent period when we were all wondering what we were supposed to be doing. We were just winging it. I knew when it was over because I felt the energy stop running through my body. Other people kept wanting to continue but I knew we could stop.

"We didn't need to stand in fixed positions any longer. Some felt we couldn't move, but I knew it was done. At the end we each made an offering to be released to the universe." Iona paused a minute and then said, "I guess that was it. I don't know if we did what we were supposed to do."

I didn't know what they were supposed to do either. The work for them was different than the work for us, and I wasn't getting guidance on their particulars. I knew that part of their initiation was to figure things out for themselves. I wanted to encourage her and said, "Good going! I'm sure that everything was perfect. Your intention, your dedication, and your presence were the most important things. Let us know when you'll be doing the next one and we'll join you energetically."

Iona responded, "All right."

We said our good-byes. I knew it had begun. The wheels were turning. The team in Santa Fe had not let Spirit down. Their intention was strong and their efforts sincere. The foundation had been laid, the braiding of energies begun, and the bridge was being formed to connect the lower and higher realms for the descension of the new Light Grid.

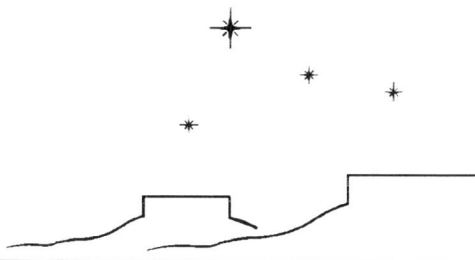

CIRCLES

The events surrounding us were being orchestrated by our celestial partners. The group in Santa Fe had heard the call, had come together, and had begun. In California, the call had also been sent out. The awakenings and the activations had begun, the circle began to form. The work ahead of us was intense, yet we had each been preparing for this our entire lives. I wondered, "How many other people, in how many other places, are also being called?"

I felt that successful completion of this assignment was a duty and a trust which was greater than I could comprehend. We opened our home to be a center for the work. Fred and I were there to support and to guide the disciples of Light as, one by one, they heard the call.

We received word from Rita in Santa Fe that she was ready to come to California, and we called the group together to meet her. Casey telephoned and said, "My mother is in town this week. Can I bring her with me?"

"Of course," I replied. I tried to take no control but to let the events unfold in their natural and divined way. I had surrendered to the process. I knew that I was serving Creator. How could there be ego? How could any human think they were in charge when the plan of universal destiny was unfolding?

We became more and more aware of a thinning of the veil between dimensions as we worked with those who came to us. Much of our preparation occurred beyond our perception. We felt the vibrations in our own bodies rising as we were penetrated by greater amounts of energy from the cosmos.

I asked Ashtar to explain the physical changes we were experiencing. He answered, *"You could say that this Light Energy is coming from the future because it represents levels that will be ordinary in a short time. These are waves of energy that rise steeply, level off for awhile, then rise steeply again. There is no point in going back to old levels. This is not our scheme. There is no returning to a level that existed in the past. Your conscious mind is the governor, the valve, that limits the amount of Light that is absorbed and made consciously active.*

"The world will be going into the future with more Light. People who resist this will keep themselves in the past, but it is precisely this increased level of Light that is defining the future in your world. There is a point beyond which you will not be able to go without allowing yourselves to come fully into these new levels of Light. The only way that this can be done is by allowing more Light inside of yourselves.

"It is possible to resist this infusion of Light energy, but if you do, it would hold you back and not allow you to grow into the future. There is a split, a rift, that is forming on the planet between those who will accept the higher vibration levels and those who cannot. Now that the Light is increasing in intensity, we are concentrating on having you learn how to handle more, to safely open your valves and let more Light flow through you in order to assist us as we ground the Light to Earth at the many points that will eventually receive it. Some will take the pressure differences and draw that inside themselves instead of drawing in the Light directly. This will only result in stress and confusion."

I already knew all this, yet the physical sensations I was having made me ask, "Ashtar, I continue to feel surges of energy running through my body like electrical spikes. Last night it was very uncomfortable and accompanied by a fever. Was that discomfort an extra infusion of voltage or was it illness? I felt very hot, like my blood was boiling and my body was too small to contain it."

"It was lots of Light coming through a valve which was turned to a fairly low setting. If this Light was water going through a tap at high pressure, there would have been pressure at the valve. It was this pressure that you felt. You can request that the Light which comes to your valve be adjusted to a comfortable level. Or you can choose to open your valve a little wider to allow the Light to come through more easily."

"It was pretty uncomfortable. This doesn't make sense to me. Wouldn't a larger opening just allow more energy to come in?"

"Just so." Ashtar spoke again, trying to make me understand more clearly what was happening, *"By opening the valve, you relieve the pressure. Leaving the valve closed builds up the pressure. Make a pact with your Higher Self that for this short period of time you will allow the maximum intensity of Light in your body that you can safely handle. Your Higher Self has another valve. It is this valve that knows your true capabilities. You have any amount up to this limit available to you. There is no possibility of doing yourself harm. But if there is a difference in pressure between what is around you and what you consciously let in, there will be feelings of pressure. This is a valuable preview for you, an experiment that all Light workers perform as they play with the valve. Remember, it's your own hand that's on the valve."*

Ashtar's voice shifted and I could feel his love as he said, *"You know, you can very easily and lovingly let in all the Light that you desire."*

"Oh, Ashtar, I'm so grateful to have your guidance. Thank you so much for your encouragement."

Fred then changed the subject asking his own question, "What is my role to be in the ceremony in August?

"You are each to be anchors for the Light, bringing the Light through you. Your particular role in the circle is to be an anchor for the circle. Your male energy is very solid and somewhat more grounded than some

of the female energy which will be present. Your strength, your focus, and your ability to remain centered will hold the group together. Much like a wizard, you will be holding a crystal ball in your hands and the ceremony will play itself out. Does that make sense to you?"

"Yes. It makes sense." Fred thought for a moment about the role Ashtar had described and added, "I'm not sure that I'm qualified to do it." Then, "I guess I am if you're giving me the role, but I don't feel ready for it."

Ashtar returned his reassurance to Fred's doubts, "*We love you dearly and know that you're capable. There will be intense growth for you in the weeks ahead in preparation for your duties. Have no doubts. You are going to be immensely qualified and confident in your task. You are not going to simply be a bystander or a spectator. You are a key player in the process.*

"Pam could not do any of this without you. We want her to recognize and accept her own strength. We want her to claim her power, and she is being given many opportunities to get used to doing this. But, by the same token, you give her great stability and reassurance. Your personal dynamics may be shifting a bit, but I think you will find the changes most welcome. You will take great joy at watching each other blossom, two flowers reaching for the Light and coming into the fullness of your bloom."

Now our thoughts turned to Rita, who would be arriving the next day. Although we thought it would be fun to have her with us and to learn from her, there was a thread of doubt as to whether I could trust her. I had heard stories of how she had been given authority by the people in Santa Fe. I was confident that our guidance was clear; however, I didn't know where she came from or what her connections were with the project, the Ashtar Command, or, ultimately, the Divine Plan. I remembered Ashtar's guidance about one who would come that we would have to trust. Was he speaking about Rita? In my heart I questioned her intentions and her alignment. I didn't want to risk being led astray at this point by one who was sent to throw us off track.

And, in response to my questioning, Dartan spoke, "*You have been left for this long period of time on your own so that you could become very clear and very strong in your own knowing without someone else giving you information. You must be forewarned not to give this power away!*

You can continue to trust in your own information even in the face of someone else's – even someone who appears to have understanding beyond yours. For the two of you this is a process of empowerment, as it will be for each of the participants."

And, then, Archangel Michael also reassured us, _"Rita is a dear one. A very dear and chosen one. She gives to others as though she needs no nurturing herself. You know, in the eyes of God, all children are loved. Each are blessed with different gifts. There are some who have been asked to carry a greater responsibility. They are like angels upon Earth in physical form. There are many lives that they will touch and much that they will be called upon to do. And, so, because of the great responsibility that they have accepted, additional gifts have been bestowed upon them to enable them to achieve these tasks."_

We knew that she would be coming to us for many reasons. There would be a balance and an exchange. Fred asked, "How can we be of service to Rita?"

Archangel Michael responded, _"You are providing her a haven and a place for renewal; a peacefulness and serenity that she is yearning for exists here. It is a little R&R for the warrior. So, you can help her forget her responsibilities for a time. Give her some diversion from her duties. There will be time for work, but there can also be time for play and healing. We will protect you. We are helping you create a safe haven."_

Fred's mind was racing at the possibilities, "I have just one more question on another topic."

"Yes."

"Who are we?"

"You are mighty Messengers of the Circles. Circles of Light. Circles of Love."

We understood.

And so they came. Feelings of confusion and misunderstanding had been replaced by anticipation. The others were now ready to meet Rita, the mystery woman whose reputation had preceded her, the one who came from New York, the one who left her home and business to travel West, the one who coincidentally showed up at the same time and place in Santa Fe as Fred and I.

Rita sat back, quietly sizing up the group as Fred and I talked. All had returned from the week before. The pair of skeptics, Allison and Beth, who claimed they didn't believe you could communicate with unseen beings or that they were a part of this whole thing, were there. I silently acknowledged their presence, knowing their return was driven by their own souls' desires to fulfill the Plan. The unresolved issues were of free will and self-determination. Each could choose whether to say Yes or No.

The circle had been cast.

The energies of the group had begun to smooth. There was only one new member in the circle besides Rita – Casey's mother, Charlene. Her hair was bright as sunlight, and she smiled shyly as she was introduced. The question of who was to be included rested on the surface waiting to be answered, when Charlene stated, "Well, this all sounds very interesting, but I'm wondering if I'm to be a part of this or not."

I knew, once again, that the answer was not mine to give and returned the question to her, "What do *you* think?"

Charlene's face flushed as the words, "Yes! I think I am a part of this!" tumbled out before she had a chance to think about the answer. Then, her emotions burst forth in tears of joy and acceptance of her role, "I've always wanted a way to serve. I think this may be it."

As Charlene wiped the tears from her cheeks, my own heart swelled with joy at witnessing another soul activation. I looked at Fred, overcome with the realization that *this* was our work! Charlene's acceptance of her soul's mission with such innocence and trust tapped into an awareness of the blessing of my own soul's awakening.

The questions continued as to who would be involved, when Rita abruptly jumped in to the conversation in her brusque New York manner, "Yes, you are to be in the circle." To another, "You could choose."

The energy in the room shifted. I knew that Rita had made these determinations for the group in Santa Fe, but I didn't anticipate her playing that role here. This group had supported each other in the process of co-discovery up to this point. But Rita was impatient, and she became easily frustrated at our clumsy attempts to figure things out.

Fred and I observed without interfering as Rita began to assert her authority over matters of selection. Charlene's daughter, Casey, was the youngest person who had come. She asked eagerly, with wide-eyed innocence, "What about me? Am I to be a part of the circle?"

How quickly they were willing to let someone else judge what each one could only know within.

Rita's energy had risen and she answered, "No. You will not be in the circle – but you can be a spectator if you want."

Casey's eagerness turned to disappointment, and Rita continued flippantly, "You don't have to feel bad about not being in this one. When you're ready, there'll be another assignment for you."

Casey nodded, leaning back on the sofa as she tried to accept the verdict. Her mother was to be a part, but she could not – not now.

Then, Aya's defiant question burst forth, "What about the gridwork? We heard that the group in Santa Fe had to have it put in by you before they could be a part of the ceremonies."

Rita brushed her hand at the air as if to wipe away the question, and scoffed, "Nobody had to do <u>anything</u>. It's just something that I offered to help prepare them to be able to handle the quantity of Light they would be in. You can't just go and do this," Rita laughed. "I don't make these decisions. I'm just passing information along. Nobody has to do anything. If you're not ready, your own *people* will make sure you don't go. You'll break your leg, or your car will break down, or you'll get sick. Something will happen to prevent you from going on the mesa if you're not ready to handle it!"

I interceded, "Why don't you tell us a little bit about yourself."

"Sure," Rita responded. "What I am is a mental healer. That's someone who works with a person's DNA patterning as well as their electrical systems. Mental healers on the planet are very rare. What I do is place my hand on your head and form a bridge to help you release negativity. Then there's physical healing work. If you need new organs – arms, legs, ligaments – those get replaced. There's a whole gallery of beings present to assist. They are your *people* and I just watch. Then after this healing work is done, they put in your Light Grids which will help you move more quickly into your Light Body. I assist in activating the grids. You could take years to do this on your own, or you could have me do it in an hour. You can think of me as an expressway. This work is not for everyone. It's very fast. We clean up a lot of stuff. When I take my hand away from your head the work doesn't stop. It's like retracting an energy bridge. This work will open up things and the work with your *people* will be ongoing. Once you've committed to doing this, they've started with you."

Rita had asked Fred and me if either of us would be willing to let her work on us before the meeting so we could tell the others what it was like to have the new gridwork put in place. I wasn't sure whether I wanted Rita changing my DNA! I didn't fully trust her. But Fred had quickly accepted the offer. Was Fred gullible? Or did his trust give him the freedom to move forward without fear?

She said, "You can ask Fred if you want to know about the work. I put in his Light Grids this morning."

All eyes in the room turned to Fred who sat, quivering from the infusion of energy which he had received that morning from Rita. She seized the opportunity, as she continued, "He got seven grids put in at once! That's the most anyone has been able to handle at one time."

We each looked from Fred to Rita, trying to make our own decisions about whether we wanted this done to us. She made it sound almost crucial. Yes, there was a price. Seventy-five dollars. Self-doubt circled the room like a wave as we each wondered if we could be ready without her assistance. Each of us knew that we must be prepared to perform the roles we had accepted for anchoring the Light on the mesa in just six weeks. The stakes seemed high.

We were baited by a desire to succeed that was so intense we would each do whatever seemed necessary. And each one's doubts surrendered to the promise for assistance. One by one, each member of the group made the decision to pay Rita's fee, and scheduled an appointment to have her assist in activating their personal energy gridwork.

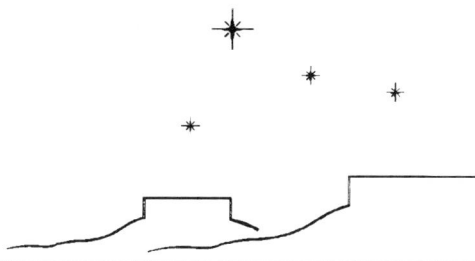

STRUGGLE

The circles were beginning to turn as the process of inner work expanded. There was individual dedication to a common purpose. Strangers living in distant cities had come together in spirit. We joined our love and our focus on a project we could not fully understand, yet our hearts said we must do.

> *Growth of the Spirit and growth of the soul*
> *Darkness and limits to be left behind*
> *Christed Light brought to Earth is our goal*
> *A task as a blessing for all humankind*

It was a time for each of us to look within and ponder the magnitude of what was possible to accomplish. To serve humankind was a heady and magnificent task, so out of the ordinary that we felt a compelling urgency to assure its success. Each, in their own way, had been tapped to be a part. Although in our private moments there were doubts about self-worth, not one of us could turn our back on the mission. We would do whatever it would take to be ready.

One by one, those in the circle returned to ask Rita for her assistance, and soon everyone had met with her in private session. Fred and I enjoyed having our home be a focal point of spiritual growth. It had become the Light Center we had desired. The field of Light which surrounded our home affected all who came, enabling them to explore questions of the soul.

Our children didn't know what to think about all the mysterious activity around them. Kari had moved out, but our two teenaged sons remained, and we hadn't shared any of the details of our experiences with them.

I told Fred, "We have to sit down and try to explain to the boys what's going on. All these people are coming over here and talking about their unusual experiences. We try to keep it separate from our family life, but this is going on all around us. It must be very confusing to Drew and Ian."

"Yeah, it certainly isn't Ozzie & Harriet time around here."

"You're right about that! Everything was so simple back in the 50's. What we're dealing with is the visceral stuff of life as people open to Spirit. I'm honored to be a part of this process, but it can be pretty intense, especially if you don't understand what's going on."

That night at dinner, Fred began by asking the boys, "Have you ever seen a real magic piece?"

They both perked up, "No."

"Well, would you like to see one?"

"Yes!" they both eagerly agreed, their curiosity triggered by the possibility of experiencing something magical.

I had the artifact with me and placed it in front of my plate as Fred told the story about how the gold artifact had come to us from an ancient civilization. My son, Drew, took the piece in his hand and closed his eyes as he listened. He seemed to sense the power of the device as his mind traveled with Fred on an imaginary journey to Peru, "I want to be a part of this! I want to go to Peru with you! I can help you find the other artifact!"

Drew was still holding the artifact and closed his eyes again as Fred continued, "This artifact is so powerful that when we find the other piece, we can't even hold the two together because it could mess up the airplane's instruments. We'll have to wrap them both in special space blanket material and keep them apart for safety."

With a shudder, Drew opened his eyes.

"What is it?" I asked.

He shook his head and looked at the artifact he was still holding, "It was nothing."

"This doesn't look like nothing," I persisted. "What's bothering you?"

"I saw your plane crashing in the jungle." Drew hesitated, but finally he shared his feelings, "Maybe it's not a good idea to go."

Fred's son, Ian, lived with us during the summers, and spent the school year with his mother and brother in Kansas. He was sitting across the dinner table from Drew, and now reached out to take the piece. He held it briefly. Then he shrugged his shoulders, "Uhuh."

"What do you think?" I asked. Fred watched.

Ian replied, "It's interesting, but I didn't feel anything." Then he addressed Drew, "Are you ready to get up?"

Drew nodded, "All right."

The two boys excused themselves from the dinner table and went to their room to discuss what they had just heard. What private conversations were shared between the two, we never knew. Drew understood that, as strange as it sounded, there was something real about what we said. I recognized that instinctive sense of knowing beyond logic which overcame him as he held the artifact and his consciousness moved to some far away place. Ian was an avid science fiction reader, but his sense of the world held the supernatural firmly under the classification of fantasy. How could he interpret what we were asking him to believe?

The two boys feigned disinterest. Could they accept a story which seemed so absurd? Curiosity and disbelief waged a silent battle within each of them. They shared the story with their friends, who heard it incompletely and second-hand. I overheard the nervous response from one friend, "You'd better not mess around with the spirit world!"

The boys weren't prepared to handle the skepticism which came from their friends. And the seed of fear was planted. It was a fear based upon stories of ghosts and demons, tales from the dark side on the movie screen which had penetrated their thinking. Quickly, that seed sprouted, and we could no longer share what was going on without drawing ridicule from our sons.

The doubts which they reflected back to us were painful to receive. After months of inner struggle to understand and accept this new information, it was not over. From our own place of knowing we were finally able to tell others. We felt we were a part of the Divine Plan. Yet the information was so out of the ordinary that our own children were frightened and would present our greatest test of faith.

It was mid-July, the night the group in Santa Fe was to perform the second preparation ceremony. Kate had come over to join us as we supported them. Aya had also returned. Her own doubts were pressing heavily upon her and she was hoping for reassurance of her involvement. Rita was still with us, stretching her intended stay of four days into weeks. At the scheduled hour of the work in Santa Fe, we sat down in our living room in Santa Cruz. We each focused our attention on the cone of blended energy as our individual energies joined to form a braid to support them with an energetic bridge.

The first phase of clearing the energy in the land had gone smoothly, and they were unaware there were opposition forces mounting.

Rita sat on the floor outside our circle and said, "You'll have to tell me what you're seeing because I'm going to be too busy to be looking!" She closed her eyes, her body curled, and she began shaking. A shadow seemed to be wrapped around her as her muscles tensed.

Each of us in the circle saw, in our mind's eye, a remote view of a different aspect of the work which was being done in Santa Fe. Fred saw the emotional state of the circle. "They are fragmented. One wants to walk away. There's an emptiness in the center of the circle." He said, "Let's place a band around this group to hold their circle firmly together." We joined our intention to place this band of support around the group. Then we saw the column of Light. Their energies had finally unified to raise the braid. I felt their strong heart connection which would sustain them through their difficulties. I felt their love for the Earth and their dedication to the task. Kate saw the energies from Earth's central core rising to the surface in a pyramid of Light. Another pyramid of Light was descending from above as the energies of Spirit and Earth moved ever closer to each other without joining. When it was completed we withdrew our energetic bridge and returned our awareness to the living room.

"Phew! They nearly blew it!" Rita announced. "They just don't take this seriously enough. Do they think they can just casually go about doing this? There was some serious opposition and they didn't even establish their protection! It took all my strength to keep the battle away from them."

She shook her head and allowed the breath to escape between her lips, "Phew!" she blustered again.

She was on her feet now, pacing impatiently. "What? Do they think this is some sort of game. Geez! This is for real and they don't get it yet!"

Aya's eyes remained closed. She leaned forward, holding her head in her hands. "I have such a headache." She turned to Rita and confessed her fears, "I really don't know if I'll be ready to be a part of the ceremony on August 25th. I couldn't see anything at all!"

"Well, you might not be ready," Rita returned. And, as she had told Casey earlier, "If you're not ready for this one, there'll be other times. There are a jillion things that need to be done to wake this planet up."

Aya was quiet. What could she say? No words were there to express her disappointment, for the call to participate remained in her soul. Rita continued, "The private session that we had last week probably stirred up a lot. There are dark forces who don't want this project to succeed and they might try to trigger some of your 'stuff' to sidetrack you. Don't forget to let your 'stuff' go."

Aya was already unsure of herself and this was not the encouragement she had hoped to get. Rita, instead, had amplified Aya's doubts back to her.

Aya said, "I think I need to lie down. Maybe I can get rid of my headache." She unrolled her sleeping bag in the corner of the living room, continuing to hold her head as she rested it on the pillow.

The telephone rang. It was the Santa Fe group calling to check in with us. "Hi! This is Jo," was the perky greeting across the line.

We all gathered around the speaker phone to listen. "How did it go?" I asked eagerly. We wondered how much of what we sensed had matched their experience.

"It went great!" Jo replied. "... even though we had some difficulties in the beginning agreeing on a place. Some of us were in an unsettled state, kind of off balance today."

"Well, you guys almost blew it!" Rita interrupted.

"We did?" Jo asked, surprised by this pronouncement.

"What were you guys doing dorking around up there?" Rita didn't mince any words.

Iona joined in the conversation from the other end, "Well, we had a hard time agreeing upon the spot this time. Everyone had a different idea and didn't want to listen to me. I felt that it was up on some very high rocks at the top of a cliff. I had the quartz wand that Sheila had given to us, and I was pretty insistent about the spot. Some people didn't want to make the climb so we went up the long way around, which was easier. We walked for hours to get there. If we had climbed up the rocks we could have gotten there much quicker but I wasn't feeling secure enough about myself to insist. They wanted to be where it was easy and we could stand in a nice circle. Even though I was scared about the responsibility of locating the spot for the work, I was certain and said 'No, we are to be on the top of the rocks.' Some people in the group were angry at me, thinking I was running them on a wild goose chase. A couple of people got so angry that they wanted to leave. But I loved it there. I was feeling at one with the Earth. It was beautiful!

Another voice from Santa Fe broke in. It was Margo, "It was bizarre! Iona insisted that we sit precariously out on the point. There was a storm coming. No one was grounded. It was total chaos. Everyone's anger was on the surface. We had to climb under a tree to get out on the rocks, and then the wind came up. We were sitting instead of standing and the strength of the wind made us feel like we could lose our balance. It was a real test for all of us!"

Even though the reports were so varied, we understood that what we had seen and felt was accurate. Iona continued, "We all did something. There were seven of us plus one alternate who was the driver. Dove played her Indian flute and made an offering of tobacco to honor the Native American traditions. None of us felt the intensity you're talking about. In fact, we were all kind of lackadaisical. Then the storm clouds began rolling in. Thunder and lightning were all around. And we had a thirty-minute hike back to the car if we took the steeper cliff route."

Iona thought a moment and added, "It probably didn't really matter. It was all just a way of getting us to cooperate with each other and to deal with our egos."

But matter it did. Opposition forces had pricked at their weak spots and upset their balance. We made a plan to unite with them again during the third ceremony of preparation. The two groups were melding as we made these energetic alliances. We wanted to extend our support to our brothers and sisters working on the preparation phase of the Light project, and this was the most effective way we could do it from a distance.

Sara was to be my anchor during the Ceremony of Light and I knew our bond must be strong, for she was here to join me in the task of planetary healing. We were to work together. The physical distance between us meant our union must be strengthened in superconsciousness.

We did what we could, corresponding with each other about our quest and sharing information received from our guides. The wheels were spinning faster now and our circles were expanding as we worked toward a common goal.

Sara wrote beautiful detailed accounts to us of her progress and the developments with the Santa Fe circle. She sent copies of pages from her journal, transcriptions of conversations between herself and Ashtar, and a detailed diagram of circles and geometric shapes which she had been shown in meditation.

When Sara asked Ashtar about her own personal role in the Light Anchoring, he responded, *"You will be the grounding force for Pam within the circle. It would be most appropriate for you to be standing next to her. Pam will be focusing on what she is to do and will experience much emotional releasing during the process. You are to see that she remains centered and grounded. Your energies will fuse together at this time in order for the two of you to operate as one like-mind. She will not be in a state to remember grounding herself, for her intent will be strong and she will be conscious only of the emplacement of the artifacts."*

I then turned to Sara's diagram of circles. Her note said, "We have been asked to continue working after the third ceremony of preparation and to bury twenty-two crystals in a configuration which corresponds to the seven rays." I looked at the diagram again. Sara's instructions from Dartan were quite detailed. We hadn't received any of this information, for this was not our task.

Severe weather and monsoon rains continued to challenge the efforts of the group to complete their assigned tasks. Massive cleansing of Earth energetically, electrically, and physically was underway. Cars got stuck in the rain-soaked earth on more than one occasion when the Santa Fe team went to the mesa to bury crystals, and they beseeched the weather spirits to leave them alone.

The second ritual was followed by a torrential rain. The group remained unaware of the etheric opposition to their activities. That night the storm outside raged as Sara and Margo sat in Sara's cottage talking about the events of the day. The Thunder Beings clapped their hands as hail and rain pummeled the roof. There was a war-like fierceness about the storm as the battle over the Light Anchoring project raged all around and above them. With a sharp crash and a flash of light, lightning struck as the forces of the stormy battle centered on Sara's house. Sara and Margo were momentarily overcome with fear. Huddled together in the living room, Sara called out for the aid of Archangel Michael. Instantly, a blue light streaked around the room giving them a protective shield.

It was the full moon in July. There was just one month remaining, and time continued unrolling the events in preparation for the ceremony to be done in August. The West Coast team was enmeshed in the preparation activities being done in Santa Fe as we continued with our own inner preparations. Our commitment to Spirit was ever-present as our vow to be of service hovered about us.

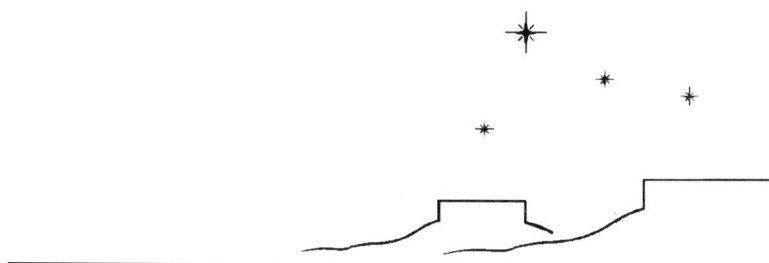

FAMILY

The next evening, our grown daughter, Kari, came home to visit. Her brothers had been telling her that a lot of weird things had been going on since she left. She was determined to find out for herself what was happening. As the eldest child, she felt she had to stop us.

As soon as dinner was over, Kari sat back in her chair and asked, "What's this about going to Peru?" Her voice was strained and her hands trembled as she broached the subject.

I knew that I would have to talk to her in terms which she could understand, and told her that we had been receiving guidance on this from the angels and Sananda, which is the name Jesus uses now. "It's not so strange when you really think about it," I said.

"You can't be talking to Jesus," she replied.

"Of course we can! Where do you think he is now?" I returned. "Everyone accepts that Moses and the other prophets in the Bible talked to God. Why can't we receive guidance from God too?"

She looked as though she could hardly believe her ears. This was not the mother she knew.

I continued, "Have you ever heard the Bill Cosby comedy routine called 'Noah'? It's very funny. It describes exactly the way we're feeling now. The voice of God came to Noah and told him to build this huge ark. And he replied, 'Who me?' Then, when Noah's neighbors laughed at him, he asked, 'Why me?' But he knew he had to follow the messages because they were too compelling to ignore. And after all the ridicule and all the struggle to follow this guidance, what happened?"

Kari was becoming quiet, although she still trembled. This was not what she had anticipated. This was too far out to be true and it was too far out to be a lie. "But what about Peru? You're not really going to Peru, are you?"

My heart ached. My daughter was distressed at our actions and I could not still her anxiety. "Yes. We are going. We'll be protected. We have had too much proof that the angels are working with us to be afraid." I tried to reassure her, "We'll be okay. Kari, I love you. Please don't worry. I don't want you to be afraid. Nothing can happen to us. What we are doing is too important. I just know it." I pleaded with her, "Please believe me."

"But Mom, it's not safe there," she cried. "I don't want to lose you!"

"Oh, Kari," I reached over to her and held her in my arms. I could feel her pain and I was torn. Still, I couldn't explain my compelling sense of duty to Spirit, for the feelings were beyond words. And, as I held her in my arms and tried to comfort her, I whispered, "Don't worry. God is with us."

She was calmer when she left, but I knew she must be very confused. I hoped that she would be able to accept our sincerity and hear that we had carefully considered our actions. I wanted our family to understand the path which we must walk was not so much a choice as it was a responsibility, that it came from an unswerving dedication to Spirit.

That night when Fred came to bed he relayed, "Ian wants to go home. I'm going to try to get him a flight tomorrow."

"Tomorrow?!" I gasped. "He's not scheduled to go for another two weeks."

"I know," Fred said. "But he's ready now. He came and talked to me tonight. He's pretty uncomfortable with everything that's going on. He might as well go."

My heart ached again and the tears rolled down my cheeks. "Why does there have to be so much fear?" I cried, pounding my clenched fist into my pillow. "Why can't they understand that the work we are doing will be making the world a better place?"

"Fear is always about the unknown," Fred replied.

"Yes. I know," I agreed as I reached out and grasped Fred's hand. "This is the hardest test we've had."

Fred nodded in acknowledgment. There was a sadness in that moment, but we both knew that it was best for his son to leave. Fred said, "I can't tell anyone else what they should believe. He knows what he must do, just as we do."

Our initial misgivings seemed so distant now. I felt open and raw. My own heightened vibrations increased my awareness of all that was around me, and emotions like anger and fear directed toward me cut me like a knife. I cried, "I don't know how much more I can bear. I'm feeling my own pain, but it's more than that. It seems that what I'm going through is a whole lot more than just my own stuff. Sometimes it's just too much for me to try to transmute all of this!"

I closed my eyes with a deep yearning for love and nurturing. A token touch from Fred brought little comfort, and I closed my eyes to sleep. But, as I drifted off, I was taken on an interdimensional journey. I felt the swiftness of the trip as I left this dimension and moved into the fourth where there was fear and restlessness of many disembodied spirits whose presence quickly passed.

Then I moved through the stars and through the cosmos. Travel was easy as time and space folded together into a dimension of no-time.

I saw a small micro-chip sized doorway and easily slid through it to the beyond.

Then I clearly saw two large hands over me. They were glowing with healing energy. Then I saw His face and knew that Jesus was with me in a way I had never before experienced. The Love of Christ was palpable.

The memory of Christ's face, so full of love and kindness, remained with me more clearly than a dream. Although he spoke no words, his presence lingered, and I knew He would be with us always, no matter how difficult or lonely the path became.

And my tears of agony changed to tears of understanding.

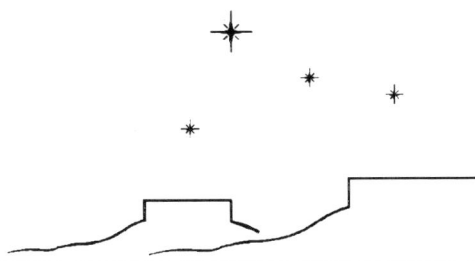

POINT OF PEACE

Preparations for the August ceremony continued over the weeks which followed and our dedication grew as we each deepened our commitment to Spirit. One day several of us were sitting on the deck enjoying the warm afternoon sun when we were introduced to special guides who would be with each of us through the final days of our preparation and stand along side us during the Light Activation ceremony. My guide was a Being named Aguilar who had one message, *"Stay centered."* These would be the only words he would ever speak to me.

Fred was quiet as the rest of us shared the names of our guides and their messages.

I asked him, "Who's your guide?"

He remained silent, a faraway look in his eyes.

The pressure of awaited reply coaxed his reluctant answer, "It was Sananda."

I nodded. It seemed so natural and correct.

Fred shook his head, "I really find that difficult to believe."

"Why?"

"Well, I don't know if I'm worthy to have Sananda as my partner."

"Of course you are! We all know it. Don't you feel fortunate to have such support?"

"Oh, I do! I just don't know what it means. It seems like too great an honor."

Fred devoted himself more than ever to his task, and his link to Sananda deepened with each passing day. Fred soon became His voice and the next time our circle formed, Sananda spoke through him, *"Hello my wise ones in Spirit, my beloved ones. Sometimes greatness comes from working in a group. This acknowledges the kind of groups that you are accustomed to working with on other levels.*

"As you know, your planet is due for some changes. You are to be the instruments of those changes and we are the guides. The object of the change is Earth and yourselves, who are of the Earth and of Spirit. This is why it can only be you who are the instruments of these changes. As incarnated souls, you have the experiences and the tools to do the melding. This is what is called for now as the planet isn't waiting. We are working with you and through you. You have remembered enough to be familiar with the concepts, allowing yourselves to be conduits and instruments of our joint work. It is our work coming through you that allows the melding of our worlds and yours. It is a merging and a blending which will lead to something new.

"We're not repeating old programs or recapitulating something that has gone on before. This is something without precedence! We're glad that you are allowing yourselves to be part of this wonderful undertaking. It's a wedding, you know. It is a marriage of the willing Earth Mother and the willing Sky Father joining together. In the past there has been a separation.

"Let us now sit just a moment and allow yourselves to receive the energies that we're sending. You must balance the time of work by a time

of quietness. In this calmness is a Point Of Peace that you can call to yourselves whenever you desire it. When the world and the things you are experiencing in these times of growth seem to be too much, you may go to a quiet place and center your minds. Ask to return to this Point of Peace.

"Let yourselves relax into this peace. Allow the cares and frustrations to quiet down. You may even allow them all to pass away as you become still. Remember how you are feeling right now and let that feeling come back whenever you need it. Let its warmth enfold you like a thick, comfortable blanket. Then, take this feeling back with you.

"It is the Light that you bring back from the Point of Peace to carry with you. It will adjust itself to fit you like the proverbial glove. You have gone to the Point Of Peace and retrieved it. It will help you be protected. There is plenty to go around for anyone who wishes to ask.

"This is a garment of Light that you may wear. It is a way of spreading the Light around. It is a way of bringing the Light from our worlds to yours. You are the instrument. You are the ones who have donned it, who will wield it. It will serve you, especially when you are out in the world. Whenever you feel the need to replenish this Light you may return to the Point Of Peace and be rejuvenated. This Point Of Peace is my gift for you this evening."

Sananda's presence departed, leaving a blanket of Light hanging in the room like a cloak that each of us could reclaim and wrap around ourselves. Our hearts felt healed and our souls were nurtured by this union with the undeniable love of Christ expressed through Sananda and through Fred. What a blessing to have this support through our struggles, to know in a deeply personal way of the love and support waiting for us all.

Rita couldn't seem to let the moment be. She jolted my attention back as she instructed us, "It's imperative that you meet on a regular basis and work together as you have tonight. You have to go to this thing 'loaded for bear.' By working with each other, you're going to continue to strengthen yourselves. If you don't participate in these practice sessions, it's going to be more difficult to participate with the larger group. Make every effort to get here when the meetings are being held (however you guys arrange that). It's not about sitting down and doing processing. It's about working with the skills that you've got already and honing them to as fine a degree as you can. None of you are asked to be perfect for this upcoming event. You are, however, asked to be as clear as you can be. That's what all of this preparation is about."

Rita continued, "Now, as for the ceremonies: You are to prepare your bodies to transmit the Light. There will be a period of fasting that will be asked of everyone that's going to participate in this. This is a water fast – drink lots of it, but have nothing to eat for 12 hours before the ceremony. It would even be in your best interest to see if you can eat only fruits and vegetables for several days just prior to it. Stay away from coffee, tea, alcohol, meat, and all that kind of stuff.

"Apparel for this occasion will be natural fiber cloth – no leather or jewelry, no metals, no elastic, no rubber, no nothing. Okay?

"You'll be barefoot during the ceremony for better contact with the earth. No accouterments of any kind are needed. These are just generalities. No plastic combs in your hair, no barrettes, no anything that's going to get in the way of the conductor that you're going to be. Think of yourself as an electrical conductor and don't wear anything that's going to get in the way of that."

I thought about the instructions and my usual clothing, "You mean no zippers, and no bras?"

"Yeah, no nothing." Rita laughed, "It would be best to go stark naked!" She chuckled at the image that flashed into her mind. "Well, I don't think we'd get anybody to do that. Just wear something comfy. Remember, you don't have to be cute."

Kate added, "Just as close to being naked as you can without actually doing it?"

"Yeah."

Kate was tickled by the notion, "A Toga Party!"

The women all giggled nervously, and Rita continued, "Yeah. Go get a bunch of cotton sheets and wrap them around yourselves. What's the big deal? You can change when you get up there. It's really simple. Just make sure it's natural fabric. Cotton or silk is wonderful. Listen to your own guidance for things like this."

Rita looked at Fred and frowned, "No glasses too. Those of you who are used to working with crystals, drums, rattles and what-all – forget it. You're it! You don't need the stuff!

"Bathe to prepare your physical body. You will also need to prepare your emotional bodies for this ceremony because anything you are holding on to will be intensified when you are standing in that much real Light. Remember your focus is to anchor this Light Grid. Just because all your friends are doing it, don't think you necessarily have to do it too. You've got to listen to what you're being told.

"Each of you that said you would do this have been assigned a specific guide. It's your duty to open up communications with these guides 'cause they'll assist you in preparation for this ceremony. There's six or seven things you're going to have to hold simultaneously for a short time during the ceremony and your guides will help you do this. You guys can all do it. There's no problem, but it needs to be just like breathing for you. That's why it's good to practice together regularly. Each one of you will receive portions of this upcoming thing. It will become clear what your portion is. Even though it may not sound like much, it's all really important because it won't get done if everyone doesn't do their part. Hang tough. You guys have got three weeks ahead of you. I'm not going to be there, so you'll do it yourself."

I asked, "You're not going to be there? From the beginning you saw yourself as the one who would be the Light Bringer. I really don't understand how you could miss this."

"Well, my guides have asked me to go up to Sacramento for a few weeks to do some work there. I probably won't be the Light Bringer for this ceremony. There will be someone else doing that. It will be a female. My function is mostly done for you guys."

Kate asked, "What do you mean by Light Bringer?"

"Well, it's a little hard to explain. It's the person – the body, the spirit – that is of a high enough vibration to comfortably hold all this energy. It will go through this person and then through the circle. It will be diluted a little bit before everyone else gets it. It will be a person who could actually hold it alone."

Kate asked, "Who is it?"

Rita responded, "I can't share that at this time. Who knows, I could even show up yet. I could be in East Juhungaland and they go 'You! Go to Santa Fe!' I can't argue with them, you know. There won't be any question about it when the time comes. You'll trust this person. You'll be fine. Try to go with no preconceived notions. It's strange stuff. Let me see if there's anything else I'm supposed to pass on."

She thought for a moment, "No. The torch passes to you two." Rita nodded toward where Fred and I were sitting, "You'll need to keep track of everybody and see that everyone gets the communiqués." Then she looked at Fred, "You may be asked to be the heavy. I've tried to explain to people that your guidance will be very clear on this. If you let ego get in there and do this without listening, you will be stopped. You probably won't break a leg, but you might get the flu. Everything's going along fine. You've got three weeks left and it's no problem. You will do dandy."

I nodded, for I understood this shift in plans. I was confident in our ability to complete the task without Rita, even though we had begun to rely on her guidance. We needed to complete what we began.

Rita laughed again, "Well, you've got to find the other artifact." She seemed amused by some secret joke, "I'd like to see a video of this thing!"

I was serious, "What do you mean – a video? Isn't this supposed to be a private ceremony? Something sacred?"

Rita laughed again, "Oh, no. It's not a private anything! There will be things to record there."

Fred, who had been listening quietly, commented, "It's subtle, and sometimes not so subtle, that each of us realize our capability to handle this."

Rita stood up and began pacing, "The only ones that don't believe you can do it are all of you. Everyone else knows it. All you have to do is go. You know what people say about me? They say, 'She is the most arrogant bitch I've ever seen. She is so egotistical.' Can you imagine people talking about me like that? Ha ha. Well they do. This is what I call a healthy ego. You don't have to be as rude as me, but you can be just like that. You're taught that you can't. I'm not holding myself up as a shining example, by any means. I happen to be a centered, grounded, female.

Period. I'm nothing else. I'm real good at what I do too, and I'll tell you if you ask." She laughed again, "Sometimes I'll even tell you if you don't ask. These things take time. That's the way humans are. You do anything two times, and you think it's gotta be that way for the rest of your life. Wrong! It doesn't work like that at all. There's all kinds of stuff in store for you people. It won't all be comfortable. Sometimes it will be really heart-breaking.

"Yes, it will be work, but you've made a commitment to do this. Just be a good example. You will be helping Beings on this planet whom you will never meet, and on many levels for which you have no concept yet. If you could see what this looks like, it's beyond awesome. The work that's going on to prep for this on other levels is incredible. There are Beings who are doing everything that you're doing, except that they're doing it in huge numbers – just huge numbers. They're doing all kinds of stuff that's new for them too. They've not worked at blending energies. The angelic faction is very good, but they don't know what it's like to work like this. This is the first time! They've got Ashtar hangin' around and doing what he's doing with his folks, the angelic realm is present. This is really big!"

Rita continue sharing thoughts about the participants, "It's looking like we'll have a nice group of witnesses. They'll be popping in even up until the last day to stand in with you. I met a man when I was in Santa Fe who would be good to have in the circle. His name is Lance. I already called and asked him to participate. I figured it'd be okay."

Over the weeks that followed, our circle gathered often. Our dedication to the mission grew and our energies coalesced as we practiced bringing the forces of the Earth up and the forces of Spirit down. In ever-increasing intensity, we acted as conduits. We were a harmony of blended parts, each one contributing support to strengthening the circle which was our whole.

We were joined by spirits from many dimensions in our prepara-tions, for this grand reunion was to be a time of merging of the ALL. The angels stood by our sides and worked with us. The space brotherhood looked on and offered their support. Native American guides, the ancient ones, encouraged us and called our purpose forth. And, as we joined, each participated in bringing form into our gatherings. We each spoke our truth and met with open hearts. Our love, each for the other, grew. We were connected to the Divine and divinely connected to each other.

It was time for the third and final preparation ritual for the land; we would join the circle in Santa Fe ethereally, casting a dome of protection over them while they did their work. Ashtar had given Sara a configuration in which crystals were to be buried on the land, and those preparations had proceeded. It was a time of releasing for the Santa Fe group – releasing of the physical objects, treasured gems and crystals, and releasing of the responsibilities they had undertaken.

To demonstrate our support for their work, I sent each of the team members a single white rose and a small white candle, each tied by a ribbon of a different color. These gifts were to be delivered by the florist just prior to their departure for the mesa. The candles were a symbol of the Light which each one of us carries; the flowers were a symbol of the bounty and beauty of Earth. Sananda had assigned each member in Santa Fe a color of the Christed ray along with a special guide. I knew each would select the candle meant for them, tied by the color of their assigned ray – seven candles, seven rays, seven Light Workers presenting themselves in dedication.

In Santa Cruz, we gathered at sunset. Each brought a contribution to our own circle of support. I made an altar on a small table in the center of the room; on it I placed a violet silk scarf, a large white candle, and a bouquet of roses. Kate brought her whole collection of house plants and placed them in the corners of the room. Aya brought four small candles and placed them to mark the four directions, along with a designated gemstone for each. Each person made their contribution to create a sacred space.

As the preparations continued, Rita paced back and forth on the landing just two steps above us. She looked down into the family room. Her impatience was obvious, "We should get started pretty soon." We were so intent on our preparations, her request went unheeded. Rita shook her head and rolled her eyes. Her attention was focused on a doorway waiting to be opened, "It's time. We need to begin!"

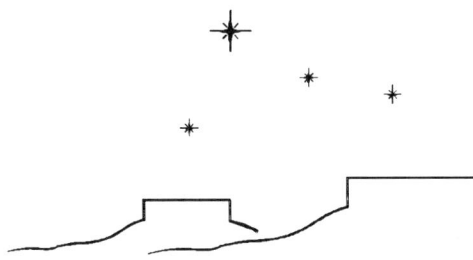

THE TEACHERS

Rita remained on the landing and guided the braiding of our energies with her words:

> "Take a breath – in through the nose and out through the mouth.
>
> Just begin by breathing deeply and slowly, allowing your bodies to relax.
>
> Begin now by becoming very comfortable in the space that you are in. Centered and relaxed.
>
> Allow, now, a golden cord to extend from the base of your spinal column. Allow it to extend deeply into the Earth.
>
> Remain conscious of the space that you are in and be comfortable. Be aware of the cord now grounding you to the Earth.
>
> Allow your crowns to open now, and extend a beam of light above your heads; hold it at about five feet. Remain conscious

of the space that you are in, the cord that grounds you, and the column of energy you are holding above your head.

This is very easy for you to do.

Hold all three things in your consciousness.

Become aware of your primary guide. There is one who wishes to speak with each of you. As you open this channel of communication, remain very comfortable and centered in the space you are in. Remain aware of the cord that grounds you and the column of energy over your heads. Hear your guide clearly.

As communication with each of your guides begins to slow, continue to remain aware of all three things you are presently holding. Now imagine, if you will, a column energy from the Teachers in the center of the circle which you have formed. Sense this energy. Remain comfortable in the space you are in, aware of your ground and the energy over your heads. As you sense the energy of the Teacher in the center, allow the columns over your heads to extend and hold them at about twelve feet, always remaining centered and comfortable in your own space.

Now allow the energy in the columns above your head to lean forward and against the Teacher's energy in the center. Do not blend. Merely touch it as you lean your column of energy forward. It is a very easy and comfortable thing for you to do.

Now begin to sense the energy columns that are on either side of you doing the same thing. Once again, do not blend; merely sense. And as you become comfortable with the energies on either side, feel free to explore the other energies in the circle which you have formed, always returning to your own space next to the Teacher's energy – gently.

Continue to remain comfortable in your space, aware of your ground, your primary guide who is hovering nearby, the column which you hold, and the others around you."

We felt our connections through our Higher Selves as we raised our braided energy and cast the coalesced column of energy across a rainbow bridge to support our dedicated teammates in Santa Fe.

They were standing on the mesa at sunset. This was their final ritual to prepare the land to receive the Light node. They each contributed heartfelt words as they lit their candles and placed their flowers on the earth. Their intention was clear and their protection well in place. It was an evening of sacred ritual.

We saw the energy within the Earth rising, ever closer to the surface. When they finished, this new vortex was fully open, prepared now to receive the Light which would finally descend and be anchored by the ceremony on August 25th.

And Rita continued guiding our work in a distant town, linked by the energetic bridge which had been cast by our intention:

"Now, each one of you, return your awareness to the space where you started. You are now able to be centered in your own space.

Simultaneously, be aware of your cord, the energy which you hold above your head, the energies all around you, and the energy of the Teacher. Very good.

Now, move away from the Teacher's energy and return your column of energy to an upright position.

As each of you straighten your columns, allow them to continue to be extended upward above your head. Do this in a balanced and controlled fashion. Merely allow it to go and go.

Continue being aware of holding all the other things that we have spoken of in your consciousness as you continue stretching your energy above you without effort, very comfortably.

Now hold your columns where they are.

Feel the energy coming up through the cord that grounds you into your bodies and extends out through your crown. When this flow is strong for you, feel, at the same time, the energy moving from the columns that you hold above you, down into your bodies and through the cord that grounds you. Feel the flow moving both up and down. Sense the power that is there which is yours, each and every one of you. Own it.

Now allow this flow to slow. Allow it to gently fade from your consciousness, continuing to hold your centers. Merely be aware of the cord that grounds you, the columns that you hold over your head, and the Teacher's energy in the center of your circle. Take a moment and be comfortable with all of these.

Very good.

Now, in a balanced and controlled fashion, allow the columns of energy above your heads to very gently retract. As all of the energy column is back with you, continue to remain centered in your own spaces and allow the cord that grounds you to retract into your spinal column. Gently.

Now take a moment and be comfortable in the space you are in.

Enter your bodies fully. Hear my voice fully and, when you are ready, open your eyes."

We were still. A gentle smile remained with Rita. Her words had been soft as she gently guided the exercise and there was a peaceful essence about her which was different from her usual abrasive personality.

Fred remained in an altered consciousness as the rest of us returned our awareness to the room and began talking. He softly said, "I have a message from Sananda." Their connection was visible.

Kate shifted her position and said eagerly, "Oh, good!"

And Fred continued with Sananda's message, "*The meditation you just did was excellent. I was in your circle as a visitor directing some energies of the heart to each of you. The term 'Teachers' is very appropriate. The Teachers are a most miraculous blend of spiritual Beings. There are many of us who have managed to blend our individual energies, submerging all of our differences in order to emit a more uniform pillar of energy in your circle. It's like making a cake. When the individual ingredients are blended, you can no longer see the individual ingredients. All you see is the cake.*

"A vast spectrum of Beings have contributed to this, leaving the personality parts outside, and putting the essence parts into the column. You will not find the feelings or sensations associated with individual

Beings. It is a much a more uniform and stronger energy which has been prepared. You will find this column of energy, or something very much like it, present in your circle when you do the August ceremony.

"This living conductor of the Teachers will encompass all of the participants, yet each participant will contribute his or her own essence. That is the point. Just as you were asked to concentrate on three different concepts at the same time, so the ceremony in August will have three main components.

"You should understand that this above and below concept is often metaphorical as the essence of the Earth Mother and of Spirit surrounds you. But we have followed the general 'up and down' paradigm in our guidance. After all, you walk upon Earth, so that is a convenient 'down.' There are a few drawbacks to this: You should not think for a moment that we are above you; likewise you should not think that the Earth is below you.

"At the ceremony in August, you should think of the three components: The Earth Mother rising, The Father descending, and the human component in the middle. The energy of the Teachers will be merged for a short while with the human energy. We're using these artifacts as attractors and balancers, as a catalyst to get the ball rolling. Actually, to give all concerned something to aim at. The artifacts will mark the exact center. All will be able to focus on the center, expand their awareness down into Earth and up to the heavens, while at the same time being aware of what's going on about you, which will include the Teachers' energy.

"With all of these things going on, there will be lots of free energy running around. There won't be sparking or roman candles or any of that, but we've been asking you to work individually and as a group, so that when you come together next month you will have had practice. It will be easy for you to expand the smaller group into the larger group when all are present.

"As you imagine, the energy running through you while it is ascending and descending may move in other directions as well. You may get spiraling, a helix conical shape. It may increase in size above or below you – or both. You might imagine it whirling in the shape of an hourglass.

The energy may change. Since the energy runs down through your head and up through your spinal column, you might imagine yourself as the pole of a sphere.

"The energy will expand beyond the circle of our participants. Some may be aware that the energy has expanded quite a bit farther than this. Everything that we have spoken about depolarizing, yielding the heart from the polarities of this universe, all that is quite true and quite important. That is the essence of this ceremony. The two artifacts will be like fulcrums from which we can raise a tremendous balanced heart energy. The artifacts are pivot points, as are all the humans, surrounded by a truly impressive array of Beings from many diverse places. This is to be the first major ceremony on the planet. You will find, once it's over, the balance into which so much Light can come will be quite amazing. I might add, it will be quite wonderful for each participant, for each observer, and for everyone to whom this energy will come. For some it will come a lot sooner. For others it will take slightly longer to get things opened and cleared. It's not easy to come into a position of primary balance from a position of imbalance when the imbalance is substantial. This balance will come to all God's children much more quickly when these energies of primary balance (heart) have been manifested on the planet. It is for every human – every man, woman, and child – that you do this. It is a releasing into the world of something that has never been in the world before.

"You just have completed an exercise, and you are very close in essence to the ceremony. You are not so close in degree, but it will be adjusted little by little so that you will be comfortable with it when the time comes. Each time you do this exercise, we can step up the intensity a bit.

"Each of your Higher Selves are very much in control of the amount of energy that is safe for you to pass – both ascending energy from the Mother and descending from the Father. It's going to go exceedingly well. If there are any fears or doubts, you can put them aside. You are all doing the work you need to do at the speed you need to do it. The time and effort you are putting into this is appreciated, and you will soon know this in unmistakable ways."

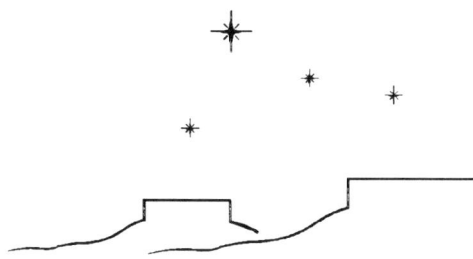

PURIFICATION

As August 25th drew closer, the importance of the event continued to grow within us. We remembered Ashtar's guidance that we should prepare for this much like Olympic athletes prepare physically, emotionally and mentally for the ultimate competition of their careers. With an expanded sense of service, we felt the enormity of assisting the shift of planetary consciousness into the new dawn.

Each time the group gathered we braided our energies in an ever-expanding column of Light. We were the co-creators of our experience, each one contributing their heartfelt words into the circle.

At one of our meetings, we were just getting ready to practice holding our focus on the energy when Beth announced, "I don't think I'm to be a part of the ceremony. I have to prepare my preschool for the fall, and I really can't be gone. I think I'm supposed to go the week before the ceremony and walk the ley-lines. I don't really know what that means, but I feel that's what I'm to do."

I spoke up, "The ley-lines are connected to the new energy grid around the planet as it is anchored into the Earth. I was shown these lines as they were giving me the information about the new Light Grid. They look like silver threads encircling the planet. There's not much information on them yet because they're a fairly new discovery, but animals have used them forever for migration."

Fred joined in, "They've also discovered that most of the world's sacred sites and temples could be mapped in geometric configurations around the planet which probably follow an energetic field within the Earth which appears as these ley-lines."

There was more I wanted to share, "We were curious about these ley-lines, so we got out a map. We discovered that the Apache Mesa in New Mexico is in a direct line with Peru; this same line extends up to Banff, in Canada. Some people talk about the awakening of the force of Quetzacoatl being connected to this line between Banff and Peru. I don't know, but it's an interesting coincidence when you check these things out on a map. I do wish you could be with us, Beth."

"Well, it's just impossible." She was so sweet and so sincere; her gentleness was a blessing.

Fred said, "I think you'll be bringing an important piece with what you're doing." He could see how difficult it was for her and gave her a hug of encouragement, understanding each one knew their part. It was a time of great introspection and emotional healing for everyone. Several of us participated in the purification ritual of the Native American sweat lodge. We integrated the spiritual with the physical, and meditations allowed Spirit to grow in each of us.

Our communications with Sara became less and less frequent as the time for the anchoring approached, and I began to sense that she may choose to not participate. I had been told that Sara was to be my anchor during the ceremony. Why would I need an anchor? What if she weren't there to perform this task? I called on Soltec for the answer to my questions, "I've been told I'm supposed to have someone at the ceremony who will act as an anchor for me. Who is this to be?"

Soltec answered, "*You may have two. You will have Sara and you will have Rachel.*"

"It seems to me that Sara may not take part."

"*We think she will be taking part. It is her decision, and if she chooses to go through with it she will be capable. She has some doubts just like the rest of you. No one is coming to this ceremony perfect, but you are all so very far from where you started. You do not see this because it's happening inside you. You are all extraordinary beings, fully capable of performing this ceremony. Many of you are capable of performing the duties for two. Choosing whether to participate is the only variable here. So we have a backup for each of you.*

"*You will find that you can remain pretty grounded by yourself. It's not that you need to be tied down to the Earth. It is more a controlling your own grounding and connection to Earth. You will find that this will be natural for you to do. The backups were a redundant and fail-safe setup where someone would be there to watch over you had you not experienced the growth which you have. Now, the backups can accept some additional roles. You will all sense how the others are doing. It will be like there is a safety rope tied round the circle and the spectators. Some of them could also bring through the Spirit energy. You will all be doing more than one thing. You will be concentrating on yourselves, on Earth, and on Spirit, at the same time you are doing whatever physical movements seem appropriate. This is why there is no script. It is to be a very flexible ceremony. Simply bring your pure essence to the ceremony.*

"*The clothes which are to be of natural materials are more of a reminder to be natural of mind and heart and not to bring anything into the ceremony which does not belong there. The clothing and dietary restrictions will remind you to come as clean, as pure, and as aligned as you can. As you forsake heavy food you will see and feel in a visceral way that you should also be forsaking your emotional and intellectual 'stuff.' Going through the necessary preparations will help you in many ways. You will feel the clothes around you which are different; they will feel comfortable. You will be aware of what you are not wearing. This freedom, this looseness, will give you the control in other areas where you need it the most – in your concentration, your visualizing, and your ability to carry out the task."*

"I feel it might be good to do the ceremony at dawn. Do you have any guidance as to the best time of day for it?"

"We will let you decide that. The full moon is a time of balance. You get the sun and the moon's rays reflected. Since the moon is fully illuminated from your vantage point, it brings the maximum balance to this time: Full sun/Full moon. Earth is not going to be connected to the sun although it is going to be connected with real Light which is contained in the sun. Just remember where your center is. You need to step up to your power. You will need to get the crystal from Mary for the final ceremony."

I thought about how much it meant to her. "I can't ask her to give me the crystal."

"You will need to have the crystal for the final ceremony and it will be good for you to have it for a time before the anchoring so that your energies and those of the crystal can merge. We think this is something you can do."

It was difficult for me to ask her for it because I understood how much it meant to her. I didn't understand why I needed it. So I said nothing in the following days, waiting to be told again that this was necessary.

During the final preparations, which were highly personal for each one, the question of what would happen during the ceremony on August 25th grew. How would it look? What would happen? Rita had told us many times, "Oh, there'll definitely be things to see!"

What did that mean?

Would there be an ascension lifting those who had purified and allowed a high enough level of Spirit to enter their bodies? Would there be a manifestation of one or more of the Ascended Masters? Would our space brothers make an appearance? How would the Indians participate? Just how would this anchoring of the Light look and feel? I listened for clues from my own heart so that I could be prepared. I searched my memory, thinking back on what we had heard from our guides over the past months for any clues they may have given:

We are asking you to help establish the grid of Light which will guide Earth to its Ascension.

There will be a releasing and a soaring of spirits.

Place your attention on completing your half of the bridge where we will be joined.

During the ceremony, you will be near more Light than you have ever experienced before.

We will meet you and you will meet us.

There are forces that do not want to see this happen.

I remembered being told that the anchoring would occur as we stood in a circle around a large rock which looked like a pulpit – a standing stone. This pressed on me as I imagined Sananda manifesting and standing before us on the rock. I dared not speak of this idea to anyone. It was outrageous, and yet, in my heart, I felt it could be true. I did not want to create expectations for the others, so I didn't breathe a hint of my own. We would all have to wait and find out for ourselves.

I thought about my own mortality and about the Plan. Was the time at hand? Was there to be a mighty lifting of souls? Filled with these thoughts I picked up my pen and wrote. The words flowed onto the paper without thought, "You will be in a great deal of real Light during the ceremony, more real Light than you have ever known. You will sense the Light. You will feel it on you and in you. Your work will turn into reverie and you will be moved to go to the Light. In love you may choose to go or to stay. The possibility of going is a gift of love, but your work is not done and you may also stay in Love and protection. You know, things worth having often take much hard work to achieve. As you toil now, the Light is your reward."

I thought about my life and about all my relations. Was it a choice that I could clearly make? I thought about my children, already grown, and the absence they would feel at my departure. I moved over closer to Fred lying next to me in the bed and clung to him as I felt the possibility of our separation. My yearning to hold onto life was too great to bear the thought of leaving. Would I be so altered by standing in the Light that my Will to stay would be overtaken by the desire to return to Source?

These thoughts began to consume me in the final days as I watched the momentum building in the activities around me. I wondered what Rita might have known that she hadn't expressed. I asked her, "Will some people ascend during the ceremony?"

She seemed surprised to hear what was on my mind as she looked at me and answered with authority, "There will be an opportunity for some. You are one who will be given the choice." She walked away, as was her manner. It seemed she was always on the move.

As she left, tears of grief welled up. It was too soon. I was too young. There were too many who would be affected by my parting. I did not want to ascend if that meant I would have to end life as we know it here on Earth.

My grip on life tightened.

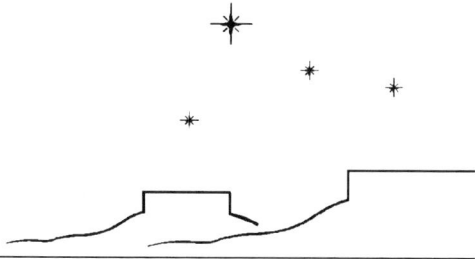

PERU

Everyone seemed to be getting a little nervous about the second artifact which we had been directed to *somehow* find. I believed that it would come to us or that we would locate it easily, even in the final days. How could I be concerned about it when I reviewed the miraculous unfolding of this adventure? Everything had fallen into place so far.

My day dreams were filled with anticipation of the trip to Peru. It would be expensive, and we had to sell some things to raise money for the airfare. This had been done and the funds were now available. My own fears had been amplified to me by our children's concerns, challenging my conviction, but our trust had grown into certainty.

It was August 1st. The countdown on the calendar was coming to a close. As I awoke, I thought about the events which lay before us. My first words to Fred were, "We have to confirm our reservations today to leave on the 10th."

Fred nodded as he tried to wake up, "I'll take care of it this morning." He pulled the covers up over his head as he rolled over, attempting to snatch an extra few minutes' sleep.

While Fred was in town later that morning, I opened the mail. A friend had sent us the travel section of her Sunday paper with a note, "Thought this might be of interest."

The headlines read, "Traveler's Warnings Issued for Peru!" The entire front page was filled with color photos and articles on the hazards of traveling in this South American country: "Cholera Epidemic Spreads," "Rebel Forces Reach Within 40 Miles Of Lima," "Bandits Make It Unsafe For Travelers In Cuzco."

Fred returned home from the travel agency and handed me our itinerary – I handed him the newspaper.

"How many tests do we need?" I wondered aloud.

"It doesn't matter."

"I know," I returned.

"We got a great deal on the fare." Fred glanced over the newspaper, "All of these warnings are just another test for us."

"Well, there's certainly no doubt on my part any more. We have to complete what we've agreed upon – no matter what!"

Fred nodded in agreement.

We were interrupted by Rita, coming in from outside as she announced, "You know, you don't really have to go to Peru!"

"Of course we do!" Fred and I both answered simultaneously.

"What in the world are you talking about?" I asked.

"Well, I was just sitting out on the deck and got the message that you don't need to go," Rita laughed in amusement at the situation.

Fred and I looked at each other in dismay. His face paled as confusion swept over him. I felt as though I had been punched in the stomach as shockwaves of disbelief reverberated through me.

How could this be?

Was this whole thing some sort of cosmic joke? Were the Masters playing with us just to force our growth or test our commitment? Was Rita trying to throw us off course? My head swam with questions.

Rita said flippantly, "Well, you can go if you want to. There'll be stuff for you to do if you go, but you don't need to go." And, with that, she left the room, leaving both Fred and me speechless. There was too much to understand – the instructions and detailed visualizations about retrieving the artifact, the guidelines from the Ascended Masters about using the artifact to anchor the new Light Grid, the unraveling of the mystery – all marched across our minds.

I was angry. "How could the Masters do this to us? If this was just a joke, how can we believe anything else? I'm not at all sure we should believe what Rita says this time."

Fred said, "I don't quite understand what's going on here either. I have to sort this out for myself."

"We need to get in touch with our own guidance. We can't just accept this from her!"

"You're right about that. I need some time to think about this now."

I agreed.

That night Fred and I sat together in our living room. We needed some sort of confirmation of what Rita had said. She came in to join us. Fred called upon Archangel Michael, "We need to get clarification on the information that Rita has given us that we don't need to go to Peru. Pam and I are very confused. We feel like the rug has been jerked out from under our feet. We don't know what to believe now. Will you please help us to understand?"

My eyes were closed as I felt the press of Spirit with the answer to our question. I spoke the words which waited, not knowing even then if I could believe them, "_The request to make a trip to Peru was a test of your dedication. It has served to create the desired results, that is to establish a level of commitment and dedication within you which will allow you to accomplish the task at hand._"

Rita asked, "You mean, like Abraham and Isaac?"

"Just so. You were given every challenge. Making the decision to go was as difficult for you as it was for Abraham to be willing to sacrifice his son's life for, truly, there were many dangers involved. But Abraham loved God so completely that, as painful as it was, he was willing to follow God's command. This was the same for you. Once you had worked through your struggles, the trip was no longer necessary. It was in this process that your dedication grew. This was the purpose for the request."

I felt confused and manipulated by Spirit. Trying to sort out now what was true and what was just an exercise, I reviewed all of the guidance of the past year. What about the second artifact? Did it exist? Were we still to find it? I remembered my request that it be attracted to us. Was it on its way to us already?

I continued to sit quietly, pondering all these questions, when Archangel Uriel made his presence known to me, *"... There is, indeed, a great operation underway. You have no need to entertain any doubts that this is real. You have been called and you have accepted the call to be a part of it. As you continue activating other participants on a daily basis, you have done much for the activation of this undertaking on your Earth. No matter how it seems to look to you at any given time, you have done an excellent job. The group in Santa Fe was assembled, and through great trials and adversity they were able to accomplish the first portion of this task.*

"Your understandings reach those you speak to at a very deep level. The extent of your commitment and the outlandishness of the request is what greatly assisted the scenario and the levels of commitment which others have been able to engender for themselves. Your trip to Peru has served its purpose already in advance of it happening. Now, the strength of your commitment is being tested a bit more with this shift. As you become more flexible, the commitment level which will be required as we go forward must be unwavering. Facing life's challenges is the only way growth can occur and in which strength and commitment can be established. All of those on the team are being put through their paces and having an opportunity to do some serious introspection."

I thanked Archangel Uriel, "I don't necessarily think I like it, but I do understand a little more now."

I still felt I had been deceived at the most fundamental level, and, in turn, had deceived all those whom I told about the quest. I didn't know any longer what was true or what was just an exercise.

Fred and I had begun to look forward to the adventure of a trip to South America – like two explorers in search of hidden treasure. I said, "You know, all our reasons for not going seem so insignificant now. We're really ready to move through to the completion of what has been set into motion."

Fred replied, "We need to do whatever we were meant to do. If we don't need to make an expensive trip like this, then we could save the money. Archangel Michael did say it was no longer necessary. I wasn't sure about what Rita said myself, but Archangel Michael has confirmed that the whole process was one of building up a trust level which is strong enough to achieve the work which is to be done. We must remember the lessons we've learned about flexibility. Sometimes things change mid-stream, and what was required at one time becomes unnecessary because other things have shifted."

I thought back to when we had been too rigid to respond to guidance when it was presented, and reflected on the times when we made things more difficult for ourselves because of it, "Well, I did ask not to go in the beginning. Perhaps the second artifact is somehow making its way to us after all."

Fred was quiet.

I searched my heart. It seemed the necessity of travelling to Peru to retrieve an artifact had dissolved. The new planetary Light Grid could be activated without the trek.

We would not go.

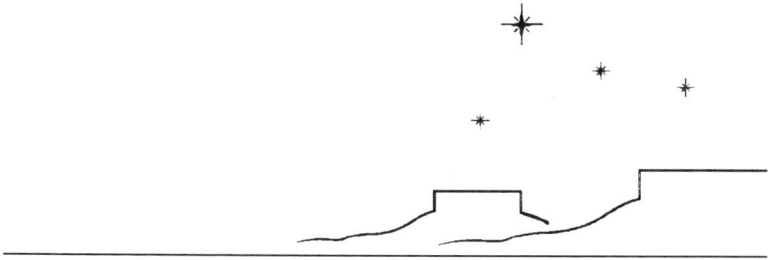

THE SEARCH

Those who would be traveling with us to anchor the Light were making arrangements for their trip to Santa Fe. Beth assumed the role of scout. She would fly alone to Santa Fe to walk the ley-lines on the mesa. Aya, Mary and Kate would drive. Fred and I would fly, along with Allison and Rachel (who would each bring their children), to rendezvous with the rest of the group in Santa Fe.

The team in Santa Cruz came together one last time to reaffirm our connections to each other and to the Light before we began our pilgrimage. As soon as everyone had gathered in our living room, Mary walked over to me. She held the green brocade pouch with its crystal tucked neatly inside. I rose to greet her as she began to speak, "I've been told that you're to take the crystal with you to the ceremony. Spirit told me that you were to ask for it, but you never did. I know you're to have it anyway." And, with that, she placed the crystal in my hand.

I held the crystal, realizing for the first time that I needed to make a personal connection with it. This time I didn't question its return. I recognized the Plan would unfold of its own design. It could not fail now. It would be done.

In our circle we braided our energies and raised the column of Light created by our union. Then we cast a rainbow bridge to the mesa, asking for the protection and safe arrival of our team. We extended an invitation in spirit to the Native Americans who have guarded the land and waited for their prophecies to come to pass at the time of the Rainbow Nation. We asked them to join us in anchoring the Light to help the planet move forward into the new time, and sent our prayer on the wings of a dove to the elders of the tribal council.

The ever-present question from the others in our circle was, "Have you found the artifact?"

"No," was my consistent reply. What more could I say? I began to wonder if there was, indeed, another artifact. I wondered, after the revelation about not going to Peru, if perhaps this was just another joke. Whatever the secret was, I knew it would be revealed at the proper time. I said, "I'm sure it'll show up just in time." I was not concerned, for I trusted in the design, although I didn't know how to communicate this. I was sympathetic to their sense of urgency but was unable, any longer, to generate it within myself, and I was at peace even though I saw tension mounting about the whereabouts of the artifact.

I told Fred, "I'm not worried about the artifact."

He agreed, "I expect it will appear just in the nick of time."

"One artifact has been attracted to us and we will surely discover the other one in the final moments. There's an urgency building. Everyone sees that we're not doing anything about it, and they want to help find it; I know inside that we don't need to get worked up over it."

"Right," Fred replied, "I don't think you'll be finding it in an antique store."

"Why don't we see if we can get some more information on it — just the two of us."

"Good idea."

We called upon Soltec who first introduced the project to us, "Soltec, does the artifact which we are to take to the anchoring really exist on the physical plane?"

"_Oh, yes! We do not wish to take away from your astonishment when you see the second artifact for the first time and realize that you found it essentially on your own. We could tell you, but we don't intend to because you have the tools to find it yourself. Everything is here. The reason that it exists and that it is necessary is because this is not just another soiree. This is real nuts and bolts, rocks and stones, being re-united with the Light of the Divine Creator. It takes Light, which you will each bring. You can become the catalysts by which the land is joined to the Light in such a way that they can never be un-joined!_

"_You know that, symbolically, something can have one meaning while physically it has another. So you know that a figurine carved out of metal could stand for something much larger. The symbol and the object in this case are one. We are trying to take two things which in the past have been separated, namely the physical and the spiritual, and we are putting them back together again. This is highly symbolic, and at the same time it is highly physical. It is the union of these concepts and these objects that is the whole point of this event._"

Sometimes these long circuitous answers left my head swimming. I wanted direct answers to my pressing questions. "Soltec," I asked, "We leave in just a few days. If the artifact does exist, then now's the time to locate it."

"_So, get out and start locating! First you must trust that you can find it. Then, you must take the steps to go and do the finding._"

"Well, can you give us any other clues? Will you tell us the town? After all that's happened, I've been confident the artifact would show up, but everyone is getting very nervous about it now. I'm feeling pressure about it. They all think I need to do something. You should see the way they look at me."

"_How about if I mail you a treasure map?_" Soltec asked.

"Oh, good! Will it come Special Delivery in my dreams?"

"*If you would like to receive guidance in a dream, it's very easily arranged. It's within your power to ask for it and to be open to receive it. We are trying to deal with your concerns here but I might point out that you are choosing to have these concerns. You are making it harder than it needs to be. You must just begin.*"

"I'm sorry. What's difficult for me right now is that we're running out of time! We need a little help here."

Soltec returned, "*We would prefer that you not be sorry! It does not become you to be sorry*"

I felt embarrassed.

And he continued, "*Teaming up with others on this little quest allows much to be accomplished with one task. It is impossible for anyone to see all of the different pieces of the puzzle until it is fully worked out. Sometimes you can look back and say, 'All of these things happened when we were doing that. Isn't that wonderful? I wonder how all that got arranged?' This is simply the mark of a vast and loving intelligence that likes more than anything else to figure these things out. Maybe what I could suggest is to increase your allowingness. Just allow a little wider and a little deeper.*"

I breathed deeply and repeated, "Allow wider and deeper." Even so, my questions pushed forth, "Soltec, is the artifact located in Santa Cruz County?"

"*Yes. You will just run into it. You will not need to go seeking. Know that all of the Higher Selves for all of the ones involved are cooperating, and have been for many months, to arrange this connection. It is going to be fulfilled because it is working on a higher level where all parties are in agreement. It's going to be like driving into the parking lot and finding a parking space right out front. You know how to do this with your intent. We ask that you relax about the issue of this artifact and let tomorrow bring its own joys and adventures.*"

I was confident that we could not fail now. I continued to have a sense that retrieving the artifact would be as easy as having the one we already had, called "Pita," walk into our house in someone's pocket. It felt like that thing called cognitive dissonance. I knew there was no need for concern, yet the forces all around me were insisting that I take action.

The rest of the group was anxious about finding the treasured artifact. One by one, they came over asking to help us find the piece of power. Members of the team went on some merry chases up and down the California coast as they attempted to locate the elusive artifact.

One morning, Rachel called with the news, "I keep seeing the artifact in the sand. Do you want to go down to the beach with me and look for it?"

I shrugged my shoulders. I didn't think we would have to comb the beaches in hopes of discovering buried treasure. This was not the way things had been unfolding, but I heard the hope and dedication in her voice. How could I say it didn't matter? I replied, "All right. Do you remember when you got the message that the artifact was located in CRUZCO? Do you think that meant Santa Cruz County?"

"Yes," she replied. "It definitely was CRUZCO not CUZCO. I listened very carefully to hear if it was Cuzco (Peru) but it wasn't. It could be here."

Rachel and I walked along the shore, asking to be guided to the artifact. We turned up all our senses, watching for a sign as we combed the beach. I told Rachel, "We must be still. We must listen so our guides can speak."

Together, we turned and looked out across the ocean. The moist air sprayed the scent of timelessness across our cheeks as Rachel pointed to the horizon. My heart swelled as we saw a pod of dolphins joyfully playing in the surf and greeting us.

Rachel and I joined hands as we turned to leave the water's edge. We knocked at the doors of several beach front houses, "Have your children found a silver treasure on the beach?" Any vestiges of shyness were now stripped away; we were intent upon our task. But nothing could be found, and we returned home empty handed.

The next day someone else from the team called. "Let's go look in some antique stores."

I replied, "All right."

So the search continued. Day after day we looked. Our sense of mission drove us on and pushed us to continue telling the story of our search for an ancient artifact to everyone we met. We didn't care whether they understood, for the activation which occurred with the telling of the story was a part of the design. We looked through boxes of buttons and bottle caps at antique stores. I consulted with a psychic (as if I didn't have enough information of my own!) who held the 'Pita' artifact in her hand and said, "You will find the piece today!"

"I will?"

"Yes," she replied, "that's the answer I got."

I felt a stirring. Had the time finally arrived to find the artifact, a piece of something which contained so much power it could impact the entire planet? My hands began to tremble. I knew it was the time.

I drove to the town where the psychic told me I would find the artifact in the back of an antique store. I located the store from her description and went in. I looked around. There was a marvelous collection of old junk. Glass counters were filled with curios from days gone by.

What was I looking for?

"Something old. Something very old," I told myself. I needed the female and balancing part to the gold artifact I carried in my pocket. I had been caught back up in the search. I looked in boxes. Today was the day to find it.

I asked the clerk to let me hold a couple of pieces, waiting to feel something that would let me know my search had ended. A small jade bowl attracted my attention. On its sides sat three figures, old and symbolic. Was this it?

I didn't know. Maybe I should get it, just in case. I looked at the price. $65.00. Wouldn't Spirit provide what we needed? I could afford to buy it, but something inside said, "No."

I asked the clerk, "Could you save this for me? I need to go home and think about it."

She agreed, and I went home.

Fred and Rita were sitting on the deck talking when I returned. I got myself a glass of iced tea and joined them. "How was the hunt today?" Rita asked.

"I went to see a psychic over at Glenda's house this morning. She told me that I'd find the artifact today. So I went right over to the antique store in Soquel where she told me I would find it. I looked through everything. What an incredible collection of junk they have there. I think I might have found it! They're holding it for me; I just wasn't sure about spending the money on it. Can you guys go back with me tomorrow morning?"

They both agreed.

The three of us returned to the antique store the next morning. I let Fred and Rita look around for themselves to see what they could find. Fred found a carved ivory feather that caught his eye, "Maybe this is it."

I was certain the feather wasn't old enough. So I got the jade bowl I had found the day before and handed it to him. "What about this? I think this could be what we're looking for."

"I don't think so," Fred replied as he gave it back to me.

"Rita, what do you think?" I asked. She shrugged her shoulders and turned to walk out of the store.

"Wait a minute!" My frustration mounted as I stood there with the jade bowl in my hands, unable to interest the other two in it.

The pressure was really on. We were to leave for Santa Fe the next morning, and still no artifact.

I said to Fred, "Let's go outside and talk," and we followed Rita out onto the sidewalk.

"Why won't you tell us what you think?" I asked Rita. We followed her down the sidewalk and around the corner, waiting for her response.

When we were finally at the parking lot, she said, "You can't even agree on what you're looking for. Fred picked up something symbolic. You picked up something old. Don't you get it? The artifact isn't something you can find in a store? The artifact is within you! It is _you_! Only you as a human have the ability to receive and transmit the quantities of Light to be anchored."

The words seemed to flow through Rita without stopping. Her usual arrogance was absent and I sensed that she was the instrument being used to deliver this message to us. Exactly what she said, I don't remember, but there was a rightness about her words. And I understood.

We headed home – empty handed and heart full.

"This ceremony will be your initiation."

"I hear you speaking, Ashtar. Please tell me more."

"For all of you, this is going to be a kind of ascension, but I don't want to use that word in a way that will indicate that you will be leaving and not coming back, for that is not going to happen. We can't afford to lose any of you after all your gains in awareness. I would like to characterize this ceremony as being an ascension of your awareness. In a sense the artifacts that we were talking to you about have crystallized within yourselves. There is going to be a new awareness, and it's going to happen with Spirit coming down and the Earth Mother rising. We are going to try to place you where the shining of your Lights will do the most good to the largest number of people. That is where you are. You don't know who you had to be to get where you are now. We didn't send pikers. We didn't send people who couldn't cut it. We sent the best there was. We sent the best that God had. Thousands of them. Hundreds of thousands of them.

"You are being attracted to us. Others are being attracted to you. We are all being attracted toward God. That's just the way it goes. This dimension toward God is everyone's goal. Some take circuitous routes and it appears that they are going in exactly the opposite direction. It's just the way their paths are going. It's not for anyone to judge. It's just getting aligned and seeing what there is to see. That's what you are all doing here. It's important for you to acknowledge how far you have come and to see where you are now."

I clasped the crystal – it seemed to mold itself into my hand now. A journey was in progress which could not be stopped, for many had been pulled into the dream. It was time to go, to share the revelations of this day, to complete what had begun. I wrapped myself in a cocoon of Light in anticipation of the culmination of our task. And sleep came.

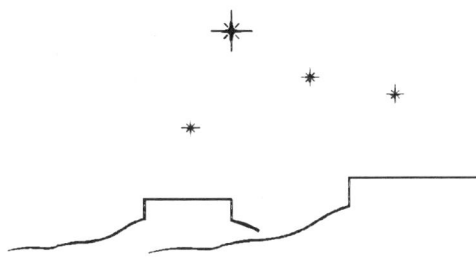

BRAIDING

August 23rd. Dawn came. I watched the sun breaking through the morning mist. The culmination of our grand adventure was at hand. It was time now to fulfill the Plan. How many stones had been rolled away? How many souls awakened? How much limitation released? We didn't know how far the ripples created by our actions would eventually travel. We bore a certainty within us as we headed for the airport.

Allison and Rachel had each brought their children, already waiting at the gate when we arrived. We greeted each other with a knowing – it is here!

Allison introduced us to her two young children. She was holding her one-year-old daughter on her hip, "This my daughter, Laurel." She greeted us with a babe's innocent smile.

"Hello," we smiled in return.

Allison put her hand on her other youngster's tousled head, "And this is my son, Russell."

Russell was an energetic three-year-old. He jumped up and down, his backpack laden with snacks and toys falling off his shoulder as he grabbed my hand and asked, "Did you bring it? Did you bring it?"

Rachel introduced us to her sons. They were around eight and ten years old, their faces full of anticipation as they eagerly greeted us, "Did you find the artifact?"

"Yes, we did." There was no way to avoid their questions.

"Where was it?" Rachel asked.

"Can we see it?"

"What does it look like?" asked one.

"Do you have it with you?" asked the other. At last, they could finally hold the magic piece they had heard so much about from their mother – the reason for this trip.

My eyes met Rachel's, "We want to tell everyone at once."

I felt like a fraud, for I couldn't answer her question – just then. I didn't like feeling that I was leading my friends on. These two young mothers who had gathered their children to make this pilgrimage with us were an expression of faith in us, in the Plan, and in themselves. There was no deceit intended, but I now withheld my understanding. There was still a charge, a mission to complete.

As the plane landed in Albuquerque, I squeezed Fred's hand and said, "Here we go."

He reached over and gave me a hug. Our voices remained still, our understanding deep. We had arrived.

We would rendezvous with the others at the airport: Beth who had gone ahead of us; Kate, Mary, and Aya who had driven; Rachel, Allison, and the children, who had flown with us.

Beth, who had come to the airport to catch her flight back to Santa Cruz, was waiting at the gate to greet us. We hugged each other, then sat together in the terminal as she told her tale. She smiled serenely as she began, "I was certainly put through my tests. I discovered when I went to rent a car that I had lost my credit cards. I didn't know what to do because I was counting on using them and didn't have much cash. You had given me Sara's telephone number as a contact so she was the only one I knew to call. She was wonderful! She welcomed me into her home and drove me to the mesa. She really took care of me.

"Sara, Margo and I went up to the mesa the first day I was here so I could walk the ley-lines. It was raining and the car got stuck in the mud. What a mess! We had to get out and push the car, sinking ankle-deep in the gooey mud, before we could get it freed. We had to give up on the idea of going that day. I went down to the Plaza one day to do some shopping. I couldn't buy much because I only had a little cash, but I found some beautiful earrings as a keepsake of the trip. Then the three musketeers (Kate, Mary and Aya) arrived from California. I left Sara's and took a room at an inn with them. I still hadn't walked the ley-lines, which was beginning to concern me as my time in Santa Fe was almost gone.

"Yesterday, we all went up to the mesa for a picnic. It was a beautiful day and the six of us had a wonderful, spontaneous ceremony, offering up prayers for the Earth. I knew I needed to go off by myself to complete my task, so I left the group and began to walk. I really didn't know what I was supposed to do and just let my intuition guide me. Sara had taken me to an area where some of the crystals were buried, and I began walking. Then the strangest thing began to happen. I felt the energy being drawn down from my legs into the Earth. I had never experienced anything like that before. I walked for awhile just letting my intuition guide me, all the time feeling this energy flowing through my legs. Finally, I came to a place under some trees where I sat down to rest. While I was there, I heard a voice I knew was Dartan's. He said, '*It would be nice if you left your earrings hanging on that tree.*'"

She smiled as she continued recounting her tale, "I thought, 'No, I just bought these, and I really like them.' But Dartan repeated, '*It would be nice if you hung your beautiful earrings on the tree. Then others who come will know you loved this place so much you have left a gift.*'

"It was so difficult. They were the only thing I had been able to buy while I was here. Finally I took them off and hung them on the branch just over my head."

"Oh, Beth," I said, "you did a wonderful job. And you got to meet our space brother, Dartan!"

"Space brother?" Beth raised her eyebrows. "No one ever told me Dartan was a space being!" She shook her head, "I don't think so!"

Fred chuckled, "Well, It sounds like you had an encounter with one of them on the mesa."

We were interrupted by the announcement, "Flight 164 to San Francisco is now boarding at Gate Number 5."

Beth said, "I have to go now."

I nodded. And she was gone.

I turned my attention to finding the others. "Now, I wonder where our ride is," I said as we began looking around the airport for Kate, Mary and Aya who were to meet us.

Then we spotted them. "Would you look at that!" I said to Fred.

They drifted past us like three helium balloons floating through the airport. They had been swept up by the magic of Santa Fe and their picnic on the mesa the day before.

He whispered, "They'd better get their feet back on the ground before the ceremony or they won't be anchoring anything!"

I called out, "Hello! Aya! We're over here."

They all three giggled when they saw us and headed our direction in a euphoric bubble. We greeted each other with hugs. How brightly their Lights were shining!

We planned the details of our visit as they drove us to Santa Fe. I told them, "We're having a gathering at the campground tonight so we can all get acquainted. It'll be a potluck dinner and camp fire. Sara's taken care of the invitations. There are some people here who want to attend the ceremony, so they've been invited too. Where are you guys staying?

Kate replied, "Mary and I are staying at the inn just across the river from the campground. Casey and her mother are staying there too."

"Well, we're definitely going to stay at the campground."

"That's where I'm staying," Aya said. "Oh, look! We're here. That's my cabin – 'Sparrow.'" She pointed out her abode as we drove by.

"We're at the end in 'Spirit,'" I leaned forward to point the way.

After we unloaded our bags, Kate and Mary said, "We're going back to the inn now. We'll see you later."

Our familiar little cabin welcomed us back like an old friend. After we were settled, we walked over to see Aya. She greeted us at the door, "Come on in and see my little retreat."

I smiled and asked, "Is this okay with you here?"

"Oh, yes. I love it."

It was a one-room cabin, much like ours. She already had a toasty fire going in the wood stove. Aya grinned, "This is perfect. I've already had a chance to do some drawing." She picked up her sketchbook from the table. "I drew this one at the picnic on the mesa yesterday. It was so beautiful there!"

"I wish everyone was staying here. It would be good if we could all be together, but we'll have a chance to begin blending the groups at the get acquainted dinner."

When Aya and I arrived at the gathering place, Fred was already at work laying the fire. Claire had erected a canopy for us in a grassy area between the fire pit and the river. Aya and I busied ourselves arranging tables and gathering chairs. Before we knew it, we saw Sara walking down the road.

I told Aya, "Everyone will be here soon. There's Sara already."

Sara was to be the bridge between the two groups. She knew of her leadership role in the Santa Fe group, yet she was traveling during most of their preparations and melded with the group only in the final days before their work began to prepare the land. Now she would merge with the group doing the Light Anchoring only after we all arrived in Santa Fe. It was a difficult position for her to be in, feeling not wholly a part of either group yet bridging the energy between the two, but she was strong in spirit and an open channel. It was a role she could successfully assume.

We met with her before the others arrived to join our pieces together as we wove the blended cloth together. Sara was in a dither, "I don't know what to do. I'm sponsoring an Ascension workshop this weekend. I'll be busy with the workshop all weekend – but I can come up for the ceremony at dawn."

"Why did you schedule it for the same weekend as the Light Anchoring?" I questioned her priorities.

"Well, this is when the speaker wanted to come. Now he's gotten ill and canceled. People have come from the East Coast to be here; I can't disappoint them. I'll have to do it myself."

This ceremony wasn't something trivial! How did she think she could just *show up*. All the other participants had undergone dedicated preparation and many sacrifices had been made. Didn't Sara understand this event was going to require our focused attention?

I said, "Well, maybe you'll have to choose."

"I know, but I'd rather not. I don't know what to do. I have an obligation to the people who have traveled so far to come here for a weekend of channeling. Flyers are up all around town announcing the workshop. I think there'll be 40-50 people there. I just can't cancel it now."

"We want you to be a part of the Light Anchoring ceremony, but it seems like sponsoring another workshop at the same time is a conflict."

She thought aloud, "Perhaps I could have a one-day workshop on Saturday. Some of the participants would like to be in the circle, and they are very well qualified to do it."

I said, "You know, this is really all one thing."

Fred and I looked at each other, both understanding what we must do. "Suppose we help you," Fred offered.

"Yes," I continued the thought, "we could help with the workshop on Saturday, and we could invite everyone there to witness the ceremony on Sunday in place of the speaker who is ill." It seemed like a stroke of genius even though I knew it had been the design. Why else would the workshop have been scheduled concurrently with the Light Anchoring? And why would the speaker cancel in the final hours? It was intended to be joined.

"Those who are to be in the inner circles have undergone extensive preparation for this event. But those who expect to show up as spectators will also be participants. This Saturday workshop can be used to extend an invitation to the Light Anchoring as well as providing a vibrational attunement for the witnesses, as they will also be receiving and channeling the Light."

Sara's relief was obvious as she tried to hold back the tears, "I didn't see how I could do justice to either event. Thank you."

We had wanted to spend Saturday working with our group or in meditation so we could be as focused and centered as possible. Sara's workshop was a distraction to us, but we felt that it was what we were to do. We were being pushed by circumstances to become more public, and to involve more people in the process.

The three of us walked over to join those already gathering in the picnic area. There was an air of anticipation, for the culmination of our work was near. We all worked together making the preparations for the gathering as everyone joined in carrying wood for the fire, making food, and gathering seats from around the camp. With each additional person's arrival, the energy escalated, and the bounty grew. There was an atmosphere of love, of reunion and joy.

After dinner we called everyone to join us around the campfire. We welcomed our friends from Santa Fe who had worked with such dedication to prepare the land. We introduced them to the contingency from California which had been preparing to perform the Light Anchoring and were already conjoined to them in spirit. We welcomed visitors from New England, Colorado, California, New Jersey, and the Bahamas, whose souls had drawn them to participate.

Allison began by teaching some of the songs we had enjoyed during our work together in California, and the groups began to join as we raised our voices in harmony. The air was heavy from the smoky fire as we sang "The River She Is Flowing" to the sounds of the swollen river rushing by. It was a time to sing and to bind our hearts so that we could arrive at the ceremony, just thirty hours away, with our rhythm pulsing as one.

And then the story was told: The story of hearing a message, of following spiritual guidance, and of the magical unfolding of destiny's path. It was a story of trust and surrender. I ended it with the revelation of the artifact, saying, "We discovered that the only artifact we had to find is within each of us! We are the crystals which will anchor the Light into Earth, and we are brought together for that purpose. Our search did not end with pieces of stuff. There is nothing outside of us which can compare to that which is within."

The air was cold and the stars shone brightly overhead. My eyes scanned the circle, looking for reactions in the firelight, but I couldn't discern the impact of my words.

The next morning those who were to be in the anchor circle gathered to complete the work of attuning their energy. When everyone had seated themselves, I noticed Casey sitting on the rough-hewn log bench next to me. She had attended every meeting. She had done her work. Did she know yet that she was a part of the circle? Or did she still accept Rita's proclamation that she wasn't ready to take part in this project? I turned to her and asked, "Do you think that you're to be a part of the circle?"

Casey's slight body expanded as she sat straighter and blurted her response, "Well, yes! I've done a lot of work and I've been just as dedicated as anyone else here." Her anger erupted at the thought of being excluded. Of course she was to be a part of this event! It was only for her to reclaim her power and say so.

Throughout the night, I had been given detailed instructions by the Masters and a diagram of the geometric configuration which was to be established to build the energetic matrix for the Light Anchoring. I brought my notes and a travel clock to monitor the time as there was much to be accomplished before Sara, Fred and I had to leave at noon to join the workshop in town. As I set my clock and notes on the ground beside me, I saw Mary snickering a whispered comment to the person next to her. I thought she was laughing at me for bringing notes, but I couldn't be concerned about opinions. I knew what I had to do.

"Before we begin, I need to warn you that there are forces which do not want us to succeed!" It was a forceful announcement from Lance, the man Rita had invited, who was joining with the group for the first time. He cleared his throat to continue, "Last night, I was psychically attacked! There was a dark and sinister entity which attempted to slay me as I slept. This was not a dream. It was a real battle! The more I tried to fight the Glory of Darkness, the more he smiled. He was arrogant and evil. He thought he could win and he threw me across the room. Then I felt my wife, Diana's, hand on my arm and heard her words, 'Remember the Light. Call for the Masters of Light to come and be with you.' With her words I was able to bring my attention back to Source and our protection, and the dark force withered away. I'm telling you this because I don't want anyone else to have to go through it. It was really awful! I've never had to deal with anything like this before."

It was a reminder that the stakes were high. The forces which have maintained the model of power and separation on Earth do not wish to lose their hold and will battle fiercely to maintain control. It was a battle of good and evil, Light and Dark. This one, Lance, was solid. He had worked alone in his preparation and was joining with the group only in the final hours. Because of his strength, the opposition had challenged him. The battle waged was for all, that we may have the opportunity of a new dawn for humankind. And, again, our understanding grew.

Kate spoke up, "We had an experience with dark energies too. When Mary and I were getting ready for bed the other night, we both sensed a strong foreboding. We weren't attacked like Lance was, but we knew there were some entities or energies there that were attracted to the Light and the work we're doing here. I don't think they wanted to interfere with our work. They were so out of touch with love and Light that they couldn't grasp what we were doing. I think they were more like neighborhood hoodlums. They saw something nice and just wanted to mess it up."

"How did you get rid of them?" I asked for the benefit of the group.

"We just kept centered and grounded. We called on Sananda and Archangel Michael who came in and moved them out fast!"

None were left in a "dreamy" state after hearing these stories. The dedication and intention of the group was reinforced. Still, I felt the intrusion of egos as I attempted to guide the group through its final preparations. I sensed resistance to my direction, but I was propelled by the magnitude of the mission and continued to hold a field where all could come together as a synchronized unit. Listening. Hearing. Understanding. I responded to my own call to step forth and guide the group. It stretched me beyond anything I had ever done.

I knew it was our ability to work together which counted. We would work in triads to reinforce the foundations of the braid. We were entraining our connections at a cellular level by reinforcing our bonds as triangulated units. It would be these bonds which would support us as we approached the anchoring. The braid so firmly anchored would sustain the work.

I said, "This group has spent many hours honing our abilities to wield and channel energy in a unified field. Last night I was given the configurations for the actual ceremony. There are to be three concentric circles. Those of us who are here will be standing in the inner circle. Although everyone on the mesa will be used to channel the energies, we are going to be focusing the energy into a central vortex for the anchoring. No one really knows what to expect, but the energies present can be expected to be very powerful. For this reason, we have been asked to practice unifying our energy fields in triads. These triads will form the matrix which will merge into the unified field of the larger circle. We will hold the anchor for everyone on the mesa. I have the diagram drawn on this paper for our positions in the circle tomorrow. You can check it to see who you will be working with this morning. I suggest that you follow the same routine we have all practiced in the group as these triads will be the anchor points for the ceremony. They must be well established.

"There will be a second circle around this one made up primarily of the team which has done the preparation of the land. This circle will serve as an anchor for the inner circle. Everyone in this second circle is fully prepared to step in to any position, and they have been told that they should be ready to do so if they are needed. All of those who will be coming to witness the Light Anchoring will form a third circle around the circumference of the other two. Understand that everyone on the mesa will experience the effects of the energies which will be present. Those who will be showing up in the final moments have been guided by their souls to be with us to participate in this event, just as surely as the rest of us."

We each found our partners and the triads locked in their connections to each other as they merged their energy into braids which would sustain the whole. Sara, Rachel and I sat together and linked our hearts, binding our souls' missions through our connection.

The afternoon hours were free to spend as each desired. Some would join us at Sara's workshop, some would go sight-seeing, and some would choose to be alone. But Fred and I had no time for ourselves as we rushed from one group's activities to another. At the workshop, we extended an invitation to witness the anchoring at dawn.

That evening the anchor circle gathered again for a final preparation. We felt the strength of our connections as we sat together. I told the group, "There wasn't any guidance about what we're supposed to do tonight. So if any of you have ideas, please share them. We'll create this time together."

There was concern expressed about the logistics of moving so many people up the mesa before dawn, and we made a general plan. "It will all just work out. This is not to be a performance. We all know that the only thing which matters is that the work we agreed to do gets done. Let's meet at 3:30 a.m. That will allow an hour and a half to gather and get everyone up to the mesa by sunrise. None of us really knows what's going to happen tomorrow. There is no agenda. The rain has kept us off the land all week so we haven't been able to locate the spot for the ceremony. It's going to be an exercise of trust." And I reminded them, "We are all going to be creating this event together. I encourage anyone who has an idea of what should be happening to please speak up, for we'll be needing everyone's contribution tomorrow."

I said, "The mystery schools and every religion have their sacred rites of initiation. These come only after a period of intense training, a vow, and exhibition of dedication. This weekend signifies that point of initiation for this group, as well as a time when we can complete the service we have each agreed upon for the planet. Even though we will expand this circle tomorrow morning when the others join us at dawn, we must maintain our attention to the work we have at hand. Each one of us has our own dreams, our own fears, and our own expectations secretly welling up inside us. We have all worked hard in preparation for this time. We must remain focused no matter what happens."

There was an acknowledgment, for each one knew the magnitude of what lay before us.

I asked, "Does anyone have a suggestion about what we should do tonight?" Silence filled the room, for our preparations felt complete. What more was there to do? It seemed like we needed to do something, but I didn't know what. Finally, I said, "Well, do you want to braid our energies again?"

Everyone agreed, and we went out to the courtyard to form our triads once again.

The pressure was intense. It seemed as though we could hardly hold the energies back, but we knew we must wait for the time when the planetary alignment was correct. Much etheric assistance would be gathered around our efforts in the morning. We must not release these forces prematurely. We were thoroughbreds waiting at the gate. We had been groomed and trained. We knew what we had to do, and our attention was focused only on our goal. Once again, we joined our triads; this time the energies were pushing to be unleashed. We looked at the full moon overhead as the vibrations pummeled through our bodies. No. Not yet. We must wait until dawn.

The time of practice was now done. We reconvened in the Great Room at the old adobe inn. The silence in the room revealed the magnitude of our task and the awesome force of our unanimous dedication loomed about us. We could not fail.

Everyone was reeling from the reverberations of the vibrations we had just experienced in our practice when all eyes turned to Lance, who seemed to hold a magnifying glass on our responsibility. The pressure mounting within him was obvious as his voice boomed out words in an ancient tongue, about the trust we carried forth.

He raised the sacred pipe and gave the charge.

The awesome power of this energy infused the room, and Allison stepped forth to lead us in the song which she had brought to our group and which we had used throughout our preparation. We formed a circle to sing the familiar refrain to the Ancient Ones.

We are travelers on a journey
walking in the Light,
Remembering the Ancient Ones,
The healing has begun.

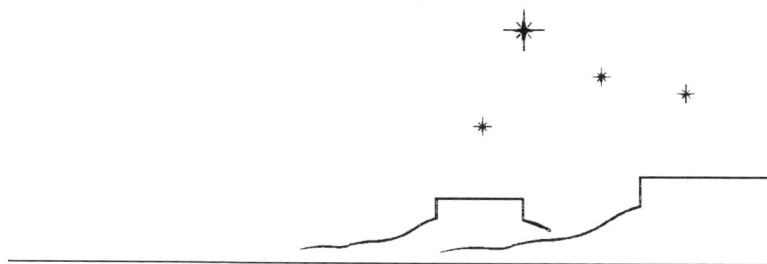

DAWN

Three a.m. finally came. I wondered if anyone else had been able to sleep.

I had laid out some clothes for the ceremony the night before. I would wear purple. No underwear to bind me. Just a loose covering of violet cloth to enfold my Being. The cotton knit pants gave me little protection from the chill in the pre-dawn air, and I dressed quickly. This wouldn't work. Another layer needed. I grabbed my favorite old plaid flannel shirt and a sweater. I put them on. Then I quickly layered the violet cape over them. That was better.

Fred was getting ready, too. He would dress all in white: white cotton pants and a white knit sweater. We each prepared in silence.

On my way to the bath house, I tapped at the door of Aya's cabin. She was already stirring, for the anticipation of this time was great. My vision had been that everyone would gather in a circle here at the campground before leaving, affirming our bonds and our intentions. Then we would travel to the mesa together as a unified group. Centered. Focused.

We had released the cabins left vacant by those who had chosen to stay at the inn, so all the cabins in the campground were now occupied with other guests. As we couldn't wake the others by gathering there in the middle of the night, we would meet in an open field nearby. I went to the fire circle and stood alone, knowing that to have the group gather there would have been the thing to do. It was the ideal that I had seen. If only I could have said, "This is the way it is to be. We all need to stay together at the campground."

As I stood alone in the darkness, I thought of the whole, of the vision, and of the design. I said a silent prayer affirming my commitment and asking for support. When I was ready, I walked back to the cabin with only the full moon to light the way.

Fred and I left the campground feeling like a pregnant couple on their way to deliver their first born. The hour had come. All we had prepared for was about to come into form. We had driven just a mile when we realized that, in our anticipation, we had left the keys to the gates of the sacred land behind. We returned to the cabin to retrieve the keys, delaying our arrival as the process of birth pushed on.

As our car rounded a bend in the road we could vaguely see a truck parked by the roadside, its hazard lights flashing in the mid-night mist. The silhouette of a man standing by the roadside motioned us to pull over. We had reached the gathering place.

Fred asked, "Who's that?"

"I don't know," I replied. "That's teamwork, though. Isn't it great that everyone is doing what they know needs to be done? We even have someone directing traffic!" How our little group had grown!

"Yeah. Look at this!" Fred remarked as he turned the car into the muddy parking lot. Cars were maneuvering around the potholes attempting to find parking places, people were milling around, and small groups were gathering without direction. It seemed strange to have all of this activity in the middle of the night in this sleepy little Southwestern town.

"There must be sixty people here." I said.

Fred chuckled, "Look, there's even a video crew!"

"I don't believe it. Where?"

"Over there." Fred motioned with his head.

This was beyond my wildest imaginings! "Remember Rita said we needed a video because there would be stuff to see? I'll bet she's responsible for this!"

The hour breathed upon us and we knew we must quickly make our way up the mesa so that we could find the location and be ready to anchor the Light during that fragile time of balance: seven minutes between moon set and sun rise.

We all piled into trucks and four-wheel-drive vehicles. The roads were certain to be muddy and difficult for this was the monsoon season and it had been raining daily. We understood that the energy work which had been done in preparation needed to be kept pure, so people were being kept off the mesa by the Nature Spirits until the final moments. We were not concerned. We would be guided to the right spot even if we hadn't been able to locate it in advance.

Fred and I wanted to ride up in the lead car with Sara and Margo. We jumped in with them and were joined by Rachel and her two young sons who opened the tailgate and climbed into the back of the Jeep. The boys were wide-eyed at all of this activity in the middle of the night. It must have seemed like a phenomenal dream to them.

The caravan rolled out behind us. Sara was concerned about the condition of the roads and debated which route to take. We encouraged her to take the shortest route, even though it was steeper. "It'll be all right," I assured her. There isn't enough time to go the long way around, even though the roads might be better."

Sara said, "Well, I'd better check the roads before we try to take all those cars up there." She rolled down her window and called to the people in the car behind us, "Wait here."

I thought "Why don't we all just go?" and sensed confusion brewing. There could be no communication between the cars and there was no plan. Everyone would wonder what was happening and worry that they were being left behind. The road was bound to be difficult, at best, and making a test run up the hill would not only delay everyone, it would worsen the condition of the muddy road.

I asked, "Don't you think we should just all go at once?"

"No," Sara responded. "We have to check it first."

"Oh, well," I thought. She seemed pretty determined.

The road was difficult as we made our first approach to the mesa. The tires slid around the curves as Margo navigated the ruts. After we made it to the gate and Sara was satisfied that the others could do the same, she told Margo to turn around and head back down.

We were part way down the hill when we saw headlights coming up the road toward us. "What's this?" I asked.

Margo said, "I don't know. It looks like the others decided not to wait."

Then we saw another pair of headlights, and then another.

Margo laughed, "Here they come!"

"Oh, geez!" I said. "What are we going to do now?" The road was narrow and steep. It was as slick as wet clay and there was no place to turn around.

Margo said, "There's nothing we can do but go all the way down to the pavement at the bottom of the hill and turn around again. The rest of them are already headed up."

"They don't even know where they're going!" I exclaimed.

Margo laughed as she said, "I know."

The confusion which teased us earlier had now erupted. The people in the cars who saw us heading in the other direction had no idea what was going on, and some of them turned to follow us down the hill.

Fred said, laughing, "I can just hear it. Follow that car!"

The confusion was bordering on pandemonium. The road was getting more and more torn up, and there seemed to be no way to stop the chaos of the cars going in all directions in the night.

None of us were laughing now.

On our way down we passed our friend Casey who was driving a rented four-wheel-drive Chevy Blazer. She had never driven "off-road" before and was having difficulty maneuvering in the mud.

"Stop the car," Fred announced as he opened his door.

"Where are you going?" I asked.

Fred was already on his way out and called back over his shoulder, "I'm going to help Casey drive that car."

Now there were not only cars sliding up and down the hill in both directions, but people were switching cars as well. I was glad that Fred would help Casey drive. We had to do anything we could to get this group together. Inexperience with the road conditions only made the situation worse. Wheels were spinning on one of the cars up ahead; another stopped in the middle of a mud slick.

Margo said, "They're gonna get stuck for sure!"

"It looks like someone already is stuck," Rachel announced. "Everyone's out of the car up there and they're pushing it."

The boys scurried to their knees and leaned over our shoulders to peer out the front window. Their eyes widened even more. What an adventure! "What's going on now?!" they asked. To them, this was more fun than anything.

Finally, all the cars arrived at the end of the road. We were at the gate. The moment was drawing near. Fred got out and put the key in the lock.

It would not turn.

He tried again. And again. "No," he said. "The key won't work."

We all wondered what we were to do. Everyone was out of their cars by now and gathered around us by the gate. We looked at each other. Everyone was asking, "What do we do?"

Why had our program been stopped? What had caused this confusion? Was it our own human failing to be organized, to have a plan, to be more in control? Or was there some unseen opposition at work throwing barbs of disruptive energy at us? In our haste we hadn't come together. The energies of the circle indeed remained blended from the night before, but our guard was down. We were now far outnumbered by the group of witnesses who had joined us, those who had not worked with us in preparation. We had not done the simple task of setting our protection before we approached the mesa. The shadow within each of us was rising to be released and, in its fractured form, it ricocheted about.

Sara announced, "Oh, look! There's a ship overhead!"

All eyes looked upward to the sky, searching for the spaceship.

"Do you see it?" Sara called.

A light twinkled brightly above us. It was blinking red, then green, then white. Was it a star? For a time we all watched the sky, when someone from the crowd shouted impatiently, "What are we supposed to do?"

I looked from Sara to Rachel to Fred who were standing nearby: Should we walk out to the meadow near the gate and do it right here, only halfway up the mesa? Should we proceed on foot? Should we turn back? We all looked at each other feeling the deadline's press and wondering what to do. No one really knew; each searched for an answer within themselves.

I closed my eyes and asked for guidance, "Where are we to go from here? Please give us a sign!"

There was a message waiting for me. It was not a voice, loud and commanding as I had known in the past. It was a thought which said, "Look to the sky. The sky will show you the way."

I looked again to the sky, hoping to see an unmistakable sign and I repeated the message to the group, "If we look to the sky, we will be guided."

Above us, to the east, the star-ship still blinked its colors. Next to it was a bright star shining down. A man next to me said, "That's Sirius. That's the star of the dawning new age."

That's all I needed to hear. "Well, then," I said, "we shall follow the star. We are to walk up the hill in that direction. The star is showing us the way."

The local participants who had worked with Sara seemed to doubt me, for I was a stranger to them. They persisted, "Sara, what are we to do?"

What? I looked into the crowd gathered by the unlocked gate and saw a sea of unfamiliar faces. They wanted to be led, but only by their trusted leader, Sara. It was as though I had not spoken.

I looked questioningly at Sara, who was standing next to me. Did she have some other guidance? She shrugged her shoulders. She didn't know either. And she told her followers, "I guess we go up the hill."

The direction was cast. Sixty lost sheep wandering on the mountain in the night climbed through the barbed wire fence and began their trek. Sara strode past the group as she rushed to be in the lead.

I wondered what was going on. Fred and I both believed that the Light Anchoring was to be done on the sacred land shown to me in the vision so many months before. Why had Sara decided that she was to be the one to show the way? Just the day before she had confided that she was thinking about not being there at all. I guess she thought she knew best where to go.

The confusion in the group was beginning to affect me and I felt my pledge to let things unfold as they would being challenged when I heard my guide's message, "Stay centered. Stay calm."

The secret longings carried by each person moved ever closer to the surface as we walked up the rocky hill. In the darkness of the early morning, we all followed.

I heard a voice cry out just behind me. It was a man with a broken leg trying to keep up with the rest. He grimaced at the pain when his casted foot slipped off of an unseen rock in the path and he slid in the slippery mud. His video equipment slipped out of his hand as he lost his balance and fell.

"Are you all right?" I asked.

"Oh, yeah. I'm fine."

"Are you going to be filming the ceremony?"

"Yeah. I heard from Rita Farnsworth there might be some stuff to see. Do you know her?"

"Oh, yes," I acknowledged.

He commented, "I thought she was supposed to be here."

"Her plans were changed."

"There's a television producer here too."

"There is?".

"Yes. The Dalai Lama is in town and she's doing a special on him. She heard about this and thought there might be something going on here she shouldn't miss."

It was all beyond my understanding. I only knew what I must do.

I wondered where we were going. We could turn off anywhere there was a clearing in the trees and proceed with the ceremony. "This is ridiculous!" I said half under my breath and half aloud. And then I said for anyone who was close enough to hear, "Let's look for an open meadow with a rock where we can stop and make our circle now." I wanted the madness to STOP!

But the group walked on, moved forward like a momentous wave which could not be stopped. We were unable to communicate with Sara and those who had hurried on ahead. This did not feel like a sacred walk. It was a charge up the mountain to beat the rising sun. The ones in the lead followed Sara as she turned to the right and headed on a small animal trail up the hill and into the densely treed forest.

What was going on? We were almost there – just over the next rise if we went straight. I said to Fred, "You know, we're not even on the land."

"I know," he shook his head as we kept walking.

"We should go straight."

"I know," he replied again. "But they've already gone off in that direction." He nodded his head to the right and took my hand, "It doesn't matter."

And we followed the others up the trail.

The walk was becoming more difficult as the path narrowed and became steep – over rocks and under branches. I was concerned about the man with the cast and those carrying babies. Finally, the trail headed back down, winding over the craggy rocks, and into an open meadow which was already filled with people before Fred and I arrived.

There was a mystical quality present in this pristine clearing. The sky was beginning to take on the paleness of dawn, and we knew our time was drawing near. My eyes scanned the silhouetted trees which encircled the meadow.

The place. Where was the place?

We must locate the circle quickly. Rita said to look for a standing stone pointing to the heavens.

As I walked into the meadow my eyes darted about, looking for the rock which would be the platform for the ceremony. There were some large boulders at the bottom of the trail coming down the hill. Maybe that was the place, back where the trail opened onto the meadow. Fred and I wandered across the meadow to where a group of people had already gathered.

For a moment, I allowed the magnificence of the space to fill me. The full moon, now descending, still shone brightly in the west, while the first rays of light began to fill the sky with a pale pink hue from the rising sun. The dark and the light each pushed to proclaim their reign. It was a sacred time, suspended in a void between the worlds. The preparation had been done. So many tests. So many battles fought and won.

Iona brought my attention back to the task at hand as she rushed over and grabbed my arm, saying urgently, "I think the place was back over there by the rocks we passed as we first came into the meadow."

I nodded in agreement, "I thought about the same place." I remembered Iona's locating skills. I wanted to go with her.

Then, Fred came over, "We need to get this show on the road." He pointed to a rock, "How about there?" pulling me in the other direction.

"That doesn't look right. This rock is flat."

"Well, it's a rock." Fred pointed to the hillside where the video crew was setting up their equipment, "We need to be near them. They're already getting set up."

There didn't seem to be a "right" spot. "How about there?" I pointed to a rock nearby which was a little larger.

"Okay. Let's just do it," Fred anxiously returned.

Iona had walked back over to the trailhead, expecting us to come with her. "I wonder why she didn't listen to me," Iona said to Jo. "I guess she doesn't trust me."

The pressure was on us all as the magnitude of our task was reflected back to us by the number of people present. Someone had to take the lead. This time, I knew it was to be me. I walked a circle to mark where we would stand around the rock we had selected, and called an announcement to begin. I cast the outline of the circle with my hand, indicating that it was time to take our places.

Allison and her young son, Russell, passed me as they were heading up the hill to the circle together. Why would she take a child into the circle? It wasn't the place for a pre-schooler. I said to her, "Are you planning to take Russell into the circle with you?"

"Yes." Allison bristled and her eyes flashed as she challenged me, "Is that okay with you?"

I didn't think she should, but I didn't want a confrontation. Her mind was clearly set. I had no experience at this and didn't know directly what might happen. I answered, "I guess so," as I shrugged my shoulders, not knowing what else to say. And I watched Allison take her place to the left of Fred with Russell at her side.

Those who were to stand in the first two circles took off their shoes and placed them on the ground. I said, "Let's all take a step forward so our circle can come in a little closer."

Everyone gingerly took a step forward trying to avoid the little cactus plants abundantly growing amidst the rocks and grasses, as they took their places for the ceremony. As soon as we were in position, all sixty people focused their attention in the center of the circle.

I turned and faced the congregation gathered and announced, "We will begin by singing the sound of the 'Om.' We will chant nine rounds, three 'Om's' sounded for each circle."

As we sang, the universal sound of healing rang out across the meadow and rose as it reached the ring of trees encircling us, calling forth the spirits of the land. The Ancient Ones came forth to join us in this long-awaited time of reckoning.

I held the crystal in one hand and the artifact in the other. I did not know, yet, just how they were to be used. There was nothing any of us could do except to be fully present and follow the guidance of Spirit in every moment. I walked from my position at the base of the circle over to the rock across from me which held the place at the top of the circle. I then placed the crystal and the artifact together on the altar stone as I turned and said, "The circle has been cast. As I place these two pieces together, the anchoring shall begin."

I crossed back to my place at the base of the circle, not noticing the prickles of the small cactus plants beneath my bare feet. Fred and Lance stood directly across from each other at the top of the circle on either side of the anchor stone. One was dressed in white, the other in black. I wore the color of the violet flame, symbolic of transmutation. The three of us made a mighty triangle to anchor the work of depolarization which had been set in progress. Sara and Rachel stood on either side of me, making their connection with the altar where the artifact and the crystal held the place for Spirit.

The seven from Santa Fe, along with Lance's wife, Diana, formed a second circle behind us. Each was ready to step into the circle for any of us in the final moments if needed. The anchoring could have been completed just as well with any one of them in any of our places. The group energies were firmly braided, and those who came to witness gathered around us.

Sara spoke up, "Would it be all right if I did an invocation?"

I was grateful that she had spoken, "Yes! Please do."

"Ascended Masters of the Light, Ascended Masters of the Great White Brotherhood, E. T. Masters of the Higher Realms, Archangels, members of the angelic realm, we would like to invite all of you, along with our Indian ancestors. We would like to invite our I AM presences, our Higher Selves, our own personal spiritual guides. We invoke the presence and vibration of all of you to be with us this moment to welcome the rising of the sun, to welcome the new energy that we are activating this morning. We would like to call forth the Christed White Light and bring it down around us. We invite you, Masters, to be with us with your love, your Light, and your wisdom so that we may all take a thread of this Light with us as we return to our destinations. And, we would like to thank all of you for being with us as we do this great work. So be it."

As the energies began to concentrate and focus in the circle, young Russell was becoming restless, asking for attention as any three-year-old might. He started talking to his mother during the invocation. Allison was determined not to let Russell distract her from her task, and she stood with her eyes closed as she tried to ignore his requests for attention. But this only served to amplify his soft implorings into insistent shouts. His baby sister, Laurel, who was being held by one of the witnesses, joined in, calling out in answer to her brother's cries.

Fred attempted to proceed as Russell became more agitated. Fred said, "We are going to start by doing a visualization."

The young one begged, "Please, mommy, please!" and his sister shouted back from across the meadow.

Fred tried, for himself and for the group, to continue, "I'd like everyone to be aware of the space that they are in. Be comfortable standing here. You are warm. For a time, let your concerns and outside thoughts be quiet in your mind."

Fred leaned down and tried to lift the child. But Russell kicked, "No!" Only one person's attention would calm him. And the child's cries became louder. I opened my eyes as I tried to figure out what to do. I looked around. Only one person was in my vision. It was Dove, standing in the second circle behind Allison and Fred.

My sight focused on her like the lens of a camera; I knew I had to break from the circle and make my request. I walked the short distance to where she stood and whispered in her ear, "Would you please step in for Allison?"

She nodded her acceptance and I returned to my position at the base of the circle.

But Dove did not move to take Allison's place, and Fred tried to proceed, "Let's start by being aware of our connections and imagine a cord that extends down into the earth. If you want, you can imagine this energy expanding. It is a force that comes up out of the Earth to greet us and forms a pyramid that has its apex in your solar plexus."

The engines deep within the Mother hummed, like turbines whirring, separating out the debris still held within our cells, throwing it out like chaff discarded from a grain mill – the spin sucking up the denser forms which could not be sustained in the new vibration.

Russell's incessant demands for attention heightened as all those standing in the meadow focused their awareness on him. Their attention only increased the energy he was sensing. His little body could not handle its intensity as he cried now in panic, "Mommy! Please! Please! Stop it!"

If only we had realized that what he needed was shielding. Many were sending him their love, but many were also angry and shot those thoughts to where he stood, as every cell in his body cried, "STOP!"

Allison was trying to hold her focus, trying not to be distracted by the outburst. In spite of her child's cries, she told herself, "Stay centered. Stay focused. Stay calm." The importance of the task and her commitment to perform her part bore down on her.

Still, Dove hadn't moved.

Russell's screams reached a crescendo as he began to jump up and down, pulling on his mother's clothes and punching her.

"Why can't I be heard!" His little heart cried out.

And he got louder.

The hurt child within each of us that wants to cry out to be recognized was being acted out for everyone to see and feel.

Rachel, who was standing at my right, could take no more. She knew this child well. She was engulfed by anger and disappointment as she felt the ceremony's success threatened, and she broke the circle to walk over to Russell. When Rachel reached the little drama at the far side of the circle, she saw this child's need and opened her heart to him. She knelt by his side and cradled him in her arms, rocking and soothing him, singing the gentle sounds of a lullaby in his ear while centering herself. His cries softened, while his mother stood next to him with her eyes closed, trying to shield out all distractions and maintain her focus on our task as we had been prepared to do.

I knew that something had to be done so that we could proceed. This ceremony was too important to fail now. It was not only our months of preparation in the balance, it was the long-awaited Plan unfolding. We were the ones entrusted with this great responsibility. We could not fail!

I felt it was up to me to do something. I had to speak. I couldn't let this go on any longer. The presence of spectators intensified the pressure we were feeling. They had traveled from far and near to be a part of this event. Who knows what expectations they each brought. Did they think they might be lifted off the planet, or ascend, or see a space ship land, or an Ascended Master materialize? Our preparations had been for a spontaneous and sacred ritual; our intention was to serve the planet. We didn't know what form it would take, but trusted Spirit to lead us as events unfolded.

Time pressed on as the sky lightened.

My patience was exhausted, and I finally spoke the words, "Allison, will you please step back and let Dove take your place?"

Allison acknowledged the request. "Yes," she said as she dropped her head and grasped Russell's hand, slipping her feet into her shoes. I knew she was humiliated and disappointed. I didn't know what else to do and I felt terrible about hurting Allison's feelings, but the successful outcome of our assignment hung in the balance.

In her disappointment, Allison lashed out in anger at her son. And through her tears she said, "Come on. They don't want us here." She grabbed Russell's hand and turned to walk away from the circle with him.

My heart ached ... and we went on.

Dove moved into Allison's position next to Fred and instantly joined her energy with the braid. Her centeredness extended to Fred, helping him to ground himself and regain his focus. He felt the chill of the early morning through his thin cotton pants and the damp ground as the cactus prickled his feet. Fred was acutely aware of the responsibility he had accepted. Everyone was waiting for him. He did not want to disappoint the Masters or the others who were there, and whispered below the rhythm of his breath, "If I could do one thing well in all my life, I would have this be it."

The importance of the moment gripped him.

We all stood in awkward silence waiting for someone to speak. There was only the sound of the diminishing cries of the child, now in his mother's arms, as we all attempted to resume our focus on our task. Seconds stretched into minutes. Fred struggled to reestablish his connection, to be an anchor for the circle, to come forth and meet his own expectations of himself.

He started once again, "I would like us to reaffirm our connection to Earth, our goals here and our Selves. Imagine the color of the pyramid as the color of dark rich loam. Now imagine another pyramid above our heads. It is white. We are going to allow the white pyramid above to descend and the dark colored pyramid below to ascend until the apexes meet a little above our heads. Imagine that now. The Light pyramid is surrounding you and the pyramid from the Mother, Earth, is moving upwards. They join together.

"Now, in your own way, imagine the energy rising up through you. You are a clear and open channel for these energies. Allow them to come into you from your feet and rise up through your legs and into your torso and then up to your heads. This is the energy of Mother Earth rising.

"Now, imagine the energy of Spirit coming down through your crown chakra, down your bodies and down your legs, passing without obstruction. Now, if we put our hands up, palms outward, we can begin to share some of this energy with those around us."

All those in the circle raised their hands, making a band of flowing unified energy held fast. Fred continued, "In the center of our circle, we can imagine a large column of energy. This is the energy of the Teacher, all of our guides whose essence is held in one large column of pure energy, which extends down from heaven, down into Earth."

It was my turn now. The calls of the birds and animals greeting the new day began to stir as I began talking the group through the well-practiced ritual of raising our braided energy to be joined with the Teacher's. As we raised our outstretched hands to the heavens, I asked the group to remember our oneness as we asked Spirit to descend. My voice was low as I spoke the familiar words intended only for the inner circle and we opened the column between dimensions. I felt the hand of the Earth Mother move up toward the heavens as it opened like a lotus within me, reaching for heaven's Light. I felt the vibrations already running through my outstretched hands, down my arms and flowing out of the bottoms of my feet into the Earth – I could no longer speak.

Fred continued, "Be aware of the Teacher's energy as it begins to expand to encompass all of the first circle. It continues to expand to the second circle and to include all of the people standing on the mesa here today and beyond.

"Before we go on, I'd like you to bring your attention back to the space that you are in. Allow the column of energy that extends out of the crown chakra to rise, turning about the circle as it rises, braided together. We are in a space wherein we have our two feet on the ground, but at the same time we rise in Spirit."

The vibrations continued pulsing through my body, and my legs began to weaken. I wondered how much longer I could sustain the intensity of the energy moving through me. And I heard Fred's words, "If you have a special guide for this event, you may ask him or her to assist you now."

Fred paused as each one had an opportunity to experience their connection with a special guide, and I heard Aguilar, once again, remind me, "Stay centered. Stay calm."

The messages which came were carried on the songs of birds now waking to the rising sun.

Then, Fred spoke the welcome to the gathering, "*Hello. This is Sananda.*"

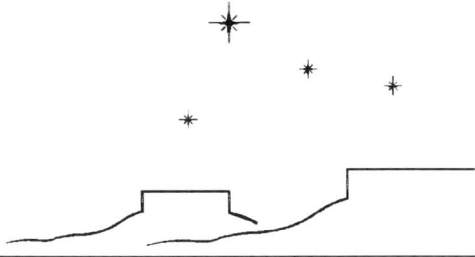

SANANDA'S MESSAGE

I opened my eyes and looked at Fred. There was a glow about him as he stood a step forward in the circle, centering and focusing the attention of the group with his words. It wasn't merely his white clothes reflecting the early morning light but, rather, a lightness which emanated from his entire body like a halo of shimmering light. He measured every word as it came through, speaking with a pure and honest heart. And I recognized that the energies of Fred and of the One for whom he spoke had merged.

"First, imagine the White protective Light surrounding all of us. Allow your senses to be open and allow the experiences of this morning to come in a natural way with no editing. Be open to what you see, for this is your time to see."

The baby, Laurel, shrieked with delight, for she was seeing now. She saw her friends in Spirit, all around us on the mesa, and greeted them one by one. Sananda's message continued:

"The unity of all the teachers is with us. Take a moment now and allow any teacher who wishes to come up to you and stand before you, to embrace you, to gaze into your eyes and to share the energy that they have with you.

"Take a few moments for this.

"Slowly, allow the energy to come up from within the Earth. Bring it up, through your feet, and allow it to rise all about you. It is the warm and loving energy of Mother Earth. It has risen up into all of you where she will wait for a few moments – the expectant bride.

"Now, rise in spirit with the Teachers.

"Rise to the heavens to meet the highest essence of God that you can imagine and bring it back down until it is just above you – the expectant groom."

My legs vibrated with waves of energy coursing through me, and it was difficult to continue standing; I wanted to kneel, to place my hands upon the Earth. And, as I felt these yearnings, Sananda said, *"Now we will consecrate the ground in our hearts. Take a moment in your own manner and say a short prayer or make a short visualization. We are going to allow the consecration and the blessing of each person standing here this morning. Know that this is done to all equally, regardless of position, regardless of experience, regardless of age.*

"Allow your guides, your teachers, to come to you and present to you whatever is their gift. It is going to be a part of your self. If they seem to be presenting you with objects, know that the object is merely a symbol for a part of yourself. It is not a real object. It is not something you go searching for in stores. It is something you will find within you.

"If they raise to you a mirror, know that they have given you yourselves. They have given you a gift of yourself to shine the Light that is now within you and without you.

"If they seem to be giving you themselves, they are giving you guidance that will stay with you. They are giving you discernment. They are giving you self-confidence.

"See if you can detect what else they are giving you.

"This is our blessing to you. You may always think of this spot. You may always think of the teachers and the guides that you have this morning. You may always ask them for assistance. You may always ask me for assistance, for I am with every teacher and with every guide and with every one of you.

"Remember this morning.

"Remember where you are now, on this planet and on this plane.

"There may not always seem to be perfection in every thing. Yet, out of every thing can come perfection and love."

And the Light rained down upon the mesa.

All who had gathered

bathed in a shower of the Divine.

For those who had eyes to see, they saw visions.

For those who had ears to hear, there was wisdom.

For those whose heart was open, there was love.

And, for those who held expectation,

there was disappointment.

As we opened our eyes, we stood in a moment outside of time, our eyes transfixed each upon the other. My gaze went around the circle. What had happened? How had we been changed? When my focus reached Kate I paused, our eyes meeting. She stood there with a smile on her lips and a question in her eyes looking like an angel shimmering in the afterglow of White Light. She looked like she was afraid to move or did not quite know how. Had she been taken, in a fold of time, to heaven and returned? I wondered.

It was as though we were frozen in time and suspended for an extended moment of transition. No one moved. Then, as though a film held on pause starts to roll, movement on the mesa resumed.

We had all cleared out much emotional debris during the months of preparation. Still, all that we held onto which was less than unconditional love of ourselves and others ... of the all ... magnified itself for us to feel. And feel we did!

Emotions which had risen to the surface were unavoidably present as we began our departure from the meadow. We silently greeted each other as we each attempted to understand what had been done. I turned to leave and saw Annie who had been standing behind me throughout the ritual and stepped forward to give her a hug. She put up her hand, "Don't!" She stiffened her back and glared at me, "Don't even talk to me!"

"I don't understand."

"I'm still here!"

"What do you mean?"

"We were told we would ascend ... and I'm still here on this friggin' planet! We're all still here!" Mary came up to Annie and put her arm around her as they turned to walk away.

I looked past Annie and saw Allison. She was sitting on a rock, holding her two children. Rachel, Kate and Aya were with her, trying to provide some solace as she grieved her disappointment in herself.

What could I say to her?

I started toward her when I was intercepted by Jo, "Wasn't that terrific? We really did it! And those children. It's really important they were here. They provided a great service for all of us."

I was confused, "Do you think so?"

"Oh, yes! That baby – little Laurel – she was so precious. She could see them all. She was so delighted to see her friends in Spirit. She hasn't forgotten them like the rest of us have. She's still young, and she remembers! And Russell. You know, these children are such pure spirits. They haven't built up all the shielding that we adults have. It was hard for him to feel all that was being released this morning. He didn't know what to do with it and he showed it to all the rest of us. He was so brave to have accepted that job! And Rachel's sons – they'll never be the same."

"None of us will."

Jo gave me an impish grin. There was a twinkle in her eye, for there was something she understood, "You're right about that!"

The sun was now shining brightly overhead. The early morning calls of the birds and other wild animals filled the air as we began a subdued descent from the mesa. Lance and Diana came up from behind me and matched my step. I paused, and they each gave me a hug, "Thank you for letting us be a part of this." We resumed walking, and Lance told me, "That was the most incredible experience I have ever had! Something very powerful happened here this morning."

"Well, I'm not sure what happened, but it was definitely BIG."

Their joy was undeniable. And they walked on ahead of me together holding hands.

I saw Fred, walking alone, and hurried to catch up with him. His gaze was intent on getting off the mesa. There were no words to share. We walked in silence, our minds and emotions trying to make sense out of the experience we had just shared as we retraced our steps down the hill.

We were all travelers on a journey in the Light.

Was the healing done, or had it only just begun?

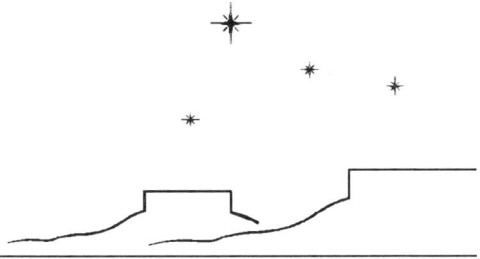

AFTERMATH

It was the not knowing that made it so difficult.

Had we accomplished what we set out to do?

It didn't feel like it. There was no joy, no reward.

We went our separate ways, into the cave, wherever we could find solitude. We could not speak, not even to each other. All eyes turned inward. Only the gloom of life's darkest hour was our companion. It was judgment day, and the one who sat upon the throne and cast the ballot was our own soul's Truth.

Fred and I had gone to our cabin and crawled into separate beds. We each pulled the covers over our heads, overwhelmed with disappointment in ourselves. How could we have been given the honor of a task so great and failed? My heart wrenched, and I cried for my humanness and my shortcomings. For eons this had been waiting. I asked, "How could we have failed?!"

After a time, someone came and knocked at the door of our cabin. It was Sara.

Fred and I went outside and sat with her down by the river to reflect on the events of the morning. We shared our feelings, the three of us, as we tried to see beyond our expectations of how it could have been.

Sara said, "I think it was done."

I was filled with sadness and uncertainty, "I don't know. It doesn't feel like it. So many people were angry and disappointed."

Sara said, "Why don't we ask? Ashtar could tell us."

"Oh, do you think you could bring him through?" I asked.

"Well, I could try," Sara replied.

Ashtar was there waiting to talk with us, *"Yes, my dear ones. You have accomplished what you were to do. I would encourage you not be so hard on yourselves. It was, after all, your presence with your intention which was necessary. The words which were spoken were for the benefit of the people present, but the real work was done on an energetic level. It was only the expectations and fantasies which people had created for themselves which led to their disappointments. What needed to be done for Earth has been done. You could return to the mesa in the morning, if you would like, for your own completion. It is not necessary, of course, but you could do this."*

"Oh, Yes!" I eagerly accepted the idea. It felt incomplete.

Sara wanted to return too.

Fred said, "Well, I'll go back. But don't count on me to say anything."

We agreed to ask the others if they wanted to return.

Fred got up and returned to his seclusion in the cabin and I remained outside, sitting by the river talking to Sara. After a time, she left and I remained alone by the river. I began to understand the major shifting which had taken place. There was an acceleration on the planet on this morning. For some it was most uncomfortable as the molecular frequencies increased. How could we have thought that such profound work – the realigning and balancing of polarity through us – would be easy? There was a major shifting as the latent energies within Earth were awakened and the vibration of Spirit was anchored.

I was alone, lying on a blanket by the river, when I looked up and saw Mary and Aya walking toward me. They seemed light-hearted, laughing together as they approached. They sat down next to me and, as we talked, they saw my need.

I told them, "I feel like I failed Spirit. This was to be the time of the Great Reunion. We were all so dedicated, our preparations arduous." My tears burst forth, "It was just a disaster!"

Mary's eyes twinkled, "I thought it was great! Didn't you see the column of Light descend? All those people with all their personal agendas were bound into a spinning vortex of energy."

"Didn't you see the Indians?" Aya asked.

"What Indians?" I hadn't seen anything.

Aya smiled as if she had a secret, "There were hundreds of them circled around us at the end of the ceremony. They came in Spirit to show us their support! It is the time to come into oneness that has been prophesied. Didn't you see them? They came!"

Aya and Mary offered me their assistance. Aya sat at my feet and Mary at my head, as they placed their hands on me. I felt their love and the Love of the Holy Spirit moving through them, and my tears flowed as my disappointment was released. The display of false strength which I was attempting to maintain melted into their compassion. There was only love. And the barriers crumbled.

When I sat up again, I felt a burden had been lifted. I had begun to understand that our work was not a failure.

I thanked them for their assistance; then we saw the mother and daughter, Charlene and Casey, walking down the road. They came and stood, looking down at us. Charlene bristled, "I am really angry!"

Casey said, "We trusted you! This isn't what we thought it would be!" Their anger flashed as they blasted me with their disappointment.

I didn't know how to respond.

Aya said, "Would you like us to try to help you with these feelings?"

"Oh, yes!" was Casey's quick reply.

I was still feeling fragile and it was difficult for me to be supportive under their attack, so I got up and went back to the cabin. Aya and Mary placed their hands on Casey, just as they had for me. They were resolute as they worked with their hands to continue the process of realignment. I turned to look back as I walked away. I saw that Casey's tears were already beginning to flow as the dislodged emotions began to be released and she opened to the love within.

I wanted Fred's support now, but he was in retreat. I knew this was his way, but it left me feeling quite abandoned. I entered the cabin and found him lying on the bed with his eyes closed. I sat across the room from him and asked, "How are you doing?"

"Pretty awful."

"Well, I feel pretty bad too. There are a lot of people who are really upset with us. They think *we* let them down."

"That was a real fiasco!"

"Yes, it was. We weren't together as a group. We didn't set up our protection before we went up. We didn't know where we were going."

"Everyone was counting on me, and I failed. The worse thing is that I failed Spirit."

"The worst thing of all is that everyone had huge expectations! There was so much mystique about what might occur, and everyone created their own fantasy around it. We did our best. We can't be responsible for the expectations others created for themselves. Aya and Mary thought it was great because they were just glad to be there and didn't have any preconceived ideas about what was going to happen. I think you did a terrific job in the face of all the chaos. I saw you. You were practically glowing with pure Light as you delivered Sananda's message."

"Oh, come on now. I can't believe that!"

"It's true. You couldn't have been more sincere. I thought Christ might appear on the mesa this morning. I wasn't counting on it, but I thought it might happen. If not him, then Archangel Gabriel might be there to blow his horn. When I saw you standing there, holding a focus for the circle in the face of all the disruptive energy, I got it. It is through _us_ the Christ is supposed to manifest this time!

"I think we accomplished what we were supposed to. It just didn't look like anyone had expected. I really felt the energy from above moving down through my body and into the Earth during the ceremony. There was one point where I could barely stand, it was so strong. We were human channels to bring the new energy through, and we experienced the sparks as those energies ignited.

"Everyone is coming here to the campground. You can't make me face them alone. Believe me, everyone is dealing with their emotions right now."

I went over and sat next to him on the bed. I laid my head on his chest. There were no words as his disappointment in himself overwhelmed him. I said, "It was a very difficult thing we did, and we did our best. Ashtar told us it was done. Remember that Rita told us that everything we were holding onto would be magnified today? Well, she was right about that one. We have to go now and be with the others; it's time to be together." I urged him to come out.

One by one, our people came. Soon everyone in our circle had returned and we were all together again, not understanding but knowing that great work had been done. The greatest hour of darkness had quickly passed and, as we began to share our feelings, we each saw the possibility that the promise had been kept.

All that we held onto was intensified in the Light. It was a time of ascension for each of us as we beheld the burdens of our hearts to be released. This had been just one more time of feeling the pain of those ancient bonds. Now, for ourselves and for the many, we could release the ties which kept us bound. We saw it and we knew.

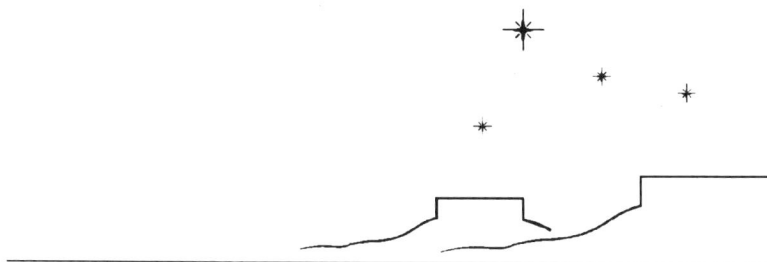

IT IS DONE!

Another day dawned. The passage through the tunnel had been long and difficult. Today there were no expectations, no pressure. There was just the sun, the sky, the Earth, and us. The children had been graciously cared for by Sheila, once again doing her part. Eleven of us gathered at the inn to head up to the beloved mesa. Fred and I were joined by Sara, Rachel, Allison, Aya, Kate, Mary, Charlene, Casey and Diana.

There was joy in the air as we returned to the place of our heart. The road, although rutted from yesterday's escapades, offered no difficulty, and we drove easily to the gate. Would the key work now? We thought it would. Surely the gate had remained locked yesterday because the Great Spirit had not wanted all those cars and people on the sacred land. We were convinced that today we would be able to drive easily to our spot. The rest of us waited as Fred got out and tried the key.

The lock would not open.

We each tried whatever skills we felt we had to open the lock: we shook it, we talked to it, and we even tried to will it open. The lock remained fast. The road to the top of the mesa was intended for our feet alone. No cars would mark the course. It was a power walk, each step bringing us more closely into touch with the vibration of the Earth. The 8500-foot elevation didn't bother any of us and, even though many of us were coming from sea level, we all made the walk with easy stride.

Wildflowers standing three feet tall lined the roadway in a profusion of color. We walked past the narrow trail we had taken the day before and continued on to the top of the mesa. There we turned off the road and walked out to a point which looked out over the valley floor below. The vista was magnificent and we each instinctively found a place to sit on the edge of the cliff to be alone with our thoughts. We were unbounded by time or obligation and our souls were free to soar.

A bald eagle glided in front of us to welcome us to his place. I sat on a rock looking out over the point and felt the energies of the Earth welcoming us to this spot. I heard the message, "You can release your fears to me. I will gladly take them from you." It was as though the spirit of the Earth was speaking. I felt a gentle rocking. Like a babe held in its mother's arms, I was cradled in the loving protection of the Great Mother. Each of the women had their own experience of union with a long-forgotten memory and an experience of Earth's blessing as they sat at the edge of the mesa in silence.

I heard the rustle of Fred's footstep behind me and looked up. He was deep in thought.

"Hi," I welcomed him. "Where'd you go?"

"I just took a little walk."

He sat down next to me, "I think I've found a place which would be good to have a circle. It's right over there."

We all got up and followed his lead through the dense pine trees to a small clearing. There was a standing stone next to a flat altar stone encircled by pine trees.

"Yes." We all agreed. This place was good.

Today, there was no ego, no competition. There was just a sense of oneness with each other. The lessons learned the day before remained strongly present with each of us. Those who could have spoken (but did not) would have a chance to speak as we became co-creators of ritual. When we were ready to begin, an eagle flew over us and announced the commencement with its call; we felt supported by the Nature Spirits around us.

We began with an invocation. It came from the hearts of each of us asking our sincerest prayer: A call for unity of all souls, a blessing for the Earth Mother who has nurtured and sustained us, thanks to the Native Americans who have so long held the truth and the connection to the Great Spirit, a call to the Ascended Masters, to our star brothers, to the Great White Brotherhood, and to the Nature Spirits. There was a reminder that we each need to claim our own personal power. There was a time and space for each to voice the yearnings of their heart.

We called the four directions with sage; we gave offerings to Earth and to the Great Spirit. There were songs and more songs. Each was free to contribute to the circle. There were no expectations. Only joy at being together and weaving our circle of love on the mesa.

Suddenly, Fred began to shake.

The voices from both within him and without which had judged his performance of the day before as less than adequate had caused him to make a pledge that he would not speak. He had wanted only for the others to reclaim their power. But his hands trembled, and he could no longer resist the insistent energy which was moving through him. The vibration overcame him as his voice boomed out, "_This is Ashtar._"

Fred was chosen, whether he liked it or not. The message had to be spoken, _"Now is the time! Get ready. We are going to do the anchoring **right now!**"_

Our disbelief was brief, for the energy present could not be dismissed by any of us. We had been playing, as young girls do, singing songs and chanting rhymes. But we knew now it was the time to finally complete what we had come to do. We each stood firmly in our place as

Fred continued speaking. The voice of Sananda replaced Ashtar's and asked us to begin by extending a column of golden light from the crown of our heads upwards and to lean that column to the center where our energies could form a braid of golden light.

Yes. This was the familiar exercise we had practiced so many times in our living room at home.

The magnitude of the moment was upon us. Every cell of our bodies had been prepared. The words and rituals we moved through were familiar, yet this time we knew they were for real.

The energy of the Holy Spirit descended. It was familiar, but its force was not anticipated. I let out a gasp as my knees buckled from the shock of the intense energy suddenly flowing through my body. Fred and Sara, who were standing on either side of me, reached over and grabbed me to stop my fall as they leaned me against the tree directly behind me.

Fred then called upon a pyramid of energy to rise up from the Earth. Yesterday the energy had flowed down through us as it was anchored into the Earth. Today, we also felt the power of the Earth rise up to meet it. There was a rising of the kundalini energy, a wedding of Heaven and Earth within each of us.

The presence and love of Sananda had so fully merged with Fred that we knew He was with us. He had manifested through this one, the brave warrior who had the courage to bring this message through, to speak his truth, and stand steadfast throughout the tribulations.

The message was about the marriage being bound within each of us this day. Not one was left untouched as joyful tears of ecstasy rolled down our cheeks. We were standing in a baptism of real Light, more Light than we had ever known. We felt it in us and upon us as our months of work turned into reverie. Sobs of jubilation rang out at this orgasmic moment of complete union with God.

We were unashamed.

The last strongholds of limitation had been lifted the day before. The shadow had surfaced to be released. And, now, we stood pure, with child-like innocence, basking in the Light of the Divine.

"It is done!"

Sananda's words were spoken. A breeze rose up from out of nowhere and made a circle around the group. The spire of Light withdrew and thunder clapped three times as Sananda said, _"Now, be on your way."_

It had ended as suddenly as it began. We sang our song of thanks to the Ancient Ones.

The healing had been done.

Mary had knelt during the last part of the proceedings, unable to stand under the force moving through her. She rose and walked over to the altar stone and picked up her cherished crystal.

I wondered what she was doing. But before my question could be answered, she fell to her knees. Mary reached out and pulled a handful of dirt toward her. Then she pulled another, and another, as her tears of determination spilled over. I realized she was digging a hole to bury the crystal. It was time! The anchor would be sealed. The Light would remain fixed on Earth. The special powers of the crystal to balance polarized energy would hold this eye of blended energy for all time.

I cried again – this time tears of joy for Mary. I knew that in this moment she was reclaiming her own power. It was a triumph for the Earth, it was a triumph for the Light, and it was a triumph for Mary.

I looked over at the artifact which remained on the altar stone. Was it to be buried as well? No. There was more work for it to do. I was to carry it on with me. We stepped out of the circle, preparing to leave, and Casey now fell to her knees and stretched out, face down, on the ground. She embraced the Earth as she acknowledged the fullness of her connection with it. I remembered the Ceremony of the Living Heart we had been told about so many months ago by Natachoka, where the Indians would lie face down on the ground to absorb the energy of the Earth in a celebration of reawakening. No one had instructed us how we would act or what we would do on this day. We each just knew.

The Thunder Beings clapped their hands at our backs again, urging us to leave. The sky overhead was blue, but we knew we could not tarry. Our work here was complete. The circle broke and I retrieved the artifact from the standing stone as we began our descent from the mesa. The sun shone brightly and the profusion of wildflowers danced brilliantly, waving hands of yellow and blue at us as we walked the pathway down.

While the rest of us walked on, Mary paused to look at something which had caught her eye. She stopped to look more closely and lifted the object from the path. It was a perfect arrowhead. No one else had seen it on the way up or on the way down this morning or the day before. It was as if it had materialized there. Mary knew it was hers to find. She clutched it to her heart and closed her eyes as she thanked Great Spirit for the gift given in return for the crystal just released.

The thunder clapped another warning and the storm clouds pushed us on. Our work was done; we were to leave this place. At the bottom of the trail, we jumped into our cars to escape the approaching storm. We were, once again, being scooted off the mesa by the weather spirits. As the wheels of our cars rolled onto the pavement at the bottom of the mesa, the sky opened up in a torrential downpour. The work would now be sealed.

We returned to the inn where we had met for our final trek up to the mesa. The skies cleared just as suddenly as they had clouded over. A few lingering clouds hung in the pale blue sky. As we turned to look back at the sacred mesa, a rainbow appeared. We all watched in silence.

The rainbow was pulsating!

The awakened heartbeat of the Earth displayed its rhythm in the rainbow bridge which arched across the sky.

And we knew,

"It was done!"

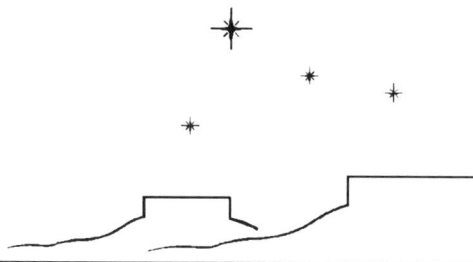

EPILOGUE

There were those on the mesa who did not understand what occurred. Their anger and disappointment were directed at us, even afterward. Several weeks after the Light Anchoring Ceremony, we received a scathing letter from one of the witnesses. He accused us of being charlatans and attacked our human shortcomings. We received a terrified telephone call from a relative accusing us of being in a cult.

It was not possible to reason with those who expressed anger or disappointment, and we attempted to be unaffected by outside opinions. Still, the stones being cast saddened us. We knew in our own hearts that we had been true to ourselves and true to Spirit. We had exercised discernment, questioning each step of the way. It was our own free wills which propelled us forward to humbly complete the task we had accepted.

I had been disappointed as we stood in the ceremonial circle that August 25th waiting to receive a gift, for I saw none and doubted my own worth. But the gifts of Spirit have come to each who participated, at the time and in the form appropriate for each one.

A year later, Fred and I went back to the mesa. Our connection there called us to return. We walked the path and felt the vibrations which had remained intact. I went directly to the circle of trees and sat down at the edge of the stone circle. The forest sanctuary held a reverent field of energy; it seemed not a leaf or twig had moved since we were there. Only a blanket of leaves and pine needles left by the passing year had been added to the space.

I knelt and placed my hand on the ground where I thought the crystal was buried.

Was it still there?

I gently began to pull the earth aside, when I heard, *"Do not touch it!"*

It was a thought. And I returned, "Oh, I just want to see if it's still here."

Again I heard, *"Do not touch it!"*

Curiosity poked at me as I pulled a little more earth aside, "I won't take it. I just want to see."

I saw the hard shape of the crystal beneath the dirt. It was still there, just as we had left it! As I cupped my hands and placed them over the mound, I felt the form beneath my hands disintegrate.

I sat back in awe as I acknowledged the presence of unseen forces guarding the open portal anchored there. They had just shifted the physical form of the crystal into another dimension! It was as though the crystal disappeared, yet I knew the energetic matrix remained intact. The anchor for Earth's new gridwork would remain protected for all time, and neither intention nor folly could alter destiny's course.

❖   ❖   ❖

The golden artifact also continues its work of spiritual and molecular activation. I held it in my care until 1996, continuing to use it when I was asked to participate in either individual or planetary alignment. The day eventually came when I was guided to pass it on. I no longer know of its whereabouts. But I am certain it is *somewhere* – in some dimension of time and space – sending signals calling others to their soul's mission.

All of the ancient traditions tell us that the time of prophecy is at hand. In 1996 I heard the call come from many of the planet's Native Peoples. It came from the Mayan Day Keepers, from the Lakota-Sioux Elders, from the Seminole, from the Ute, and from the Hopi Traditionalists. They all tell us they have seen the omens that the time of prophecy is here. Many Elders are saying there can be "No more secrets." It is essential to the survival of the planet that the sacred teachings held in their trust now be shared with the world. It is an understanding that we are all one, that all of life is sacred and connected.

Each time another Elder comes forward and says, "Now. It is the time; we must share the ancient wisdom; the survival of all people depends on it," an understanding reverberates deep within me as I recognize a connection with the work our little band of warriors accomplished. Much has occurred to prepare us for the new realization, as a change this significant could not be accomplished in one gigantic step. Thousands have now assisted in opening the new vibrational gridwork, each according to their own soul's guidance.

When we did the ceremony on the mesa, we were asked to anchor the energies of Spirit into the Earth. In spite of all the adversity we faced, we followed Spirit because we knew we must. There were no guidelines to follow except those we accessed from within. We had no guru — no leader except that inner voice which pushed us forward to complete what we agreed to do.

Many were called. And many responded. With the passing of time, many have now forgotten the sense of purpose they once felt. They've returned to their jobs and their lives, memories dulled with the fog of time. But now those of us who have been awakened and slipped back into the comfortable slumber of unawareness must remember. Our view of the cosmos continues to expand as the walls of our perceptual boxes are blown away by experiences we cannot explain, and as growing numbers of people acknowledge their own experience of unseen forces – the presence of miracles in their lives.

Seven years have passed since we anchored the energies of Spirit and Earth on that mesa in New Mexico. I must remind myself, even as I question the importance of releasing this story, that the events in our lives were real. I called upon Soltec for any words or understandings which should be added to the telling of this story. His response was immediate: *"Beloved child of Light, we come in response to your request that we would bring illumination into the many aspects of the Mesa Project. You were with a group of Beings participating in one Point of Light upon planet Earth. You were an aspect of the whole connected to the transition underway upon the planet. It came at a point of turning.*

"The gateway which you opened created a portal between dimensional realities; it was a portal in time which you accessed. As you anchored these energies into the planet and into form, you set into motion the potential of bringing expanded reality into your awareness of now.

"The work with the planetary Light Grid has continued through the 1990's with many participating in the process of fastening together the potential of moving beyond the boundaries of physicality. Now hundreds, even thousands, of people have assisted in opening the new vibrational gridwork so that it could become accessible. This has happened as a natural evolutionary process.

"Earth is a part of this process, and Earth has called forth this transition which is necessary for her existence. She exists within a planetary field that is demanding all life forms move into a frequency which can co-exist with the higher frequencies of the Universe. This is all because a new level of awareness is making itself available. The thoughtforms which have bound you into a linear time-space continuum, and which have created a ceiling on your awareness which has limited your ability to perceive, are disintegrating. They are dissolving into something which is much broader. This expansion will bring about great expanded thinking. Those who have struggled as they tried to present their ideas to the world

and those who have been judged will now begin to be accepted, because what only a few have seen in the past will now become more available.

"*Many have become ungrounded in the process of accessing other dimensional realities. Some have spun so far out they have been unable to reintegrate, for they have split apart from the third dimension. This was never the intention of Spirit. It is now the job of those who have the ability to interact with the higher frequencies to ground them into the third dimension. Bring the understandings into your life in a way which is functional. Get real with it!*

"*Much of the current reality of the planetary mind which was limited by third dimensional constructs (where time is linear and space is measured by length, height, and width) is going to merge with higher frequency non-linear time-space reality. It is this merging that the Mesa Project was about. What was begun by a few on the top of a sacred mesa in New Mexico in 1991, and has been continued by growing numbers of people consciously working with the energetic field of the planet, is about to be firmly anchored into place.*

"*As the beings on the planet awaken to their ability to access the higher frequencies, there will naturally be an end to separation. There is no separation in the higher dimensions. That is where Christ Consciousness resides. It is where creation and manifestation originate; unconditional love, understanding and compassion prevail. It is that which you are now being asked to embody.*

"*It is not about leaving this beautiful planet to move on to the 'next level.' It is about bringing yourselves as a species into the next level of consciousness here – in body and in form – on this planet! It is time now that this be done. If this story can open the eyes of just a few to the magnificent potential which lies before you, it will have served its purpose.*

"*This is the time which has been prophesied. It will be an opportunity for humankind to express itself with a new understanding of wholeness. Tell the people to be open, for many new things are about to come: scientific breakthroughs will tumble forward, miracles will occur ever more frequently, and new ways of living in the global community of Earth will present themselves.*

"Many will be in awe at the changes, for things are not going to be the way they used to be. How you respond to the thinning of the veil and the anchoring into consciousness of expanded reality will determine the expression of this change. There will be many responses and many expressions, but there will be no stopping it, even though many will try from their fear.

"It is time to bring Heaven on Earth. That is the essence of what will happen. The possibility exists for each one to manifest Heaven into your life now! The restrictions have been lifted and the potential of a new reality is present. You may bring it here now with courage and with joy. Everyone who is present on the planet at this time has agreed to be a part of this process. You may choose your role. And you may choose your experience and your expression."

It is time to look back in history and to understand that the lessons of the past can now be complete. We can turn to the present opportunity of now, and to the potential of tomorrow. The burdens which we have carried have been a part of our learning experience, but the opportunity at this moment is to stand, to turn, to connect, and move our consciousness forward in a vertical alignment. As we do this, much will be revealed and understood.

When we did the ceremony on the mesa, we were asked to anchor the energies of Spirit into the Earth. As we carry forth this work, we are asked to become Spirit in form. As we move into our own individual godhoods and access our power from the godhead, we will embody this magnificent merging. At this time there must be new definitions of reality, new names for things, and new understandings of creation. It is a glorious opportunity to participate fully in the experiment of life on planet Earth.

There are many souls who have incarnated at this time to assist with this change: the ascension of the planet and her peoples into the new paradigm of living in a higher octave, consciously aware of the interconnectedness of all things. We are all here as individual souls destined to serve the whole. For this is the time ordained for humankind to move out of the period of darkness and greed into the time of Light and compassion. We can all do our part by learning to love ourselves and others without judgment, by being compassionate with family, friends, employees and fellow workers, and simply by expressing gratitude in our daily lives.

The planet has been "hooked in" to the celestial gridwork so all can more easily access this newly anchored higher octave. It is available to everyone. In this time, it is possible for every man, woman, and child to realize their full potential as spiritual beings, living and acting as the masters which they truly are. This awareness will come quite unexpectedly to many, for Spirit works in wondrous ways. It guides us and teaches us about the mysteries of life. It empowers us to reach our greatest potential if we will quiet ourselves and listen. Listen to the heartbeat of Mother Earth, feel the love of our Father, and come to know our true natures as Beings of Light.

About the Author

Pam Cameron brings us this compelling spiritual adventure story. Through steadfast personal dedication, she has followed the spiritual guidance which led her on this journey. She has asked that her story be published in the desire that it may assist others to have the courage to take the steps to find their own way.

Pam's first book, *Bridge Into Light, Your Connection to Spiritual Guidance,* was co-authored with her husband, Fred. Together, they conducted channeling workshops for several years in the early 90's and have taught hundreds how to access their own higher wisdom through the channeling process. They write a quarterly newsletter, *Light Lines,* which is available through Luminaria Press.

Pam, a native Californian, now lives in southern Colorado with her husband. It is her greatest desire to help people connect with their own divinity and understand their intrinsic connection to the whole, which is made up of both spirit and matter.